Life and Action

Life and Action

ELEMENTARY STRUCTURES OF
PRACTICE AND PRACTICAL THOUGHT

MICHAEL THOMPSON

HARVARD UNIVERSITY PRESS

Cambridge, Massachusetts
London, England

First Harvard University Press paperback edition, 2012

Library of Congress Cataloging-in-Publication Data

Thompson, Michael, prof., 1959–
    Life and action : elementary structures of practice and practical thought /
Michael Thompson.
        p.   cm.
    Includes bibliographical references and index.
    ISBN 978-0-674-01670-5 (cloth : alk. paper)
    ISBN 978-0-674-06398-3 (pbk.)
    1. Ethics.   2. Conduct of life.   3. Life.   4. Agent (Philosophy)   5. Act
(Philosophy)   I. Title.
    BJ37.T49 2008
    191—dc22   2007043818

Contents

Life and Action

Introduction

THIS WORK COMPRISES three philosophical investigations, each pertaining to a different sphere of concepts, and through this sphere of concepts to a different stratum of being, as we might say. The first investigation, "The Representation of Life," is organized around the concepts *life, living being, vital process, vital operation* and, above all, *life-form* or *'species'*. The second investigation, "Naive Action Theory," is similarly organized around the concepts *action, intention* and *wanting*, and certain elementary appearances of the concept *reason for acting*—or, equivalently, certain elementary ways in which an action can depend on a thought or consideration. The theme of the final investigation, "Practical Generality," is fixed in turn by the concepts *practical disposition* and *social practice*, and by certain *further* distinctive appearances of the concept *reason for acting* that are specially allied to these concepts—or, again, with correlative forms of dependence of action on thought. The investigations might perhaps be read independently, but they share a common purpose, a common method, and a mass of substantive interrelations; my purpose in the three following sections of this introduction will be to bring out these connections in a preliminary way.

The three ranges of topics are nested in the obvious sense that phenomena coming under concepts in one sphere are presupposed in the constitution of phenomena coming under the concepts in the next sphere: a practice is not possible except where action is possible, and

1

action is not possible except where life is. Though the phenomena registered in any one sphere fall into every prior sphere, nevertheless the move from one sphere or stratum to the next involves a kind of break, at least in the form of representation employed. My thought will be that the break is in each case properly logical or categorial—a matter, that is, of the fundamental *forms* of thought and being at issue in each case. What this means will become clearer later in this introduction and still more in the detailed execution.

If my approach were less essayistic, these relations of dependence might have been complicated by the interpolation of certain further spheres or strata, each—I think—involving a parallel categorial break with its predecessors. Some of this interpolation occurs in passing in the articulation of the material I have taken as properly my own. Thus the essay on the peculiarities of the representation of life might have been preceded by two others. I might first have attempted an investigation of the sphere of concepts that includes those of *object* and *concept* in the exceptionally thin senses attached to the words by Frege— together perhaps with those of *truth* and *objectivity*. This would have been followed by an investigation of the narrower sphere constituted by the concepts *individual substance, actuality* (Frege's *Wirklichkeit*), *process, event*, etc., at least as these figure in ordinary commonsense conception. A rock and a number are both Fregean objects, but a number is for sure not an individual substance or an "actuality". (These two particular spheres are in fact developed a bit in what follows, in accordance with the method I am everywhere attempting to employ—even a bit in the last section of this introduction.) The materials of Part One, the discussion of the stratum defined by the concepts *life, life-process, life-form*, etc., would then have followed the elaboration of these: life, we may say, is a categorially distinctive form of substantiality or actuality *(Wirklichkeit)*, just as substantiality is a specific form of objecthood.

Next, before approaching the topics of Part Two—of agency, action and wanting—one might have interpolated an investigation of the specific type of life or being that gives us scope to apply concepts such as *animality, self-movement, consciousness, perception, sensible quality* and *appetitive desire*. This sphere of concepts is nowhere developed here. The agency, action and wanting under discussion here are something "higher" and more special than these. I am taking them as phenomena of specifically self-conscious life—a life with concepts, a life that resolves into subordinate processes, as every life does, but where some of these processes are actions founded on potentially articulable considerations or "reasons". (Thus in a sense the second investigation belongs to a wider study of self-conscious, self-knowing life in general, though this wider investigation is not pursued, and concepts like *judgment* and *concept* are taken for granted.) If the method I am following is sound, there is a categorial shift in our thinking here—and, if you like, in the form of being we apprehend through these thoughts—just as there is a break in the move from the representation of actuality in general to the representation of life. The capacity to be the subject of such phenomena and the capacity to grasp such thoughts will come together; to frame a third-person judgment bearing one of the shapes that will be discussed in Part Two is inter alia to represent the object of thought as capable of entertaining the same thought in a first-person form.

Thus far the strata I have distinguished amount to those of a familiar Aristotelian *scala naturae* erected on top of a Fregean infrastructure. The ladder in question may be summed up in the narrowing sequence of formal concepts *object, substance, organism, animal, agent.* Notice that the abstract expression "a being" can be used in any of these registers. Thus we have the perfectly intelligible vegetarian slogan "All beings are created equal," in which animals—feeling, desiring organisms— are what count as "beings". And in science fiction we have imagined meetings with "alien beings"—that is, with non-human but intellectual organisms, and not, for example, the Venusian equivalent of oysters. (Note that the word "life" admits a similar diversity of gear settings. In Kant it characterizes perceiving, desiring beings—that is, animals— while "organized being" is used for the concept most of us express with the word "life" or "living thing". Similarly, in another familiar use, "a life" is what is described in a biography, and characterizes only intellectual organisms.)

But this *scala naturae* ends in the idea of an agent, and this, I am thinking, is the beginning of a sort of *scala practica.* The specific form of *dependence of action (or wanting) on a consideration* that is at issue in the second investigation—the specific form of mediation of the general 'life process' by judgment and concept—is more or less that usually called "instrumental" (though if my account is sound this expression is not really appropriate). This is, I think, the only form of dependence of action on thought that is contained in the idea of concept-mediated life in general. As Kant points out in the *Religion*, we cannot analytically preclude that some self-conscious self-knowing agency might perhaps be merely Humean in character. In such an agent what is not founded on an instrumental consideration or thought is simply governed by appetite or the pleasure the agent takes in the thing. But, as Kant immediately notes, we know that further fundamentally different forms of agency and thought-dependence are nevertheless possible. Here again, that is, there is scope for a categorial break, perhaps for several. It falls then to Part Three to elucidate *some* of these higher forms of agency, or thought-dependent operation, or have a go at it. (Neither form that I discuss in Part Three is anything Kant would condescend to elaborate on; his attention here as everywhere turns immediately to what is most exalted: to a nexus of thought and action that is allegedly governed by what he calls "pure practical reason" and the associated form of agency and life; I will return to this point briefly in the next section.) The associated forms of explanation of action or wanting by thought will be explanations of final objectives—explanations of final objectives by thought, not by appetite—and they will be governed or underwritten by what I bring under the terms "practical disposition" and "social practice". I will suggest that the capacity to bear items coming under either of these headings marks a complete break in the form of agency and its description. Strange as it may seem, the difference between *such* an agent and a merely Humean agent is on the present account akin to the difference between a rock and a number.

This, then, is the scale or ladder I am working with, though my three essays overleap certain rungs.

Any of the concepts in the three spheres that I have isolated as setting my proper themes might of course be deployed in some form of empirical investigation—an investigation of a biological, psychological or sociological character, as it might be. In view of this fact, the impression might form that in truth these concepts are all constructions of those special sciences, and are properly the possession of them. A philosophical inquiry into any of them would thus come under the heading of philosophy of biology, or philosophy of psychology, or philosophy of social science. None of our spheres would constitute a space for the operation of philosophy pure and simple. One of my chief ends in composing this work is to contest this thought. The distinctions in question are not empirical. Of course, I do not propose to stop at this negative judgment. My more general purpose is simply to elucidate these concepts—to orient myself and the reader among them and the things they capture, together (as will emerge) with certain associated *forms of thought, judgment or predication* and the concomitant forms of representation in speech.

1. The Practical-Philosophical Tendency of This Work

Though the discussion will mostly have something like a metaphysical character, my remarks will already have suggested that the point of achieving the orientation we are after is ethical or practical-philosophical. Movement up the ladder I am envisaging ends, or would end, in properly ethical and related reflection. This we might characterize provisionally as reflection on the questions *what is to be done, how to live, how to live together,* and so forth, taken as possessing the widest generality they may admit. Nevertheless, the three parts of this work are strictly preliminary and never really reach this last rung, though occasionally ethical materials intrude, especially in limiting the scope of the last investigation. We may say, again very provisionally, that the intelligibility of those great questions is internally related to our possession inter alia of a higher conception of a mode of dependence of action on thought or consideration, and thus a higher conception of agency, than is articulated in this book.

This is a point Kant would immediately emphasize, rushing in to fill the breach with his special conception of action as determined by "pure practical reason", *Wille* and so forth. My thought, though, is that an approach to these great questions, and to any more exalted conceptions of agency and the role of thought in action, must come from below. In this respect, I am operating in accordance with the program of G. E. M. Anscombe's 1958 essay "Modern Moral Philosophy." That essay claimed that practical philosophy had been spoiled by its emphasis on the contentless words "moral", "morally ought", "morally permissible", etc., and that it "cannot usefully be practiced". For starters, she thought, the word "morality" should be replaced by the word "justice", and "morally wrong" with "wrongs someone"—these are terms that may bear conceptual content. But the best path is to "banish ethics totally from our minds" and busy ourselves preparing the ground for possible reconstitution of it. It is in this same period that Anscombe published her monograph *Intention.* That work studiously avoided ethical categories, though it was aimed at elucidating objects adequate to be brought to them, as we might say, and was not simply a scholastic development of the material for its own sake. In the second, "action-theoretic" part of this work I attempt to reinterpret and radicalize some of the thoughts contained in Anscombe's monograph. (Anscombe's general 'analytical' Aristotelianism, as we might call it, is a pervasive influence on all parts of this book, as I will note in a moment.)

In any event, the approach I take to this basically metaphysical material is constrained by two convictions pertaining to the ethical purpose with which I write: first, the thought that any developed ethical or practical philosophy will have to employ the concepts I have taken as setting my theme, or some belonging to each of the three spheres they define; and second, the Kantian thought that an investigation or use of these concepts can only have this orientation to the chief questions of practical philosophy if we can first see our way past the empiricist conception of them outlined above. We must see how it can be that concepts like *life*, *action* and *practice*, or at least some in each sphere, do not acquire their content by the sort of direct association with experience that is possessed by concepts like *rock*, *oak* and *ape*, nor by some more mediate association akin to that possessed by concepts like *quantum state*, *selection pressure* and *mode of production.* If there is anything in the approach I adopt, it will follow that concepts like *life, life-form, action, practical disposition, social practice*, etc., have something like the status Kant assigned to "pure" or *a priori* concepts. I will give a somewhat clearer account of the status in question in the last section of this introduction. The hope, we might say, is to win a right to paraphrase Frege's lyrical remark about the natural numbers (which in that particular case was perhaps ill-advised): the distinctions at issue in the present investigation "are not given to the reason as something alien, from without, through the medium of the senses, but as its nearest kin are utterly transparent to it." This is not to say that it will not take a certain labor to bring this alleged transparency out, or to regain it.

I have said that the ladder we are climbing reaches toward the ethical without really reaching it. But it may help orient the reader if I make one further remark under this heading, namely, that the particular program in the light of which I originally contemplated these studies was a reconstitution of something like a specifically Aristotelian ethical theory: a 'neo-Aristotelianism' of the sort outlined at the end of Anscombe's "Modern Moral Philosophy" and lately defended in Philippa Foot's monograph *Natural Goodness* and in the last part of Rosalind Hursthouse's *On Virtue Ethics*. Anscombe counseled a general retreat from ethics for the sake of ethics. But in outlining the possibility of an Aristotelian practical philosophy, she noted that the hope of reaching such a thing must confront the fact that "there is philosophically a huge gap, as present unfillable as far as we are concerned, which needs to be filled by an account of human nature, human action, the type of characteristic a virtue is, and above all of human 'flourishing.'" Though I had not intended to act in obedience to this advice, it is no accident that, of the four topics Anscombe mentions, the first three are taken up in precise succession in the three parts of this work.

Thus one implicit purpose of the discussion of the concept *life-form* in the first investigation is to make a particular life-form concept, viz., *human*—the concept, if you like, of *the life-form I bear*—safe for practical philosophy, and to say something about how one might rightly work with it. One mark of Aristotelianism is the special position it gives to the concept *human* in practical philosophy, in particular the preference it gives to this concept over the abstract concepts *person* and *rational being*. It is an essential characteristic of the Kantian approach that it makes these latter concepts central. I do not think we are practicing anything that merits the title of Kantianism except where we are led into the project of articulating a conception of how to live, and how to orient oneself in life, and how to reason practically, that would apply as much to the Martians or Venusians carefully described in Kant's "Universal Natural History" as it does to us. If my action is properly linked to a thought or consideration—that is, if my will is 'morally' determined—then a 'law' is operating in me that can also operate among the imagined Martians, just as a single law of gravitation operates in me and them considered simply as bodies. Of course the law in question is specifically different from any ordinary law of nature, operating as it does through the agent's at least implicit conception of it. On an Aristotelian view, the closest one could come to such a thing—somehow to be found "in" many agents and in some sense potentially linking consideration and action in them—is the specifically human life-form itself, which is *ex hypothesi* not found in the imagined Martians. If I hazard a few general remarks under the heading "how to live", supposing them to have application in my own case, then, for the Aristotelian, the life-form I bear provides the measure of widest generality I can intelligibly aspire to attach to them. Of course a life-form that occupies this position will be very different from that exhibited in a turnip or tarantula: its bearers will have to operate with an implicit intellectual conception of it. (This question of the generality to be assigned to a practical proposition seems to me one of fundamental importance. It is a striking fact about received casuistical literature and the received literature about 'practical reason' that authors are prepared to weigh in on the question when, morally speaking, 'one' should or shouldn't do something—turn the trolley onto another track, say—or to declare on what reasons 'we' have, and to offer 'arguments' for various positions, but nowhere specify the scope of the generality contained in this 'one' or 'we'. I cannot see that the discourse is in either case any less devoid of content than would be a succession of tensed predicates deprived of any subject.) Though the positions share much structure, the Aristotelian view of the sorts of background element or explanatory factor that can underwrite a connection of thought and action might be judged to be skeptical in relation to that of Kant, who believes in a practical law that can break through anywhere in the cosmos and underwrite particular actions. A radically Humean position—that the only form of dependence of action on thought is instrumental and underwritten by a further particular objective—is similarly skeptical in relation to both of them, and indeed to the intermediate sub-ethical possibilities outlined in the third part of this book.

It will emerge from my argument, I think, that all of these 'modes of dependence of action on a consideration', real or imagined, and the diverse views of the sorts of explanatory factor that might underwrite them, share a common abstract structure, and the perception of this might help to bring the dispute to resolution. For all I can argue here, it may be that Kant has found the true approach to ethical theory. But his principal argument for overleaping the Aristotelian possibility rests on a true premise about the proper role of empirical concepts in practical reflection and its philosophical representation, and the false premise that there is no way of explaining the concept *human* or *the life-form I bear* or (on a certain way of taking it) *what I am*, except as an empirical or, as we would say, biological concept. (This is Kant's "favorite insight," as Schopenhauer says, and he loses no occasion to repeat it.)

If the case against Aristotelianism is to be made, it must be on other grounds.

The discussion of the concept *practical disposition* in the third part of this book has a similar relation to the so-called neo-Aristotelian project; it makes a limited start at the project of saying what sort of thing might come under the concept *virtue*, a concept everyone agrees is central to that approach. Of course the concepts *practical disposition* and *virtue* make crucial appearances in other quite different accounts, for example, as we will see later, in that of Gauthier, whose neo-Hobbesian program is, I suspect, the only real alternative to the neo-Kantian and neo-Aristotelian projects that is not basically skeptical about the idea of justice. My discussion of the concept *practice* or *social practice* has a somewhat different relation to the imagined neo-Aristotelian program. It arises from the difficulty an Aristotelian or indeed any non-subjectivist account has in handling what we might call the historical character of any case of sound human practical thought—and thus also the historical or 'practice-mediated' character of the more determinate virtues that would ideally underwrite the associated dependence of action on thought. I think that none of the neo-Aristotelian writers I mentioned have properly come to terms with this aspect of the matter.

Though the hope of a modern but specifically Aristotelian ethical theory provided the impetus for some of these thoughts, still, as I have said above, my official posture in this book is one of agnosticism about the prospects of such a position. *Any* sound practical philosophy must get clear on the concepts in question. Moreover, I am thinking, if we do get clear on them, we will be familiar with certain structures of thought that might equip us to move further into fundamental practical philosophy.

2. The Aristotelian, or Quasi-Aristotelian, Character of the Substantive Doctrines Propounded in This Book

This text might be related to Aristotle not just by an aspect of its extrinsic practical orientation, but also in terms of the detailed content that is actually defended in each subordinate investigation. Here, though, it is Aristotle's theoretical philosophy that is of interest, and not the *Politics* and *Nicomachean Ethics*. Scholars sometimes maintain, with justice, that Aristotle makes little use of his metaphysics or 'natural philosophy' in his ethical theory. But the significance of these other aspects of Aristotle for the present investigation rests precisely on the difference in historical situation. What Aristotle could take for granted is often problematic and disorienting for us. For him the pursuit of practical philosophy did not pose metaphysical problems.

We might approach the point as follows. This book is a kind of exposition of certain aspects of the "manifest image", which Wilfrid Sellars familiarly contrasted with the "scientific image" to the alleged discredit of the former. (The expression "image" is inept; Sellars is contrasting certain systems of concepts.) This is no surprise: if anything is clear it is that 'the practical' happens precisely in this so-called manifest image; the categories with which the reflecting and deliberating agent operates and conceives herself belong here; a discourse that breaks with them completely will be alien to the agent and will simply not be practical philosophy. My hope, of course, is that my procedure will do something to defend the possibility of attaining truth here and there within this supposed image, and thus to oppose the globally fictionalist attack Sellars mounts. But, now, it is a commonplace among philosophers who use such terms that Aristotle is a philosopher of the manifest image, or of 'the ordinary', or of the world of rustic common sense. Indeed, the conceptual structures through which we apprehend *these* things he extends to everything. But the situation is in a sense even worse than that. Nature in general, we may say, he approaches with the categories derived from the representation of life and action. This is very bad news if you are envisaging, say, a mathematical physics. But if your topic is precisely life and action, and these as objects of philosophy, then things are evidently otherwise. It is in the sphere of action and life that we find legitimate place for the forms of philosophical reflection that led Aristotle to introduce his peculiar concepts of *substance, capacity, activity, form, matter, unity, process, final cause,* and so forth—even if these particular concepts are not just exactly the ones we ourselves need. It is in the sphere of action and life that we might find use for a conception of, say, a 'whole' or 'totality' that precedes its parts or phases; it is in the sphere of action and life that we might find use for a conception of a special nexus of particular and general through which we might see the former as accounted for through the latter, or through something the latter contains. Again, it will be necessary to detach all of these ideas from some of the material in which Aristotle has wrongly buried them, and subject them to further violence.

But, cleaving to Aristotelian jargon, my effort in this book might be provisionally characterized as an attempt to show that certain leading concepts in our various spheres—*life-form*, *action-in-progress*, *intention*, *wanting*, *practical disposition* and *social practice*—are all 'form concepts'. Anything that falls under any of them will exhibit some of the attributes Aristotle attaches to form/*eidos* in his general metaphysics and natural philosophy. Each concept catches a particular type of 'unity', as we might equally say: a unity through which the things united can at the same time in some sense be understood. Philosophical comprehension of the concepts in question will come from grasping the specific character of this form or unity in each case. Thus, for example, in the treatment of action in the second part of this work, everything will depend on viewing action as something that has parts or runs through phases; a grasp of the nature of action will reside in a grasp of the specific type of unity these phases exhibit, and moreover on our seeing that a certain rustic kind of understanding comes precisely from bringing the manifold phases to this unity; thus, I hope, we will lay our hands on the peculiar mode of dependence of (some) action on instrumental thought. In general we may say—again, with the facile phrasing characteristic of prefatory remarks—that this text is always steering between a kind of atomism or individualism that rejects the element of form or unity, on the one hand, and a kind of Platonism or Cartesianism that puts this element at a distance from the things united. My hope is that this is happening in accordance with a method that will actually produce progress, and not a jargon like the one I have just now been using. All such jargon is a desperate attempt to capture something that emerges ineluctably from the most elementary forms of human thought, and which must be grasped if specifically human life is to be grasped.

I mention Aristotle not of course because I propose to produce any learned or even unlearned exposition of him. My effort might better be characterized as aiming to bring my own thoughts about the matters at hand—however unworthy these thoughts may be—into what we might call the Aristotelian tradition in philosophy and practical thought. And here there is after all a genuine tradition: the antecedents to whom we must "look up with grateful awe," as Frege said of Kant, would include not just Aristotle but also St. Thomas, Hegel, Marx, and even indeed Kant in certain respects. Kant's third critique and the pure 'psychology' that pervades his work clearly bring him under this heading. They exhibit a profound re-appropriation of the Aristotelianism he met with in the "schools", despite his ambiguous relation to the actual Aristotle, and despite the fact that for a more orthodox Aristotelian he frequently emerges as the enemy. The other thinkers I mentioned all worked with a deep knowledge of the actual Aristotle, and, I think, it is only by seeing this that we can make a beginning of understanding them or making use of them. The project of an "analytic" or "analytical" Hegelianism or of an "analytical Marxism" (however well- or ill-advised such a thing might be) must see itself as aiming at a form of analytical Aristotelianism, and thus at a form of what Anscombe was first to attempt and is also here attempted. I mention these writers to bring out the generic and undogmatic character of the Aristotelianism propounded in this text, and because particular doctrines we may associate with each of these thinkers appear on or just below the surface at various points in it. The interest of these writers resides in the fact that in them certain very abstract thought-structures or forms of reflection are employed in diverse materials and connections, and thus we become accustomed to them through the comparison, arriving at a sort of Galton picture we can apply to our own problems. In Aristotle himself these thought-structures are, as I said, partly buried in an ill-fated reflection on nature in general; in Marx they are submerged in a possibly botched quasi-empirical reflection on a specific form of organization of social life; in Hegel they are given a kind of independent logical representation, but one fused with a (for me) ungraspable method and a completely indefensible form of expression in writing. If it is wondered how I can bring such diverse authors under one heading as "Aristotelians" and make them relevant to my task, it will be enough to remind the reader that in textbook accounts they are all inevitably accused of a dark holism or organicism, a doubtful essentialism, and a dubious use of teleological locutions. My thought, though, is that if our material is to be grasped, we must comprehend what it is in our most basic forms of thought that leads a thinker to propound propositions of the sorts that inevitably attract these dismissive epithets. We must, that is, ourselves risk attracting these epithets. Under the fraught heading of "teleology", in particular, it may be worth remarking that one of the Hegelian features of the present book is that teleological judgment is not made central, but is always related to the element of form—even in the case of intentional action, where teleological thinking seems to have its proper home: here and everywhere it is necessary, as Hegel says, to advance from the 'external' point of view of teleology to the standpoint of 'inner design'.

One strand in contemporary Aristotle scholarship prides itself on making Aristotle's theoretical philosophy out to be as alien and incredible as possible; it is a system that must fall without remainder at the first breath of modernity. But we must keep in mind that the scholar is an empiricist, *hōs epi to polu*, and that this was not the view of Hegel and Marx, both moderns who use Aristotle on every page. It is a puzzle how it can be held that thinkers of their stature—or even that of Martin Heidegger and Elizabeth Anscombe—might already have shown a complete misunderstanding of Aristotle simply in holding that every philosopher must devote herself to the study of him.

3. The Fregean or Post-Fregean Method That Is—or Would Ideally Be—Followed in This Book

I have said that this work might be characterized as a sort of attempt at 'analytical Aristotelianism'. What 'Aristotelianism' there is to be found here emerges in the substantive things I say in each part of the work—about *life*, *action*, *practice*, and so forth. It is the *method* with which I approach these matters that is analytic or analytical or, as we might say, Fregean. I am supposing that Frege has the same relation to any philosophy that can be called by this name as Aristotle has to the tradition in philosophy that I was calling Aristotelian; otherwise I have no idea what the expression "analytic philosophy" means. My idea is that a sound contemporary representative of either tradition must also fall into the other. This is the circle I am squaring, and I suppose it will inevitably involve doing a bit of violence to each line of thought.

I will thus end this introduction with a few remarks on the sort of method I am attempting to follow and in particular on its relation to Frege.

The concept of a *form of judgment* will be all-pervasive in the development of the material under discussion. What really marks off my three different spheres of thought one from another, I think, is precisely the distinction among the *forms* of judgment (or thought or predication) that prevail in each of them—and not, in the first instance, in the *things that are thought of* under each heading. In advancing into a new sphere, as I frequently say, thought as thought takes a quite specific turn. The elucidation of the *concepts* that I have taken as setting my theme—*life-form, action, practice*, etc.—the concepts that capture the diverse 'things thought of'—will reside principally in bringing out their connection to the associated stratification of forms of judgment. This use of the idea of a form of judgment is closely associated with a feature of the discussion that might be found odd, namely, the frequent claim that the distinctions we are interested in are fundamentally *logical* in character. But I think my argument does turn precisely on forms of reflection that were traditionally brought under that heading, certainly in Frege and Kant. Other things that are also rightly brought under that heading—discussion of logical constants, inferential rules, formal systems, etc.—are not much in evidence here; if these are taken as definitive of specifically logical discussion, then I will need some other expression to characterize the type of reflection I am attempting, however haltingly, to carry out. But I have no doubt that there is something Frege and Kant were doing that I am attempting to do as well. (What is missing here, from the point of view of more familiar forms of logical inquiry, is the element of iteration; the distinctions that will interest us are exhibited only in "atomic" and other very simple forms of thought.)

Now, in his mature phase, Frege did not use expressions like "form of judgment", or the language of form in general. But it is clear, I think, that he is the philosopher of forms of judgment or thought or predication *par excellence*. This might be overlooked for the simple reason that many of the things that Kant, for example, boldly ascribed to the "mere form of thought"—for example, whatever is expressed by the words "some" and "all"—belong for the mature Frege to the content judged. At the same time Frege's procedure shows how it can be that some quite particular concepts—concepts that are in a certain sense contentful—can be explained or comprehended precisely through a reflection on forms of thought or judgment. And this is a crucial aspect of the program I am attempting to prosecute. In Frege, of course, the 'contentful concepts' in question will not be our own—*life-form, action, practice*, etc.—but rather the leading concepts of Fregean ontology, viz., *object/Gegenstand, concept/Begriff, relation/Beziehung*, etc.

If we simply pick up the term "form" from the tradition and apply it to "judgment" or "thought", the resulting expression "form of judgment" or "form of thought" will inevitably exhibit a certain ambiguity.

We might, for example, say, employing Greek letters after the fashion of Frege, that we are faced with a particular "form of judgment" in, say, ξ *ran over* ζ. Concrete thoughts that share this form would be, say, that *Jones ran over Smith* or that *Smith ran over Jones*. Only an intellect that has attained to this form of thought—one that has grasped the concept *running over*, as we ordinarily say—can properly apprehend these complete, judgeable, concrete thoughts. But, as Frege would promptly note (if we could convince him to adopt this vocabulary), any judgment or thought that exhibits this form will exhibit another, namely, $\Psi(\xi,\zeta)$. *This* form is shared by the two concrete judgments mentioned, but also with the judgments that, say, *three is less than seven, Damascus is the oldest city in Syria* and *Burma is identical with Myanmar.* The diverse more particular forms ξ *ran over* ζ and ξ *is less than* ζ and ξ *is the oldest city in* ζ and ξ *is identical with* ζ we may call contentful or *inhaltlich* forms of thought. Though they are contentful, they are still forms, since they need to be "completed", as Frege says, or "enmattered" or supplied with further content, as we might say. Only then will we have a thought proper: something for which the question of truth arises. But these four contentful forms obviously stand opposed in character to the more general form $\psi(\xi,\zeta)$, which we find enmattered in any thought that exhibits *any* of those more determinate forms. In the former, $\psi(\xi,\zeta)$, we have reached a pure form of judgment, as Kant would say, or a logical form, as we might say—the form, as we all do say, of a two-place relational judgment. That is, in attaining to the conception of this form, and in reaching this pitch of abstraction, our reflections have now made their way into the logical element, as they had not in the conception of the thought-form ξ *ran over* ζ. In relational judgment thought as thought takes a quite specific turn. In grasping this we have become logicians, in our small way.

One of Frege's chief thoughts, which, again, he would not express in quite these terms, is that a single complete communicable thought can exhibit a variety of such pure or logical forms. So, trivially, any of the several complete judgments mentioned above exhibits the form $\phi(\xi)$, which is also found in, say, *Smith is a fool* or *Damascus is beautiful* or *three is prime*, as the form $\psi(\xi,\zeta)$ is not. Indeed, any of those concrete relational judgments exhibits this form $\phi(\xi)$ in two ways: the thought that *Jones ran over Smith*, for example, may be taken as an enmattering of either the contentful form ξ *ran over Smith* or the opposing form *Jones ran over* ξ. It is another favorite point that in the judgment *Thompson healed Thompson* the form $\phi(\xi)$ appears in three ways, in one of which ξ *healed* ξ is taken as the predicated contentful form. That it yields these phenomena is characteristic of the specifically Fregean approach to the question of the form of judgment or thought or predication.

Another decisive Fregean thought is of course that a contentful form that appears as enmattered in one judgment can itself enmatter another higher contentful form. Thus in the thought that *five of the people mentioned on George's list healed themselves* or *five of the people mentioned on George's list are beautiful*, the contentful forms ξ *healed* ξ and ξ *is beautiful* enmatter a single higher contentful form; the thoughts share that form, which makes its appearance in language principally in the words "five of the people mentioned on George's list". A different higher contentful form, the unrestricted existential quantifier (considered as something that figures in thoughts), is similarly enmattered in the thoughts that *some object healed itself* and *some object is beautiful*. These four concrete judgments share the common pure or logical form $\Phi_\alpha \, \phi(\alpha)$. This is something that belongs to them just as thoughts, apart from any content they may carry. They may exhibit other forms as well, of course. The thoughts about George, for example, also presumably exhibit the form $\phi(\xi)$. Though a single thought may exhibit both forms, the conflation of the forms themselves would for Frege be as gross a confusion as is possible.

In the examples $\psi(\xi,\zeta)$, $\phi(\xi)$ and $\Phi_\alpha \, \phi(\alpha)$, we are beginning to articulate a familiar system—a "table of forms of judgment", if you like. The complaint registered by Hegel against Kant's table, that it is a decorative assemblage based on external experience of sentences and without a genuine principle, could hardly apply here: it is child's play to extend the table indefinitely, rapidly arriving at forms one would have trouble filling with content—and rapidly running out of Greek letters. It is just the fact that this table of forms is so evidently founded on principle and is unlimited in scope that generates the illusion I am most anxious to combat in this work, namely, that it gives complete coverage. Once we are in possession of this principle, which is perfectly genuine, it is easy to think that there are no other pure forms of judgment or predication to be considered. It is easy to think that the form of reflection that engendered it has been brought to a close by Frege.

It must be emphasized that the list of forms of thought or judgment we have so far developed can indeed be called a list of *forms of predication:* the first Greek letter always corresponds to something predicated in the thought in question, and the letters enclosed in the outermost brackets correspond to what it is predicated of, the "subject" or "subjects". In a typical thought, something is thought of something, or of some things; our list is precisely a list of forms that a thought's being-a-thought-of-something (or of some things) can take. Again we must emphasize that the same concrete thought might at once exhibit many such forms of predication. No one thing need be "the" subject or "the" predicate of a given thought. This is one of the grounds for Frege's allergy to these expressions. None of this speaks against the point that the diverse Fregean "analyses" of a given concrete thought are each represented by isolating a single *predicative* element, and one or more elements to which it is attached.

We might then further note that our assemblages of Greek letters—$\phi(\xi)$, $\psi(\xi,\zeta)$, $\Phi_\alpha \phi(\alpha)$, etc.—could find a second use representing irreducibly diverse forms shared by contentful things predicated in thought, rather than forms of the complete thoughts themselves. The question we ourselves are posing would thus be whether there are other unlisted and un-Fregean forms of predicative element.

Now, the Fregean forms of thought or judgment we have been considering are in the first instance forms of the thoughts we grasp—thoughts that are independent of any individual's grasping them, and still more of anyone's actually judging that any of them is true. But we may also say that they correspond to basic intellectual powers possessed by each of us. These are capacities that are exercised in any case of grasping suitable thoughts, though perhaps inarticulately, and in 'acts' of judging them to be true. Our list of assemblages of Greek letters might thus find a third use as distinguishing irreducibly diverse but interrelated capacities that find their seat in our intellects. Or, if you prefer, taken together they characterize an aspect of the power of thought, which is itself single. In the elaboration of this system of forms of thought the individual subject might thus be said to gain inter alia a certain sort of intellectual self-consciousness.

At the same time, though, I can hardly represent myself as a bearer of intellect, that is, as a potential grasper of thoughts, unless I can think myself capable of registering what could be *true* through the exercise of this power. I must hold myself at least capable of grasping a particular thought through which, in accordance with some given predicative form it possesses, I might be said to think of something, and to think that it is something—where this latter is something that the former indeed is. (In relational cases I will think *of some things* that they are something, that is, are thus and so related.) I must hold this even if I frame the hypothesis that maybe everything I actually think is false, or indeed that most of the operations or would-be operations of my intellect fail even to grasp thoughts, because, for example, they are linked to the reception of empty words. None of these skeptical possibilities are any offence against the diverse forms of predication we have considered, taken by themselves, or their aptness to contain truth.

Pressing the copula into service after the fashion characteristic of Aristotle's *Categories* and ensuing "metaphysical" enquiry, we can hardly then fail to find a fourth use of our list as denominating diverse inassimilable *forms of being*—forms, that is, of something's being something, or (in the relational cases) of some things' being something. These reflections will also lead us to the familiar division of Fregean 'categories', a division to which Frege attaches the highest importance. The distinction of categories corresponds to the distinction among the Greek letters our table employs (as we have so far developed it). The category *Object/Gegenstand* corresponds to "ξ" and "ζ" as we were using them; *Concept/Begriff* corresponds to "φ"; *Relation* corresponds to "ψ"; *Second-level concept* corresponds to "Φ"; and so forth. This division of categories is a division of *forms of what can be*, that is, *forms of what can be something*. Given the iterative character of Frege's approach it will follow that all but the first are also forms of *what some thing or things can be*. Our own question will thus be whether the resulting table, or tree, of categories is complete.

Note that the category-word "object", as Frege uses it, itself names a perfectly good particular occupant of his category *Concept/Begriff*; a content to be placed alongside, say, the one expressed by the words "slightly warm". An object can *be slightly warm*, and, on the other hand, an object can *be an object*. Similarly, the word "concept", as Frege (rather ill-advisedly) uses it, names a perfectly good particular occupant of his category *Second-level concept*. (The case is quite different with the word "category" as I am using it: it cannot be assigned a content that falls into any of the categories under discussion; my use of the word thus raises the sort of difficulty Frege addresses in "On Concept and Object" and which so much exercised Wittgenstein in the *Tractatus;* but the point that the word "category" might belong to a ladder that must be thrown away does nothing to affect the particular category-concepts Frege introduces; the *Tractatus* has an objection to these concepts, too, but it has a quite different basis.) Despite the fact that "object" and "concept" can thus be assigned particular determinate (higher) category-occupying contents, the procedure through which the words are introduced shows that the concepts (in our contemporary sense) expressed by them—the concepts through which we grasp those particular (higher) category occupants—are not empirical concepts. We may say that Frege's implicit account of our possession of these concepts rather depicts them as arising in any given subject from reflection on the pure or logical forms of the thoughts or judgments she is capable of grasping—the forms of truth that she is capable, on a happy day, of receiving. The division of 'categories' will thus be resistant to the sort of empirical criticism that might be raised against a taxonomy of fundamental particles or of terrestrial organisms; opposition to the division, like elucidation of it, must take place entirely within philosophy.

This is exactly the status I am aiming to claim for the (very partial) division effected by the concepts that I am taking as setting my theme: *life-form, organism, agent, action, practice,* etc. Each concept captures a "category of being", if you like, and is certified as pure or *a priori* by its connection with a certain sort of reflection on the peculiar turns that thought, as thought, can take. Frege's system enforces a restricted or impoverished 'interpretation of being'—that is, an impoverished conception of the formal possibilities of something's being something— and thus a restricted doctrine of so-called categories. The success of my own program will thus turn on my capacity to convince the reader that certain classes of complete contentful thoughts share forms not found on a list like Frege's, forms which, unlike ξ *ran over* ζ and like $\psi(\xi, \zeta)$, are nevertheless pure. It is clear that we should not let ourselves be distracted by the fact that many of the concrete thoughts we will consider in this light will *also* exhibit this or that Fregean form. If a thought can exhibit two or more Fregean forms, as Frege insists it can, there is no reason for thinking it cannot exhibit a Fregean form but also another, non-Fregean form of a type we are proposing to uncover.

Any detailed development of this idea must be left for the three appended investigations themselves. But we may say that the thoughts exhibiting these alleged non-Fregean forms of thought or predication will mostly be marked off in the first instance by the peculiar types of *generality* and *temporality* they exhibit. The peculiarities of these types of generality and temporality will emerge especially from a meditation on the relation the thoughts in question, and their elements, bear to other thoughts exhibiting these same and other forms—it is here that the allegedly Aristotelian aspect of the material will emerge.

Thus in the discussion of life, much will turn on the status of so-called *natural-historical judgments* and the connected systems into which such judgments are fitted to enter, as well as the diverse related forms of judgment into which the elements from which they are constituted are themselves fitted to enter. Natural-historical judgments can be formulated in human languages in diverse ways, for example, "bobcats breed in spring" or "the domestic cat has four legs" or "it belongs to a Texas bluebonnet to carry nitrogen-fixing bacteria in nodes on its roots." The judgments just expressed evidently differ in content, but they intuitively share something as well—and this, I think, cannot be shoehorned under any Fregean rubric. I will argue for the naive view that thoughts expressed in these sentences exhibit a common form of predication: I am thinking "of" *bobcat* or *bobcats* or *the bobcat* in the first judgment—it doesn't matter how you say it—and of *Texas bluebonnet* in the last. This un-Fregean form of predication is just as direct as that found in parallel predications about individual organisms, as when I say, for example, that *this* bobcat bred last spring or that *this* bluebonnet has nitrogen-fixing bacteria in its roots. The natural-historical judgment registers a novel and un-Fregean shape that something's being something can take. The category occupied by the 'thing thought of' in such thoughts (and which thus enters potentially into cases of being something that takes this shape) may be expressed by the word "life-form". Thus even if our actual possession of the concept *life-form* arises with experience, it need not be thought to arise from it; its content is rather supplied by reflection on certain possibilities of thought or predication.

⟶ THOUGH THEY SHARE SOME features with singular judgments, natural-historical judgments are clearly also in some sense *general.* For example, they can enter into what we might call judgments of exemplification, as any Fregean generality could—that is, their linguistic expression can be continued with the words "for example . . ." If we think of the totality of possible "examples" appendable to a general judgment, we may think of the general judgment as bringing what is expressed in these many judgments under a kind of unity; thus the deviant generality of the natural-historical judgment brings into our thoughts a specific *form* of unity of one thing with another. The peculiar *temporality* of the natural-historical judgment makes a crude first appearance in just this connection. Even where the natural-historical judgment intuitively contains *absolutely nothing* pertaining to the past, still, the exemplifying judgment *can* pertain to the past: we say, "bobcats breed in spring—for example, this bobcat bred last spring." Frege's generalities cannot exhibit this phenomenon, though others, not of this specific kind, do—for example, the judgments articulating practices and dispositions that will be met with in the last part of this work.

The discussion of action will similarly turn on the peculiar *temporality* of the judgments in which it is recorded. I might at the moment express any of the three very different thoughts *Jones is walking across the street, Jones was walking across the street* and *Jones walked across the street.* Any account of these thoughts must exhibit them as containing at least two elements in common, viz., those expressed in language by the word "Jones" and the verb phrase "to walk across the street". The problem for Frege is to give a Fregean account of these common thought-elements, and then to press the respect in which they differ into Fregean form. It is natural to suggest that the first judgment contains a reference to the present moment, and relates Jones to it, and then to suggest that the second judgment contains quantification over temporal instants or past temporal instants. (One might then affirm, quite reasonably, that quantification over a structured manifold of temporal instants must involve empirical materials, and thus that the difference between these judgments rests on something empirical.) Such an account, I suggest, will have difficulty accounting for the existence of the third judgment and its difference from the second. Meditation on the third form and some of the inferences in which it figures might lead to the doctrine that it involves quantification over a manifold of events (understood perhaps as an empirically given class of objects): the judgment says that one of these objects is "by Jones" and a "walk across the street". Such a doctrine, I suggest, will run into difficulties accounting for the other two judgments—which are, on reflection, consistent with the non-existence of any such event. The conclusion toward which I aim is again the naive one that we have to do in such judgments with three distinctive but coeval forms of thought or predication. The 'thing thought of' in true thoughts of these three forms is thereby marked as falling under the category *individual substance*, as we might put it; meditation on the single element diversely predicated in these diverse thoughts will similarly lead us to introduce a category of *event- or process-form*. (How I propose to develop these ideas further, toward an account of the concepts *agent, action, intention* and *wanting*, will be seen.) That *the three thoughts differ though the two contentful elements joined are exactly the same* is part of what blocks the way to a correct account. It is a fundamental feature of the Fregean approach to what I am calling predication, founded as it was on an analogy with the formation of functional expressions in mathematics, that nothing like this can be found in it. There are never two ways of combining a numeral and a one-place functional expression without further contentful material. There is a sense in which the whole idea of a Fregean syntax, or of a 'categorial grammar', in the sense of Ajdukiewicz and Lewis, must tend to exclude the phenomena we are interested in. If, in an extended *Begriffsschrift*, I attempt to mark the threefold distinction of judgments by introducing three signs to distinguish the sentences expressing them, these signs will be syncategorematic in the classical sense—a status unknown in Frege's actual system of representation, in which every elementary sign purports to have a reference.

Nevertheless, I want to insist, the reflection that leads to the doctrines I am propounding belongs to the same order as Frege's reflections did, and thus the Aristotelianism I hope to develop is a Fregean or analytic one. In any case, this is my struggle.

~ PART ONE

The Representation of Life

∼ 1

Introductory

1. Logic and Life

Among the many scandalous features of Hegel's table, or 'system', of logical categories, we would nowadays want, I think, to accord high rank to this, that he finds a place for the concept *life* on it. Hegel is of course not blind to the counter-intuitive character of his teaching on this point. In his *Science of Logic*, the chapter headed "Life" begins by considering an objection to any specifically *logical* treatment of the notion of the sort he proposes to give. Something in the objection, at least, might still find favor today:

> The idea of life is concerned with a subject matter so concrete, and if you will so real, that with it we may seem to have overstepped the domain of logic as it is commonly conceived. Certainly, if logic were to contain nothing but empty, dead forms of thought, there could be no mention in it at all of such a content as the idea of life.[1]

1. *Hegel's Science of Logic*, trans. A. V. Miller (London: Allen and Unwin, 1969), p. 761. (I have omitted certain initial capitals.) Hegel's response to the objection he is posing is unfortunately of doubtful value, or in any case too little developed. He says that logic is concerned with cognition, and that cognition is life; therefore, etc. This gets us nowhere unless the first premise means that *cognition* is itself one of the logical categories, alongside, say, *being* and *quantity*. This may be true, but the premise is only uncontentious if it expresses the weaker traditional view that the logical categories are the forms of thought or cognition.

25

We may set aside the lyrical opposition of life's golden branches and poor, gray, lifeless theory, a favorite object of Hegelian ridicule. Even if there *are* special 'forms of thought' allied to the concept of life, it is anyway hard to see how they would be any more or less *dead* than those linked to the concepts of, say, being and quantity.

If the tendentious rhetoric is dropped, the objection Hegel is contemplating can be expounded in a series of apparent truisms. For logic, if tradition can be trusted, relates to the *form* of thought—a form of inference, for example, or the 'logical form' of a judgment. 'Form' here is of course opposed to *content*, a distinction that begins to become explicit for us when we learn to use schematic letters of different types and to substitute other expressions for them. How the distinction is to be further elaborated, and how exactly logic is supposed to 'relate' to the associated notion of form, are admittedly matters for dispute. But let them be resolved as one likes: how can anyone pretend that *thought about living things* differs in any such respect from, say, *thought about planets?*

After all, *living things, organisms, are just some among the concrete individuals we think about, marked off from the others in quite definite ways.* The word "life" is meant to capture these points of distinction. It therefore expresses one of those "particular characteristics of objects" which, according to Frege (here following tradition), logic must "disregard".[2] We could hardly have said the same about the ultra-abstract, bare-bones distinctions of category that Frege himself introduces, for example, that between *Begriff* and *Gegenstand,* concept and object. If the former sort of thing were marked out within a wider class (the class of *entities*, as it is inevitably called) by the possession of some 'particular characteristic' (which we express, maybe, by calling the things "unsaturated"), then there would have been no problem about the concept *horse.*[3]

If, then, we conceive or judge or infer differently in connection with the living, it is just that we conceive and judge and infer different things. It is no use to affirm that life is an 'essential property' of whatever has it—or that maybe 'being' is a basic category of thought and

2. Gottlob Frege, *Begriffsschrift,* trans. Stefan Bauer-Mengelberg, in *From Frege to Gödel,* ed. Jean van Heijenoort (Cambridge, Mass.: Harvard University Press, 1967).

3. See especially "On Concept and Object," trans. Peter Geach, reprinted in *Collected Papers,* ed. Brian McGuinness (Oxford: Blackwell, 1984), pp. 182–194.

vivere viventibus est esse. "Metal" and "monocotyledon" arguably express essential properties of whatever satisfies them; and if 'to be, for living things, is to live', then presumably also being, for a cockroach, is being a cockroach, or living a roach's life. If any of these concepts sets the theme for a theoretical discussion, then the discussion must fall under one of the special sciences. A properly *logical* discourse would have to be carried on under some more abstract heading, for example, "individuals", "relations", "properties"—perhaps even "being" or "essential properties"—but "life" and "organism", never.

I propose to attack this sort of conception, and to make a beginning of what amounts to a logical treatment of the idea of life, and its near relatives, and their expression in language. Hegel, I think, was so far right. Thought, *as thought*, takes a quite special turn when it is thought of the living—a turn *of the same kind* as that noticed by Frege in the transition from thought of an object to thought of a concept, from *Aristotle is wise* to *The wise are few*.[4]

2. Ethics and Life

But why treat such an abstract and apparently extra-practical topic in a work that claims an orientation toward the ethical? The simple answer is of course that an appeal to notions of life and organism and life-form would seem to be implicit in all departments of ethical thought. For example: intentional, thought-applying, concept-exercising *action* is on any view the principal theme of ethical theory. But action in this sense is a specific form of *life process*, as we may say, and a proper comprehension of it will surely rest on seeing it as coming under the latter category, and thus on an elucidation of the wider category itself (the beginning of such an elucidation is attempted in the following chapters). *Will* we may call the capacity to be the subject of life processes of that more determinate type; *practical reason* is the inevitably concomitant ca-

4. Throughout this discussion I take Frege's above-mentioned remarks on concept and object as a paradigmatic elucidation of a 'distinction of logical category'. It may be that this commits me to a somewhat eccentric employment of the phrase, though I believe my usage merely develops a certain aspect of the traditional idea. It is one of the lessons taught by Ludwig Wittgenstein, if I understand him, that we must recognize many intuitively more determinate distinctions *of the sort Frege introduced*. Wittgenstein of course calls the corresponding sort of distinction among *signs* a "grammatical difference".

pacity for one's thoughts to bear suitably on *such* life processes. It is moreover natural to think that these interwoven powers, like the capacity to perceive, can only belong to an individual thing, the agent, as the bearer of a specific *life-form*—or, as we might say, according to its 'species'.[5] Thus it seems that an elaboration of the nature of action and agency will at the same time be the elaboration of a certain turn that determinate life-forms can take—namely, where they are determinate forms of rational life, such as the specifically *human* form, a phenomenon of terrestrial evolutionary history, is forever being said by its bearers to be.

A meditation on agency that developed this line of thought would belong to practical philosophy broadly construed, but not to its specifically ethical aspect. It would not reach the question of what makes the will good, or action fine, or what reasons we have to do or want to do things, at least where these are not simply a matter of the orientation of the prospective action to some further objective already in view. But concepts like *life* and *life-form* inevitably enter even into the properly ethical parts of practical philosophy. Kant's supreme practical principle is supposed to attach to practical reason somehow generally considered—that is, as something that appears in people, Martians, God and angels alike. But in order to get much of anywhere in ethical thinking, Kant is forced, in the *Metaphysics of Morals*, to consider systematically how this principle 'applies' to specifically human beings, that is, to fellow bearers of the terrestrial life-form or species that he himself exhibits. So even here concepts allied to those of *life* and *life-form* make themselves felt.

A more interesting, because more radical, appeal to these concepts—especially that of a life-form or species—is made in a certain tendency

---

5. I will be using the words "life-form" and "species" more or less equivalently in what follows, with some ambivalence noted as the occasion arises. The latter expression is used in empirical science and might reasonably be given over to it, but it should be remembered that the English words "form" and "species" arise from philosophy, in particular from Latin translations of Aristotle's *eidos*. The principal difference between them, from the present point of view, is in associated ideas: in thinking of a particular species, I will imagine a manifold of individuals outside and alongside one another; in thinking of a particular life-form, I will imagine one individual, the image having the standing of, say, a picture in a field guide. This difference does not affect the underlying mode of conception contained in either expression, and arises from the fact that what falls under them cannot really be an object of *imagination* at all.

in contemporary ethical Aristotelianism.[6] We may view this line of thought as beginning with the idea, just mentioned, that will and practical reason are on the face of it just two more faculties or powers a living being may bear, on a level with the powers of sight and hearing and memory. The second crucial thought is that an individual instance of any of the latter powers—sight, hearing, memory—is intuitively to be judged as defective or sound, good or bad, well-working or ill-working, by reference to its bearer's life-form or kind or species. So, for example, a house cat's visual capacity is, one gathers, not to be remarked upon, if it cannot apprehend the ripening of a banana, though that of a human being would be. This is not simply because the individual cat in question is unlikely to share its owner's interest in the ripeness of bananas, but because of the difference in kind or form or species, or because of what each of them is. In estimating the soundness of an individual cat's vision I do not bring it to a measure or standard appropriate to all beings, or all perceiving beings, or all visually perceiving beings, but to a measure or standard appropriate precisely to all domestic cats.[7] The neo-Aristotelian idea I am considering proposes to bring these two thoughts together in order to provide an interpretation of the fundamental 'normative' concepts with which human practical thought inevitably operates.

Now, in the works of will and practical reason we have to do with movement in quite different categories, in some sense, from those of mere sensibility. But, then, sensibility seems to differ just as radically from the sub-psychical, merely vegetative aspects of life; and yet absolutely parallel remarks could be made about the criteria of soundness and defect in the parts and operations of individual plants. Why, then, should the novel character of will and practical rationality prevent our again according to the *kind* or *form* or *species* some of the status that it seemed to possess in respect of the 'lower' faculties?

6. Here I am thinking especially of the concluding pages of G. E. M. Anscombe's essay "Modern Moral Philosophy," *Philosophy* 33 (1958): 1–19; the last part of Rosalind Hursthouse's *On Virtue Ethics* (Oxford: Oxford University Press, 1999); and above all Philippa Foot's book *Natural Goodness* (Oxford: Oxford University Press, 2001).

7. It will be plain that this is not to deny that we might have use for some such judgments as that the visual capacity characteristic of one kind of sighted animal is better, because more discriminating, than that characteristic of another kind of sighted animal.

And so, for example, if we care to contemplate kinds of reasoning animals other than our own, as Kant constantly implicitly did, shouldn't we be prepared also to imagine different shapes of practical reason, subject to different standards of defect—that is, of *irrationality* or *practical unreason*, which on an Aristotelian sort of account are particular forms that defect may take in this sort of case?[8] And similarly, moving in the other direction: whatever place is to be given the picturesque customs of the world and to peoples' 'projects' and the like in reckoning what is rational or practically sound in individual cases, mightn't there be some larger, thinner, more generic measure of practical rationality that is the same for all who are of our same kind? Certainly we seem to presuppose our possession of such a measure in our willingness to criticize certain projects and customs as completely unreasonable, or as unsound or twisted. But, given the possibility opened up by this sort of Aristotelianism, there would seem to be no reason to insist on interpreting ourselves as in possession of any measure that could be granted a further cosmic or even supra-cosmic scope, as Kant did. And if something in the way of justice, for example, is perchance a part of the life characteristic of the specifically human kind—and this, on the imagined account, would be what we commit ourselves to in assigning some kind of 'normative authority' to certain types of *consideration about other agents*—then won't its presence in a person's thinking be among the marks of a sound practical reason that are associated with our kind—associated, that is, with *what we are*, taken in a certain life-related sense?[9] It will perhaps be impossible, after all, to effect the separation required to make it a great question whether morality in general is rational.

---

8. It is sometimes said that we do not envisage bumping into thinking animals who exhibit fundamentally different forms of theoretical reason and that this must be a ground for rejecting the idea that forms of practical reason might differ radically from one another. This is to forget that in representing a given animal as a bearer of theoretical reason, I represent it as representing the same world I do; I do not represent it as living the same life I do, or as exhibiting the same form of life.

9. I attempt to say something to characterize a specifically Aristotelian approach to the virtue of justice, distinguishing it from Humean and Kantian accounts, in "What Is It to Wrong Someone?," in *Reason and Value*, ed. R. J. Wallace, M. Smith and P. Pettit (Oxford: Oxford University Press, 2004).

3. Ethics and Logic

It would take a treatise or two to develop such thoughts properly, but one need not enter into details. The slightest movement in such a direction is enough to set off alarms in many quarters. Some of the likely objections are notoriously difficult to understand: for example, that when it comes to treat moral questions such a line of thought must inevitably commit the naturalistic fallacy, or pretend to supply materials for a would-be derivation of 'ought' from 'is'. Other types of resistance involve a wrong idea of the place of controversy—it will be thought, for example, that the tendency must aim not at an elucidation of the fundamental normative concepts we inevitably employ in practical thought, but rather at an axiom from which particular practical principles (inevitably illiberal ones) would then be derived, and that the proponent's next step will be to prove that, say, usury and contraception are 'wrong' because 'unnatural'.

But the objection I think I understand and want to take seriously starts from the thought that in employing such notions as *life* and *organism* and *life-form* or *species* we introduce something *foreign*, in particular something 'biological', or crudely empirical, into the elements of ethical theory. Any such view, one thinks, must involve either a vulgar scientistic dissolution of the ethical, tending maybe toward an 'evolutionary ethics', or else the covert substitution of an outdated metaphysics for what we know to be empirical. Each path leads to its own absurdities. Together they may be thought to betray a yearning to view our practices 'from outside' or 'from sideways on' in hope perhaps of providing them with a foundation or an external grounding.

It is, I think, to be granted that ethical theory, in all its departments, is in a certain sense conceptually fastidious, and that there is here again a sin of 'overstepping' akin to that Hegel noticed in connection with logical theory, and that the formulation of basic ethical principles, for example, is contaminated by concepts that come our way through a purely scientific and empirical development. This, if it is right, is not a consequence of some more general crime of struggling to 'get beyond our practices' or 'outside our language' or what you will, but a specifically ethical truth. It is what Rousseau meant when he said that one shouldn't have to make a man a *philosophe* before making him a man,[10] and what Kant presupposed in shrugging off the criticism that his *Groundwork* proposed no new moral principle, but only a new formula.[11]

But suppose that the concepts *life*, *organism* and *life-form* really are logical determinations, and that some such primitive practical concept as, say, *action* belongs to the sphere they govern, and is not itself to be castigated as a novelty or a foreign body, something that is alien to the point of view of practical thought. Then the employment of such concepts within ethical theory would merely make articulate something already implicit in *pensée sauvage practique*—and it might seem that a so-called neo-Aristotelian is looking at things head on, not sideways on.

10. *Discourse on the Origin of Inequality*, Preface.

11. "Who would want to introduce a new principle, and as it were, be its inventor, as if the world had hitherto been ignorant of what duty is, or had been thoroughly wrong about it?," *Critique of Practical Reason*, Preface, trans. Lewis White Beck (Indianapolis: Bobbs-Merrill, 1958), p. 8.

～ 2

Can Life Be Given a Real Definition?

1. 'Signs of Life'

I want to begin by raising difficulties for one of the thoughts I took for granted in articulating Hegel's objection to his own proceeding—namely, the apparently innocent idea that *living things are just some among the concrete individuals we think about, marked off from the others in quite definite ways.* If this is right, then the word "life" expresses a 'particular characteristic of [those] objects', in Frege's phrase, and presumably not their logical category.

The question forced upon us by this thought—what the supposed characteristic marks of the concept *life* might actually be—is not one that much exercises contemporary philosophers as philosophers. We may say of the problem what Frege said of investigations into the concept *number*—another 'concept fundamental to a mighty science':

> Admittedly, many people will think this not worth the trouble. Naturally, they will suppose, this concept is adequately dealt with in the elementary textbooks, where the subject is settled once and for all. Who can believe that he has anything still to learn on so simple a matter?[1]

---

1. Frege, *Foundations of Arithmetic*, trans. J. L. Austin (Oxford: Blackwell, 1980), p. iii.

33

I want to consider just such an *Elementarbuch*, a typical college freshman's biology text.

In her book *Biology*, Professor Helena Curtis supplies us with a special illustrated section, separated off from the main text and labeled "The Signs of Life":

> What do we mean when we speak of "the evolution of life", or "life on other planets" or "when life begins"? Actually, there is no simple definition. Life does not exist in the abstract; there is no "life", only living things. We recognize a system as being alive when it has certain properties that are more common among animate objects than inanimate ones. Let us take a look at some of these properties.

Here the apparently innocent thought is frankly expressed, and the associated task of expounding *Merkmale* is gladly shouldered. There turn out to be seven of them. "Living things," she tells us, "are *highly organized.*" They are "*homeostatic,* which means simply 'staying the same.'" They "*grow and develop*" and are "*adapted.*" They "*take energy from the environment and change it from one form to another,*" and they "*respond to stimuli.*" Finally, of course, "[l]iving things *reproduce themselves.*"[2]

It may seem a bit odd to take casual remarks from the opening pages of a textbook and make them the starting point for one's reflection, but consider Frege's remark quoted above, and his method throughout the *Grundlagen*. Professor Curtis's discussion is not really casual. A random survey of college bookstores will show that her list is one of many, all of them apparently distant progeny of some *Ur*-list, a Q-document for which one searches in vain, but which we find repeated again and again, subject to whatever improvements occur to the immediate author.[3] A certain type of context, at once introductory and reflective, seems to at-

2. Helena Curtis, *Biology*, 3rd ed. (New York: Worth, 1979), pp. 20–21. I choose this book for sentimental reasons, but, as I remark below, any number of others might of course have been chosen.

3. Moritz Schlick introduced such a list into philosophy already in lectures of 1927, attributing it to "Wilhelm Roux, the founder of so-called developmental mechanics [who] says: A body is living if it possesses the following characteristics: 1) Metabolism . . . ; 2) Growth; 3) Active movement . . . ; 4) Reproduction . . . ; 5) Inheritance . . . ," but he unfortunately supplies no reference to Roux's works. The idea of such a list must have arisen during the vitalist-mechanist debates. See Schlick's *Philosophy of Nature*, trans. A. von Zeppelin (New York: Philosophical Library, 1949), p. 73ff.

tract this kind of thing. Perhaps there is no Q-document to uncover, but even if there is one, possession of it would only supply a superficial explanation of this peculiar tradition. We would still have to explain the fact that the list gets *repeated*, with variation, and that no one worries where the idea of such a thing came from, and that it all seems so obvious. The source of the repetition of such lists—a certain form of philosophical unconscious, I suppose—is the true original of any one of them, as also of the rare more learned account, and it is, I hope, the real focus of my remarks.[4]

But let us return to our token of this type, Professor Curtis's list. Troubles begin even before we consider the several properties adduced: what does she mean to be saying about them? She is linking an expression for life or organism with a number of predicates in unquantified propositions: "Living things are F." What form of judgment is being expressed? One of the hints she gives us is clearly mistaken—*baldness*, *bad manners* and *home ownership* are all "more common among animate objects than inanimate ones," but presumably none was a candidate for inclusion. She seems to allow that the properties she retails are neither collectively sufficient nor severally necessary for the 'system' that bears them to count as alive; are they meant to illustrate a system of 'family resemblances'? And are we doing metaphysics or epistemology? She calls the properties "signs" of life, and speaks of how "we recognize a system as being alive"; but the inner tendency of such a list is surely toward a real definition, a metaphysical analysis, a teaching about 'what life consists in'—in any case, something on the order of criteria, not symptoms.

We may prescind from this obscurity: the reasons for it will emerge, I think, from a discussion of the individual members of the list.

2. Organization

Nothing is more common than to make *life* a matter of organization, order, structure or complexity. Professor Curtis will be no exception. She writes: "Living organisms are highly organized, as in this cross sec-

---

4. The idea of using this tradition of list-making as a clue to the typical contemporary *Lebensweltanschauung*, so to speak, is also employed by Gareth Matthews, who rightly contrasts these lists with the familiar and seemingly similar list produced by Aristotle. See his "*De Anima* 2. 2–4 and the Meaning of *Life*," in *Essays on Aristotle's De Anima*, ed. M. Nussbaum and A. Rorty (Oxford: Clarendon, 1992), pp. 185–193.

tion of a pine needle. It reflects the complicated organization of many different kinds of atoms into molecules and of molecules into complex structures. Such complexity of form is never found in inanimate objects." It is worth enquiring, though, how the intended notion of organization is supposed to work. Is it meant to cover the organization of parts in an animal, of parts in a car, of words on a page, of people in a factory, of molecules in a crystal? If the notion is so abstract, then I think we can have little reason to think that there is any one consistent measure of more-and-less in respect of it. Is the administration of the University of Pittsburgh more highly organized than, say, a Buick or the Hope diamond, or more complex than the rules of chess? Any of these would at best make an unhappy metaphor. But I suppose the lament of a 1950s auto mechanic, faced suddenly with a recent Volkswagen, would have straightforward content.

Now, Professor Curtis mentions that atoms and molecules are among the elements organized, and later on that "living things take energy from the environment" and so forth. This might suggest that we have to do with a determinate conception of organization after all, namely, that sometimes said to be implicit in thermodynamic theorizing. This interpretation would perhaps supply a determinate scale; and, if it does make sense, we can happily allow that the physical contents of the regions of space occupied by terrestrial organisms tend to take on its higher values—I mean, in relation to other things we know of.

Is it perverse, though, to remind ourselves that fresh corpses are not alive, and yet have presumably lost little in the respect measured on the relevant physical scale? Suppose we freeze a bunch of camels' corpses, and arrange them for art's sake in a sort of flying wedge, hurtling toward Alpha Centauri; could the adventitious *arrangement* supply, for the whole, what the individuals lost with death? The thought seems perverse because, but for a camel's life, we have no camel-carcass, and anyhow the additional arrangement sprang from the allegedly awesome degree of order or organized complexity exhibited within our skulls—a part, that is, of *our* life. Should we say, then, that living things are *sources* of thermodynamically highly organized lumps of stuff? The 'living body' of an organism would be just one such highly organized precipitate of its life processes, alongside the nest or honeycomb or house it helps to build, and the dry leaves, paw prints or corpse it leaves behind. We would be characterizing the life-process by its physicalistically intelligible and salient results.

But do we really know that nothing else can bring the results about, or that if something else can, it must be rarer, on a cosmic scale, than living things are? Even if we do know these things, or managed to find them out, it would be wrong, I think, to incorporate this knowledge into a list of the type we are hoping to construct.

To see the difficulty, it may help to consider another proposed list-occupant. Professor Ernst Mayr, in a somewhat differently motivated "tabulation" (as he calls it), puts our present topic, "Complexity and Organization," just ahead of something he calls "Chemical Unique-ness." In explaining the latter he says: "These organic molecules [to wit, those from which terrestrial organisms are composed] do not differ in principle from other molecules. They are, however, far more com-plex than the low molecular weight molecules that are the regular con-stituents of inanimate nature. These larger organic macromolecules are not normally found in inanimate matter."[5] Now, it is true that if we were sending a probe to Mars to search out 'signs of life', we might have it test for the presence of 'large organic macromolecules'. But then, we might have it test for the likes of *DNA* in particular. One sup-poses that "Living things contain DNA" might hold good even on a cosmic scale—perhaps we could discover that there is no other way to get this sort of thing going, given the physical constitution of 'our universe'; it has to be exactly so. But even then no one would hope to improve on the tradition by incorporating mention of DNA into one of these lists. The judgment about DNA, if it were true, would only show how resource-poor the physical world really is. It could make no contribution to the exposition of the concept of life, or to a teaching on the question, what life is—except perhaps as pointing to a few gorillas and turnips might. The ends of our sort of list, however obscure they may be, point to something more abstract and would clearly be contravened by it.

But does mention of DNA differ fundamentally from a sparer appeal to 'large organic macromolecules'? Not at all, it seems. Appeal to what is, after all, a *particular physical quantity*, thermodynamic order or orga-nization—though it be that much more abstract—is evidently in the same boat as either of them.

The point would be easier to make if we could say that God and the

5. *The Growth of Biological Thought* (Cambridge, Mass.: Harvard University Press, 1982), p. 54.

angels are 'living things' if they are anything, and that physical concepts hardly have a place in the analysis of *their* kinds of life.[6] But in the
context of the present essay, and the relevant sort of list, "living thing"
means *organism*. This narrower focus does not, however, supply a pre-
text for the importation of empirical physical concepts—as a further
narrowing to, say, *mammal, primate* or *gorilla* might. I do not know
whether the theological proposition *Not everything that lives is an organism* is really coherent; but on the tradition according to which it is, and
is true, the specific difference of the organism was marked in a number
of ways, hands left clean of the empirical. One said, for example, that
organisms *are composite*, or *have parts*.

Let us return, then, to the thought from which we started—that the
unsubscripted notion of order or organization is a very abstract or generic one, and that, left abstract, it does not make sense to think of a
standard of more-and-less in respect of it. We have, on the one hand,
the concept or idea of organization, and, on the other, a number of
conceptions, determinations, types or genera of it. If a remark of the
form "A is organized," or "A exhibits a more complex organization
than B," is to express a definite thought, it must isolate one of these.
Which do we have in view in making our list, then, if not the allegedly
thermodynamic one—and if it is 'quality' and not the 'quantity' of order that matters? The obvious answer is that the relevant conception is
simply equivalent to the idea of life: to be alive is to be *organ*-ized; to be
alive is to be a subject of, say, 'vital organization'. Or if, as we were just
imagining, a living thing needn't be an organism, then the thought
should rather be that *organisms* are in that sense organized; or, equivalently, that if a life is a life-with-parts, then this form of order must prevail among these parts. Whatever else our list of criteria may contain,
then, it is plain that this one is adding *nothing* to it.

The formula "Living things have parts," which has seemed a little
too obvious to merit a career as a list-occupant, is evidently closely
related to the thought that living things are organized: the parts are
the elements that are arranged or ordered. But if the notion of order or
organization is abstract, the notion of part is as much so: we need to
supply a subscript before the suggestion that living things have either
of them can express a definite thought. Our language, feeling this need,

6. See, e.g., Aquinas, *Summa Theologiae*, I, q. 18.

sometimes permits the subscripts to be supplied non-contextually through certain uses of the words "organ" and "member" and "tissue"—though these terms are all perhaps most apt in connection with sensitive or animal life, as words for *partes animalium*.

I said that no one would append the like of "Living things contain DNA" to a list of the sort we are considering, even given suitable physical hypotheses. No one would add, "Living things have parts, in the sense of organs" either, but for another reason. Will he or she follow the cautious Professor Mayr and remark, in the scholium, that organs are "not normally found in inanimate matter"? My suggestion will be that *every* candidate list-occupant must strike the sub-metaphysical Scylla of "DNA" or else sink into the tautological Charybdis of "organs", and that every such list may as well be replaced by the empty list.

3. Stimulus and Response

Before pausing to reflect on these matters, I want to move on to some of Helena Curtis's other criteria. Two of them seem to me to belong together. First, an underwater scene:

> Living things respond to stimuli. Here scallops, sensing an approaching starfish, leap to safety.

And now the forest, as an owl descends open-clawed upon a mouse:

> Living things take energy from the environment and change it from one form to another. They are highly specialized at energy conversion. Here a saw-whet owl is converting chemical energy to kinetic energy, thereby procuring a new source of chemical energy, in this case a white-footed mouse.

Again there is a problem of understanding. Are we to say, for example, that the asphalt on a summer day "takes energy" from sunlight, and "converts" it into heat? And is an avalanche, on the other hand, the "response" of a snow-covered hillside to the "stimulus" of, say, excessive yodeling?

But before considering what can be made of these rhetorical questions, I want to raise a few objections to the given formulations. First, it is clear that the notion of 'response' employed in the first criterion *must* apply not just to *the leaping of threatened scallops*, but also, for example, to *the effect of spring warming on the buds of maple trees*. Otherwise the notion will be left covering a phenomenon merely of sentient or animal life. It would thus acquire the standing of baldness and bad manners— it would be a property uncommon even among the living, but all the same 'more common among the living than the non-living'. And notice further, in connection with the second criterion, that there is nothing really special about taking *energy* from the environment—she could as well have characterized the living as taking *stuff, matter,* from the environment, and converting *it* into other forms. Energy is after all just another physical quantity; if the considerations of the previous section are sound, then it is vulgar anyway to drag an expression for such a thing into the sort of account we are hoping to produce. Curtis's formulation of each of these particular criteria seems, then, to be defective. But what is the thought that tempts one to propound them, or anything like them?

Let us consider just the first criterion for the moment, the thought that living things 'respond to stimuli'. *The warming of an asphalt roadbed* and *the train of photosynthetic events in a green leaf* are both of them, in some sense, the effect of sunlight. And *the thawing of icy ponds* and *the opening of maple buds* are each occasioned by rising spring temperatures. It is natural, though, to think that the two vegetative phenomena belong together as instances of a special type of causal relation, or a causal relation with special conditions, distinct from any exhibited in asphalt or water. (The corresponding phenomena of sentient or animal life, those most aptly described in terms of 'stimulus' and 'response', belong to a subdivision of this type that need not specially concern us.) On the other hand, though, the effect of *the hydrogen bomb* on a rose, and on a roadbed, will be pretty much the same—at least if they are both at ground zero. I mean not only that the effects will be similar, but also that the type of causality will be the same. It is in a more restricted range of cases that we seem to see a difference, if the affected individual is an organism. I mean: sunlight makes the asphalt warm; moisture and cold make it crack; the H-bomb turns it to a vapor. These things are all on a level. The asphalt is in a sense passive in the face of any of them. But, in the familiar metaphors, the rose or maple is ready for certain of these 'influences'—rising spring temperatures, for example—it is already on to them, it takes advantage of them. Green leaves are not *subjected* to the light, if it is not too strong; they are not in the same sense passive in respect of it; the access of photons is not to be understood on a model of bombardment—that is, as it would have to be if we were discussing the fading of a book cover or the warming of a stone. This, I think, is the contrast one is trying to register, in placing 'responsiveness to stimuli' among the characteristic marks of the concept *life*.

If we attempt to put the thought less metaphorically, in terms of a notion of process, we come upon some surprising appearances. The arrival of spring, on the one hand, and of the photon, on the other—these events are meteorological and physical, and we can trace them back to their antecedents in the relation of the earth to the sun. But they are also phases of larger processes *in the plant*, just as the replication of yeast cells is part of a larger culinary-technical process, if it takes place in some sourdough. The rose and maple are subjects of processes of their own, which the meteorological or physical events merely complete or continue: the formation of leaves of a certain character, come spring, and the fixation of carbon in those leaves, once illuminated.

In learning of the various cellular processes unearthed and described in biochemistry—photosynthesis, for example, or the Krebs cycle, or the replication of DNA—one is inclined to think, It's all getting boiled down to chemistry and physics, isn't it?, and in some sense of 'boiling down' this is of course true and very desirable. But it is interesting that if the only categories we have to apply are those of chemistry and physics, there is an obvious sense in which *no such succession of goings-on will add up to a single process*. In a description of photosynthesis, for example, we read of one chemical process—one process-in-the-sense-of-chemistry, one "reaction"—followed by another, and then another. Having read along a bit with mounting enthusiasm, we can ask: "And what happens next?" If we are stuck with chemical and physical categories, the only answer will be: "Well, it depends on whether an H-bomb goes off, or the temperature plummets toward absolute zero, or it all falls into a vat of sulfuric acid . . ." That a certain enzyme will appear and split the latest chemical product into two is just one among many possibilities. Physics and chemistry, adequately developed, can tell you what happens in any of these circumstances—in *any* circumstance—but it seems that they cannot attach any sense to a question "What happens next?" *sans phrase*. The biochemical treatise thus appears to make implicit play with a special determination of the abstract conception of a process, one distinct from any expressed in physics or in chemistry proper.

If these traditional though perhaps rather metaphysical meditations are sound, then it is not just that 'the rose and maple are subjects of processes of their own': they are also subjects of a special type or category of process—'biological' processes, if you like, or 'life-processes'. The possibility of a biochemical discourse uniting large sequences of purely physical and chemical descriptions of things and events is enough to show that the illustrated 'life-processes' are not marked off from others by their *content*, which is here entirely physical or chemical in character, but precisely and only by their *form*. Whether such processes share a form of the sort to interest us in a logical investigation is a matter to be considered later.

The list-occupying notions of stimulus and response (which, as I have said, must be construed broadly so as to cover phenomena in the life of maple trees and blue-green algae) can be explained in terms of this type of process. The simplest explanation would involve a prior idea of events as coming respectively 'from outside' and 'from within' the thing stimulated and responding. Let us leave this commonsense distinction momentarily unanalyzed. Then, roughly, events will add up to stimulus and response if the first comes 'from outside' and the other 'from within' the subject of the events, and they are joined as elements of *this* form of process, a life-process, as I was calling it.

The receipt of photons and the formation of glucose, the rising temperature and the unfolding leaves, the apprehension of a starfish and the leaping away are all of them bound together in this sort of nexus— though the lattermost pair of events is also caught up in certain more determinate (psychological) categories. But the radiation cast off by the detonated H-bomb and the evaporation of a thing, whether it be asphalt or an organism, will not be so joined or united. This particular type of process or nexus, this *form of unity of events*—which, by the way, need not be sorted into those 'from without' and those 'from within': the phases of, say, the Krebs cycle or glycolysis are not—this is, I think, what is really at issue when 'stimulus and response' make it onto our kind of list. But, again, it is clear that with this thought we lose another list-occupant. A philosophical account of this form of unity and a philosophical account of life are at bottom the same: *such* processes are after all what goes on as life goes on.

4. Vital Operation

The same thought will perhaps be supposed to underlie that other list-occupying formula, "Living things take energy from the environment and convert it into other forms." For it is in the nature of our sort of enterprise, I said, to recoil from words for particular physical quantities. If we cleave to this principle and delete the reference to energy, we are left with a general schema of 'taking and converting'. And this, it might be argued, is itself only worth mentioning as an illustration of *events as bound together in a life-process.*

But perhaps everything that follows the word "energy" depends on it and should fall with it. The remaining thought would then simply be that *Living things take.* This is more a thought-fragment than a thought, but it suggests what is at least *prima facie* a different account of the idea that underlies the criterion we are mutilating: it is not that living things are the subjects of events falling into a certain form of process, but that they are subjects of a certain form of *agency.* It is the element of activity that is intended. We have to do, that is, not with a special *nexus of events,* but with a special *nexus of thing and event.*

The topics are obviously closely related, and another of Curtis's criteria, "Living things grow and develop," would seem to split itself between them. "Development" is another word for process, and it can only be a life-process that is intended. *Growth* involves a notion of increase in size, which, given certain very general but philosophically unmentionable facts of physical nature, would seem to be entailed by the demands of reproduction (a matter to be discussed latter). The rational kernel of such a criterion is just the *difference* between the growth of a chipmunk or a pine tree and the growth of, say, a trash heap—which difference has of course nothing to do with growth. The relevant nexus of thing and event is the one we intended above in speaking of an event as 'coming from within' a thing.

Now, the tactic of marking off a class of things by the special relation they may bear to some of the things they do—which doings are *ipso facto* 'doings' in some restricted and italicizable sense—is a familiar one.

Suppose, for example, that a certain thing can be said to will or intend some of what happens to it or some of what it does (in some broad sense), or that some of these happenings can be said to be caused by its intention or judgment in suitable ways. Then presumably we can call the thing a *person* or an *agent proper*, and dignify the events in question with a title of "intentional action" or even simply "action".

The notion of an animal and the notion of 'behavior' or 'animal movement'—*motus animalium*—might be given a parallel treatment, as forms of agent and agency. How does a bird's progress out of the stadium, where it has been mistaken for a fast ball, differ from a progress out in search of better food? It is usual to say that, in the one case, the bat moves the bird, and that, in the other, the bird *moves itself*. If this account of the difference is sound, then we may perhaps go on in good conscience to introduce some new expressions, granting a title of "animal" or "self-mover" to whatever is 'such a source of things', and applying the words "behavior" or "animal movement" to any event with that sort of source.

If, arguably, person = subject of intentional action and animal = subject of animal movement, then perhaps what the fragment "Living things take" really means to tell us is that living thing = subject of (say) 'vital operation'; this is our deeper reading of Curtis's intentions, or rather those of the tradition she represents.[7] And as person and animal are metaphysically distinctive forms of living thing, so presumably also *intentional action* and *animal movement* are metaphysically forms of vital operation. The traditional hierarchy of forms of life appears to correspond to a hierarchy of forms of agency.

I don't want to object to any of these identities. The question, once again, is whether anything like the third identity can rightly contribute anything to a real definition of its subject. As I have formulated them, the second and third equivalences would give an appearance of circularity if advanced as definitions, a fact that may be put down to my ten-

---

7. Gareth Matthews quotes a list of so-called basic characteristics of living things that includes the *responsiveness* we have already discussed, but also—and at first glance completely mysteriously—*movement* (Matthews, *De Anima*, p. 185). That the author Matthews quotes must have heard of the laws of falling bodies, on the one hand, and of deep-rooted trees, on the other, suggests the necessity of such a deeper reading; it is only the present broad form of 'agency' in respect of changes that can be intended. In the list Schlick quotes from Wilhelm Roux, the place of movement is thus taken by something called 'active movement' (see n. 3 above).

dentious nomenclature. After all, we have an explanation of 'animal movement' as *self-movement*. But is the explanation any good?

There is no question that a misunderstanding about which of the two sorts of bird-out-of-stadium cases one had intended can be cleared up with the words "No, no, it moved *itself*." If, however, we ask in philosophy what the difference is between the cases, then we mean to find the difference between such cases generally, and an appeal to 'self-movement' is not illuminating.[8] The reflexive is simply one of the means our language gives us for marking the different relation posited between subject and predicate, thing and event. It does not by itself tell us what this relation is.

It will perhaps help to see this if we remember that the relation of the bird to its movement was supposed to be somehow higher or more exalted in character in the no-bat case than in the other, and that, of course, the same special animal-event nexus can bind a bird and the movement of *something else*, a piece of straw, for example.[9] And, more obviously, the special relation between a bird and the movement of its own parts need not be severed if the movement can be said in some sense to spring from something other than the bird, suitable prey up yonder, for example. And in general, if A moves B, then the mereological sum of A and B in some sense moves itself, or some of itself. Some 'self-movement', then, is other-movement; some 'self-movement' is movement-by-another; and some non-'self-movement' is self-movement after all.

We are considering the special case of animals and animal movement for purposes of analogy, but in truth, I think, any attempt to mark the character of organisms in general by an employment of such prefixes as "self-" or "auto-"—as in, say, "self-reproduction", "self-organization" or "auto-regulation"—is for the same reason completely empty. The phrase to which the prefix is attached is always a distraction, and the whole problem is already contained in the reflexive; it should be re-

8. See a parallel remark in G. E. M. Anscombe, *Intention*, 2nd ed. (Cambridge, Mass.: Harvard University Press, 2000), p. 3.

9. It may be objected that a bird never moves straw, except by moving itself—that is to say, parts of itself. But if we refuse to take the idea of the limits of an animal's body for granted, and ask how it is settled *what is a part of it*, and *what is just stuck to it* or *what it is just holding* or *what, come to think of it, is really on the other side of the room*, then we will, I think, be forced to import the notion of 'animal movement' as something already understood.

placed in each case with some such transparently circle-making expression as "bio-", "biological" or "vital". The emptiness of a *philosophical* appeal to this reflexive is already shown by the fact that we incline to it in so many places—to distinguish the two types of growth, the two types of bird flight and even, in Kantian moral philosophy, two types of rational agency. At each link in the great chain of agency, activity, autonomy or spontaneity we employ the reflexive to introduce another 'higher' link; it is a finger pointing upward, yes, but we want to know what's up there.

If we must drop the special emphasis on the reflexive, then we might think to make progress in some other way. It is natural, for example, to explain the special nexus of animal and event by appeal to sensation or appetite. Our account of the concept *motus animalium* would then mirror the sort of account of the category of willed, voluntary or intentional action that takes such notions as desire, intention and judgment for granted, together with some abstract conception of cause.[10] Something must fall between the would-be agent and what it does—something that, as 'cause', in a pre-given sense, of the latter happening, gives the whole ensemble the special character of rational or intentional agency in the one case, and of animal movement in the other.

I am not certain what to make of these ideas about rational agency, but in the case of our present quarry, the extremely wide category of vital operation, or life-functioning or vital agency, the picture must fail. *The materials for constructing a 'causalist' account (as we might call it) are simply unavailable in this more general case.* What individual happenings will 'fall between' a tree and its getting larger, thereby potentially distinguishing this nexus, as living agency or vital operation, from that involved in a crystal's or flame's or trash heap's getting larger? Well, no sap runs in a crystal, you might say, and there is no photosynthesis in a flame; but then no sap runs in an amoeba, and there is no photosynthesis in a human being. Nothing has the position in respect of organisms *generally* that sensation and appetite have among animals and that judgment and intention have among persons. There is no general *type* of event or state, X, of which we will be tempted to say: whenever an individual event is to be brought back to the 'vital operation' of an organism, there must be some other event or state of type X that predates the

10. See especially the first five essays reprinted in Donald Davidson, *Essays on Action and Events* (Oxford: Oxford University Press, 1981).

attributed event and causes it—unless of course the prior phenomenon is simply *more vital operation*. An account of *this* type of 'agency', 'activity', 'substance-causality' or 'spontaneity' in terms of a prior abstract notion of cause and a particular kind of prior state or event is thus I think impossible.

5. Summary of Results Reached So Far

A number of abstract categories—that of a concrete individual; of a thing's being a part of something; of order or organization; of one thing's following another in a process; of a thing's doing something—are all together determined or specified, or thrown into a higher gear, to yield the concepts: *organism; organ,* 'part' or 'member'; *vital order* or *organ*-ization; *life-process;* and *vital operation.* The abstract notion of existence, in the sense of actuality (Frege's *Wirklichkeit*) evidently bears the same relation to that of *life:* 'to be, for a living thing, is to live'.[11] I will later suggest that this same shift of gear will turn the abstract notion of a kind or of a 'natural kind' into that of a *life-form*—the notion, that is, of a living kind, or of a species (on one reading of that expression).

These concepts, the vital categories, together form a sort of solid block, and we run into a kind of circle in attempting to elucidate any of them, a circle much like the one Anscombe found at a higher stratum of things:

Why is giving a start or gasp not an 'action', while sending for a taxi, or crossing a road, is one? The answer cannot be "Because the answer to the question 'why?' may give a *reason* in the latter cases", for the answer may 'give a reason' in the former cases too [e.g., where the 'reason why' you gasped is that you misheard "It's satin" as "It's Satan"]; and we cannot say, "Ah, but not a reason for *acting*"; we should be going round in circles. We need to find the difference between the two kinds of 'reason' without talking about 'acting'; and if we do, perhaps we shall discover what is meant by 'acting' when it is said with this special emphasis.[12]

11. Aristotle, *De Anima*, II, 5 (415b13).
12. Anscombe, *Intention*, sec. 5, p. 10.

Our circle may of course be larger: "Why is a taxi not an 'organism' while a tarantula is one?" The answer cannot be, "Because a tarantula has *members*", for a taxi has parts as well. . . . We might go on to explain the intended notion of part in terms of vital organization, say, but in the end the flypaper will have to stick somewhere. It is of course useless to attempt a 'holistic' account, seeking to elucidate the several categories together by describing their interrelations: the relations that hold among the vital categories are presumably the same as those holding among the more abstract ones I mentioned.

Anscombe escapes her circle by fixing on the relevant sort of *reason*, and then rejecting what may be called a purely metaphysical approach to it. It is the hope of giving a real definition that sends us reaching back into the circle and then from pillar to post. She takes refuge instead in the *representation* of 'reasons', 'explanations' or 'accounts' *in general*, in the asking and answering of questions "Why?" If, now, she can isolate a certain particular 'sense of the question "Why?"', she will have exposed the more determinate kind of *reason*, and with it a whole ensemble of practical categories: action, intention, end, means, will, motive, etc.

My method in what follows is meant to be the same. To apply it, though, we must first expand our circle to include the concept of a life-form or a species as I suggested above that we might; this, I think, is the weak link. A species or life-form is just a certain kind of kind—the sort of thing to be the subject of a general judgment or a general statement; it is the sort of thing that is said of something and about which something can be said, in the sense of Aristotle's *Categories*. Our problem will then be reduced to one of isolating a particular form of general judgment or statement—a *natural-historical judgment*, as I will call it. What is fit to be the subject of such a thing we may call a species-concept or a life-form-word. A species or life-form, then, will be whatever can be conceived through *such* a concept or expressed by *such* a word—not a real definition, alas, but not a circular one, I think, and not egregious organicist metaphysics either. It is because in the end we will have to do with a special *form of judgment*, a distinct mode of joining subject and predicate in thought or speech, that I am emboldened to say that the vital categories are logical categories.

～ 3

The Representation of the Living Individual

1. Sameness in the Sphere of the Living

This discussion has so far focused on the metaphysical ambition of the list-making approach to the question "What is life?" But there is another hope evinced by that tradition, a hope bound up with a certain extreme *individualism*, as I think it can rightly be called. An acceptable answer to the great question is implicitly required to tell us *how things must be in a given region of space* if we are to say, "A living thing is there"—or, perhaps better: what a *region of space-time* needs to be like, if it is to be occupied by a four-dimensional object corresponding to an individual organism of the sort we meet in experience.

That Professor Curtis is not managing to pull the trick off becomes painfully clear in the text for her final "Sign of Life," which she illustrates with a photograph of a mature pair of ostriches and twenty head of little ones. It is a traditional favorite:

> Living things reproduce themselves. They make more of themselves, copy after copy after copy, with astonishing fidelity (and yet, as we shall see, with just enough variation to provide the raw material for evolution).

Problems of understanding again arise, this time from the apparent accident that she has put her definiendum, "living things", in the plural.

49

conatus ad perseverare

It is not just that living things generally 'take energy from the environment'—I, Thompson, do this as well; and I, Thompson, 'react to stimuli', I suppose. What would it be, though, for me, Thompson, to make more of *myself*? We are not envisaging an increase in portliness.

Let us say that it means: to make a copy, indeed "copy after copy". We might forestall mentioning that I seem to have spent many years of apparent life not having done this, if we adopt a backward-looking formulation of the criterion, as say "Living things *are made by* more of themselves," or "Living things are copies of what they are made by." This raises the problem of a beginning, but, putting that aside, the question must still arise: in just what respects am I supposed to be copied, or to be a copy? Or again: more of *what*? It is of course no use to say that the formula means simply that *living things come from living things*, so that the words "living thing" themselves express the respect of sameness. This need not be circular; it might be an implicit definition, requiring us to solve the equation in order to arrive at the content of "living thing". But again *material object* will make as good a solution as *living thing* will.

The same difficulties must beset another of Professor Curtis's properties, the last I will mention. "Living things," she tells us, "are homeostatic, which means simply 'staying the same.'" Now, of course, on one way of taking these words, they would formulate a fairly sound criterion of death. *What*, then, do we have to 'stay', if we are to 'stay the same' in the sense intended?[1] One is familiar, after all, with fairly radical phenomenal and physical alterations, 'metamorphoses' as they call them, in the typical life of various sorts of animal. It is clear that the concept of life is plastic enough to allow *such* 'changes of form' to be as thoroughgoing and frequent as one likes, consistently with the thing's being the same and alive. What happens once in a typical butterfly's life might happen a hundred times in the typical life of some yet-to-evolve quasi-butterfly.

I want to say that in neither the case of reproduction nor that of so-called homeostasis is the requisite sort of sameness fixed or determined

---

1. I take it that the word "homeostasis" has been supplied with a rather extended sense in this context, so that it does not cover mere maintenance of body temperature or the ratios of things dissolved in cells, but the whole 'reproduction of the individual' in the sense of Kant, Hegel and Marx. Her criterion is a form of the traditional slogan that substance has a tendency to keep itself in being.

by anything in the individual itself: whatever else may come from a thing, and whatever becomes of the thing itself, the upshot will be in some respects the same and in other ways different from what we had before. If we call the relevant sameness *sameness of form,* then that a thing *has* a given such form will not be an 'individualistically' determinable fact about the thing; it will not, for example, be simply equivalent to any collection of physical or phenomenal facts about the thing itself or the region of space-time occupied by its perduring double. The imagined example of a sort of poly-metamorphic butterfly makes this obvious in the second sort of case: the superficial, changing *morphē* may be taken in by the eye, or the constitution of the thing registered by a physical apparatus—each of which trades in what is present here and now; but the shape of things that really must be *maintained,* according to the criterion, is realized in radically different ways at different times, or may be; it is "form" in a quite different sense from phenomenal character or physical structure. But the case of reproduction bears some further discussion.

 SINCE A THING needn't *actually* reproduce itself to count as alive, one wants to say that it must at least be *able* to, or *have it in it* to do so. Even this is not quite right, given any ordinary understanding of the words "able to"; but let this pass. Our thought would seem to be that if a thing is to count as alive, it must fall under some universal U where (a) an individual's falling under U is an individualistically ascertainable fact about the thing, and (b), some general truth approximately formulable as "From a given U, another U can come to be" holds. I have already remarked that this proposition will come out true if we substitute "material object" for "U"; but let us suppose we have a principle for ruling out such trivial readings.

Now, "Another can come from it" doesn't mean: *another can come from it, whatever the circumstances.* We can at most require that we get 'another' in *some* circumstances. The necessary weakening must bring the whole naive picture to ruin. One is acquainted, after all, with the astonishing works of some of the 'large organic macro-molecules' that characterize terrestrial life, enzymes, for example. Now there must be many chemical substances C, such that for some appropriate stew of *other* chemical stuffs, S (some of them no doubt 'large organic macro-molecules'), the following holds good: if a bit of C is introduced into a vat of S, then a bit *more* C will be produced, and so later on a lot more C will have been produced, until in the end we face a parody of 'environmental collapse'. This is the principle of the polymerase chain reaction, for example. Perhaps we can find such an S for any chemical substance C. And why shouldn't it be true of *anything*, whether it be held together by chemical bonds or not, and under any of its physical descriptions, partial or complete? There is some 'environment', also physically describable, in which, if there be one of that description, another will come to be. If it isn't so, then this is just another empirical fact about this vale of dross and tears, the 'physical universe'. From the point of view of physics, after all, a text in a scrivener's shop is like an amoeba in the sea, or a bacterium in my bloodstream. And so perhaps everything has 'reproductive fitness', and under any description, and all things are full of souls. It is just that most of them are starved of the highly specific circumstances that would express the trait.

What we miss, or miss most obviously, in the flat physicalistic picture of reproduction, is any conception of the unity of a thing and its circumstances as potentially *non-accidental*. An organism's coming to be in such circumstances as tend to its reproduction *is itself typically a vital operation*, or a phase in a life-process, and therefore, in a certain sense, 'no accident'. A dandelion seed's falling on reproductively apt soil may seem fortuitous, but its parent, by a kind of ruse of vegetation, makes such an accident no accident, most obviously by producing so much seed. The reproduction and staying-the-same that are put down as "Signs of Life" are really just *'self'-reproduction* and *keeping 'oneself' the same*, where the reflexive expresses, not an abstract relation to the subject, but vital operation; or they must be restricted to such forms of reproduction and self-maintenance as come under the heading of *vital process*.

And so in the final analysis these criteria might be thought to take us nowhere we haven't been. It is enough that the thing should exhibit *any* vital process or operation—why should reproduction and 'homeostasis' in particular be among them?

But though the conception of the relevant sort of 'form'-transmission or 'form'-maintenance is a notion of vital operation, it may yet be that a grasp of the category of vital operation, or of any conception of a particular vital operation, must presuppose a grasp of the appropriate category of *form*. And this, I think, is what really gets registered in criteria of self-maintenance and reproduction—that is, of the 'reproduction of the individual' and the 'reproduction of its kind', as Hegel says, or of *threpsis* and *genesis*, nutrition and reproduction, as Aristotle says. But the transition to this category will, I think, inevitably destroy the individualistic ambition implicit in our sort of list.

2. The Mediate Character of Vital Description: The 'Wider Context'

Rather dark, that, but let us make a fresh start, in hope of explaining it, with some quotations from Anscombe's discussion of contraception. The points are unsurprising and I think familiar, but their formulation is suited to our purposes and method; it is interesting, too, to see them formulated in a distinctly earlier epoch of the analytic tradition:

> Acts that are pretty clearly defined biological events, like eating and copulation, may be said to be by nature acts of a certain kind. Eating is a useful example to illustrate further the concepts I am using; it is a biological example like copulation, but on the other hand we shall not here be confused by controverted moral judgments. Eating is intrinsically a nutritive act, the sort of act to be nutritive; this would be an essential mark of eating if we wished to identify it in an animal species differing very much from us in structure.

And she also says:

> In the same way, we may say that . . . the eye is as such an organ of sight: consider how we would identify eating and the eye from one species to another. And it is in this sense that copulation is intrinsically generative—though there are very many copulations which in fact do not generate.

And best of all she says:

> When we call something an acorn, we look to a wider context than can be seen in the acorn itself. Oaks come from acorns, acorns

come from oaks; an acorn is thus *as such* generative (of an oak) whether or not it does generate an oak.[2]

Anscombe is mostly interested in the idea of an action's bearing an 'intrinsic nature'; having attained the conception, she puts it to work in an eccentric classification of sexual acts. But I am interested in the matter of a 'wider context', a matter she promptly drops: *When we call something an acorn, we look to a wider context than can be seen in the acorn itself.*

"Acorn", I suppose, means "oak-corn" or "oak-seed", and this might seem to make the point about the look to a wider context pretty trivial. In thinking of something as an acorn, we tie it up specifically with *oaks*, none of which need be present here, and so of course we 'look beyond' the individual lump of stuff. But the remarks about eating and the eye show that the point is not trivial: the 'look to a wider context' occurs already in thinking of the acorn as *seed*.

But that materially different things can add up to the same—be it seed, or eating, or eye—is of course not enough to vindicate a non-individualistic account of the thing that *is* the same; thus, for example, *copper* and *iron* and *silver* are all equally *metal*. That the reverse is also true in our sort of case may however be seen if we expand on Anscombe's example of eating.

We can readily enough imagine the genesis of a novel kind of shark—one nourished, not by the flesh of smaller fish, but by plankton and the like. Certain elaborate structures have developed on the sides of these sharks: they continuously filter the water and extract the nutritious elements. All the same, we may suppose, these newly developed sharks or quasi-sharks can sometimes be seen to chase after smaller fish and incorporate them. No part of this flesh ever enters the bloodstream; rather, it makes a hideous brew and is spewed out occasionally to frighten predators. The operation looks very much like the hunting, munching and swallowing that actually existing sharks go in for, and no doubt some of the genetic basis of the latter will have carried over to the former. Someone might take the movement for the same sort of thing, and call it eating; but it is clear that it isn't eating. When we call something eating, then, we appeal to something more than is available

---

2. All of these quotations are from pp. 85–87 of "You Can Have Sex Without Children," in *Ethics, Religion and Politics* (Minneapolis: University of Minnesota Press, 1981).

in the mere spectacle of the thing here and now. 'Philosophers can arrange', in Philippa Foot's phrase, that the spectacle should be there with or without the phenomenon of eating.

Another example may be constructed from the familiar textbook facts about mitosis and the accompanying process—the doubling, sorting out and splitting up of chromosomal material. It may be happening here, under the microscope, in an amoeba; and there in a human being. In the first case, an event of this type will of course be a phase in a process of reproduction—one of the forms of generation available to that kind of thing. But in the case of the human it will rather be a part of growth or self-maintenance; reproduction is another matter, and has another matter, among humans. The distinction between the two cases of mitosis is not to be discovered by a more careful scrutiny of the particular cells at issue—any more than, as Frege said, the closest chemical and microscopic investigation of certain ink markings will teach us whether the arithmetical formulae they realize are *true*.

It is pointless to say that, after all, the *DNA* will have a different structure in the different cases—as pointless as it would be to say that the quasi-shark's quasi-eating will not really *look like* that of a proper shark, what with the repulsive feeding apparatus the quasi-shark carries about with it. Philosophers can arrange that the apparatus should have fallen off moments before in a lover's quarrel. The 'look to a wider context', then, is not a look to the left and right.

This will perhaps be more obvious if we consider another sort of case involving DNA. Lab technicians keep lines of human cells of suitable types multiplying in vats for ages; suppose then a lake in South America, one maintained by nature in such a character as the lab solution is by art, and shaken perhaps by frequent earthquakes to keep things from sticking together; and now—it does not matter whether it be by a process of evolution from something else, or a quantum-mechanical accident, or an act of God—something as alike as you like to a human cell of the appropriate type appears in that sinister fluid. At some point we will have a race of one-celled vegetative creatures, to be given a Latin binomial name and investigated like any other. This kind is evidently not human-kind, and its mode of reproduction is not the human sort. The division that takes place in the lake has a characteristic, *reproduction of the species*, not exhibited in the laboratory vat or flask. More surprisingly, in the one case we have a collection of *individual substances* and *organisms,* and in the other case nothing of the sort. Yet if we ladle up a bit of the lake and take it back to the lab in New York, no test, however subtle, will ever disclose the difference. The example is maybe a bit wild, but it shows, I think, that the same sort of DNA might chance to 'control' the operations of merely vegetative and of rational life. It follows that a proposition running "This DNA contains *in itself* all the information . . .", though sound enough in its place, cannot bear a metaphysical emphasis—and that something on the order of a Human Genome Project can no *more, or less,* uncover the 'real essence' of the human than could a study of the anatomy of the human hand.[3]

3. The 'Wider Context' Is the Life-Form

If a thing is alive, if it is an *organism,* then some particular vital operations and processes must go on in it from time to time—eating, budding out, breathing, walking, growing, thinking, reproducing, photosynthesizing; and it must have certain particular organs or 'parts'— leaves, legs, cells, kidneys, a heart, a root, a spine. But we have suggested, following up Anscombe's clue, that if any of these things *is there,* or *is happening,* then this is not something fixed or determined by anything in the organism considered in its particularity or as occupying a certain region of space. That they are there or happening, and thus that we have an organism at all, presupposes the existence of a certain 'wider context'; it is this that stamps these several characters onto things.

This is a purely metaphysical formulation of the thought; let us move on to the matter of representation. It is obvious that a language cannot contain any representation of *objects,* in the thin Fregean sense,

---

3. A tamer example may be of some use in exposing 'the fetishism of DNA and the secret thereof'. Different individual plants falling under the same species and with the same parents will often present quite dissimilar appearances if grown in different soils and climates, especially if these are in either case intuitively deficient in some respect. Let us then suppose *two* species to have evolved independently, one in the Arctic and one in Brazil. One has red flowers and one has white; one is compact and creeping and one is tall and upright; one is pollinated by bees and one by a special sort of moth; etc. The various segments of genetic material will thus carry widely different bits of 'information' in either case. It is of course consistent with this, and with every physicalistic slogan, that the *seeds* they form, and thus their *genetic material,* should be alike in every physical detail. The 'phenotypical' differences would then arise solely from the differences in soil and climate. Though physically identical, the seeds and the genes will necessarily attract quite different descriptions.

unless it also contains predicative expressions. And, perhaps more generally, an intellect cannot have a power of apprehending objects unless it has a power of thinking something *of* them—that is, if you like, of apprehending Fregean concepts.

We may also say that a language cannot contain any representation of things in the narrower but richer class of *concrete particulars*, Frege's 'actual objects', unless it also contains some of a narrower but richer class of predicates—for example, verbs expressing special causal concepts possibly applicable to such particulars. "A small selection: *scrape, push, wet, carry, eat, burn, knock over, keep off, squash, make* (e.g., noises, paper boats), *hurt.*"[4] And, again perhaps more generally, an intellect cannot receive a power to judge of concrete particulars, unless it also receives, inter alia, some such special causal concepts.

Perhaps this last will not be accepted, but it is in any case only a model for what I want to say, namely, this: if a language contains any representation of members of the yet narrower class of *organisms*—'actual objects' for which actuality takes the form of *life*—it must also include a battery of what we may call "life-descriptions". Such would be, for example: representations of parts as organs or 'members'; representations of particular sorts of goings-on as vital operations—a class subordinate to that of which we had a "small selection", just as organisms constitute a class subordinate to that of concrete particulars; and so forth. And, again, an intellectual capacity to think of individual organisms will have to involve possession of some of the corresponding concepts.

But, of course, what falls under such descriptions and such concepts will be different in different 'wider contexts'. And so, if there is to be thinking of organisms or a representation of life at all, then the thinking and speaking subject must have some means of apprehending the various sorts of 'wider context'—the various 'life-forms', as I will call them. Even the most pedestrian case of life-description, say, that the cat is drinking the milk, must make an implicit claim about the relevant 'form' or 'context'—that *for it*, or *in it*, the events before us add up to drinking; or that what the creature is doing is drinking, *for such as it is*.

But still, what *is* this supposed 'wider context', this 'life-form', as I

---

4. G. E. M. Anscombe, "Causality and Determination," in *Collected Philosophical Papers*, vol. II, p. 137.

am calling it? The doctrine into which these ciphers enter has a structure in common with other more familiar ones: it is to be compared, for example, with that familiarly expressed by John Rawls in the decisive passage of "Two Concepts of Rules" (which is itself, of course, intended as an application of certain thoughts of Wittgenstein):

> Many of the actions one performs in a game of baseball one can do by oneself or with others whether there is a game or not. For example, one can throw a ball, run, or swing a peculiarly shaped piece of wood. . . . [But no] matter what a person did he could not be described as stealing a base or striking out or drawing a walk unless he could also be described as playing baseball, and for him to be doing this presupposes the rule-like practice which constitutes the game. The practice is prior to particular cases: unless there is the practice, the terms referring to actions specified by it lack sense.[5]

Rawls claims that the sort of 'wider context' intended in the description of an individual action as one of stealing a base or striking out is a *practice;* and we may say that Anscombe, by contrast, in her remarks on "eating" and "eye", implicitly claims that the 'wider context' at stake in particular applications of those words is a *species.*

This suggests, though, that we know what it means to speak of a practice, on the one hand, and of a species or life-form, on the other, before we come to advance such claims. Do we take the concepts over, maybe, from sociology in the one case, and empirical biology in the other?[6] But we are practicing philosophy, or mean to be, and so if we accept the equation *the 'wider context' of vital description is the life-form,*

5. "Two Concepts of Rules," *Philosophical Review* 64 (1955): 25.

6. On practices see, for example, Max Weber's classification of 'empirical uniformities of action' in *The Theory of Social and Economic Organization,* trans. A. M. Henderson and Talcott Parsons (New York: Free Press, 1964), pp. 120–123. On species, see Mayr, for example, *The Growth of Biological Thought* (Cambridge, Mass.: Harvard University Press, 1982), pp. 270–275.

It is remarkable that contemporary moralists, many of whom uncritically employ notions of 'practice', 'social practice', 'custom' and the like, yet view any notion of species or life-form with suspicion, as a sort of foreign scientific intruder. But each concept can seem to spring from empirical science. And where either is given a more properly philosophical employment, it can seem to involve a metaphysic of 'inner *nisus*' and so forth, unless it is approached correctly.

then we must, in a phrase John McDowell once used, 'enter it on the left side'. Vital description of individual organisms is itself the primitive expression of a conception of things in terms of 'life-form' or 'species', and if we want to understand these categories in philosophy we must bring them back to that form of description.

If this is right, then, of course, we are wrong to think of the concepts of the various life-forms as reached through abstraction from features of their particular bearers. *That* notion takes for granted a picture of the terrestrial biosphere as offering us a magazine of living individuals, which we then carve up in accordance with certain principles. The error is not overcome, but only complicated, by the Realist notion that, after all, we 'carve at the joints'. What is wrongly called *carving* is already a part of thinking of individual things as alive, as organisms available for 'classification'.

This is not to say that the category we reach in the explanation of "species" or "life-form" as 'wider context of vital description' cannot be further specified or schematized with a view to empirical terrestrial employment. The thin category that is accessible to philosophy must, for example, leave many questions of sameness and difference of life-form unsettled, questions that might be decided by a 'definition' in terms, say, of interbreeding populations (at least among things that breed). It may be that the word "species" is best left to express some such more determinate conception, and only the word "life-form" retained for our properly philosophical purposes, but I will not so leave it. The resolution of these fine points, of course, presupposes an accretion of empirical content—so that, for example, the formula "It is a merely empirical fact that any organisms fall into species" will come out true on the empirically schematized reading and false on our own. But even this, I think, does not entail that in the central range of cases a sentence containing a particular kind-term that has been introduced in association with the definition in terms of (say) interbreeding populations must express a *thought* different from one expressed with a term that has been given a sparer, philosophical exposition. (The thought that it *must* entail that is perhaps just a Fregean prejudice: "Different concepts touch here and coincide over a stretch. But you need not think all lines are circles."[7]) I think, then, that Anscombe was not

---

7. Ludwig Wittgenstein, *Philosophical Investigations*, 3rd ed. (New York: Macmillan, 1963), II, x, p. 192. (If circles coincide for a stretch, they coincide.) So also, if Wittgenstein is right, and I understand him, his favorite signs, "non" and "ne" (where "non non p = p" and "ne ne p

wrong to import the word "species" into this context, but at most a bit uncritical.

A species or life-form of course *determines* a class of individuals, its bearers. But if the only possible account of the concept of a species or life-form were in terms of ensembles of individuals bound together by certain external relations, then our remarks about the 'wider context', read accordingly, would be completely absurd. We may see this if we consider a more radical illustration of those remarks.

What should we say about a creature who comes to be from sand or swamp muck by the agency of lightning or quantum-mechanical accident—a creature part for part the same as I am, standing nearby, and just considered physically? One wonders whether the limits of philosophical imagination have not been transgressed in such a fable, but let us waive the suspicion. Philosophers have doubted whether such a thing could have thoughts, or whether its thoughts would have content.[8] If my friend N.N. shouts the name "Thompson!", my double and I will each *hear something* and each *turn his head*, it is supposed, but while I am *wondering, "What's N.N. doing here?"*, the newcomer will not be.

We must accept this skepticism and carry it further: the thing has no ears to hear with and no head to turn; it has no brain-states, no brain to bear them, and no skull to close them in; prick it, and it does not bleed; tickle it, and it does not laugh; and so forth. It is a mere congeries of physical particles and not so much as alive.[9]

In the other cases we considered, physically or phenomenally similar events took place in different 'wider contexts'. The opposing life-

---

= ne p"), may each express the category of negation involved in, say, philosophical difficulties about being and not-being; here, and in the simplest cases of affirmation and denial, the thoughts expressed in either vocabulary will be the same, though of course the thoughts expressed by the doubling of the signs will differ. (See *Philosophical Investigations*, secs. 547–557, and *Remarks on the Foundations of Mathematics*, 2nd ed. [Cambridge: MIT Press, 1978], pp. 102–110.) Similarly, strictly philosophical discourses in different cultures that involve words like "species" might express the same philosophical thoughts though the words are associated with different empirical accretions in their extra-philosophical employment.

8. Donald Davidson, "Knowing One's Own Mind," in *Proceedings and Addresses of the American Philosophical Association* 61 (1987): 441–458.

9. Thomas Aquinas seems to take a similar position in *Summa Theologia*, q. 51, art. 3, "Whether the angels exercise functions of life in the bodies assumed?" His answer is "No." Thomas is thinking of supposed appearances of people to, say, Abraham and Sarah or to Lot and his family; it was traditionally maintained that these involved angels rearranging matter in the shape of a human being. There could, he thinks, be nothing properly called speaking or walking in such a thing, only sound and spatial movement.

forms or wider contexts put divergent interpretations on these out-wardly similar events, sending them in different directions; and so different vital descriptions applied. In supposing my imagined double to be a product of sheer accident, *we have severed all links with any specific such wider context;* we can associate it with no *determinate* life-form at all; and so the ground of all vital description is removed. We can say, in the light of *my* form, which is the specifically human form, that *these* are arms—a bit weak maybe, but fairly together. Are *those*, which 'he' 'has', maybe *legs*, after all—only horribly deformed and not much good for crawling with? Or are they mutilated wings? Is his tail missing? We cannot link my supposed double with anything that would decide these questions; as far as the physics and phenomenology of the case go, any answer would be possible. It may be thought that these specific matters might be settled by a look to 'his genes'. But suppose we grant that he has genes: are they defective? Even the purely biochemical description of the cases is affected: suppose we are each now turned to jelly by a land-mine left from the last war; *those* micro-events, happening just be-fore the blast, were the opening stages of (say) glycolysis in me—a pro-cess unfortunately left hanging, glucose unsplit. But nevertheless it was precisely glycolysis that was happening. But in 'him'? That physical conditions were present for what was in my case 'the next stage' or 'what happens next', in chemical succession, is by hypothesis *accident*, in every sense, just as 'his' origination was; they have no more bearing on the description of what was happening with him than the proximity of the bomb itself does. Thus we cannot say in his case, as we can in mine, that glycolysis was happening, though it didn't happen, in that the glu-cose remained unsplit—and similarly, I think, with any other vital pro-cess we might have been tempted to ascribe to 'him'.[10]

---

10. Compare again Ludwig Wittgenstein, *Remarks on the Foundations of Mathematics*, p. 336. Wittgenstein is, alas, merely ambivalent about describing the denizens of his two-minute mid-Atlantic simulacrum of a part of England as, say, *adding* or *subtracting*. (The am-bivalence may spring from the fact that he imagines a God in this connection, so that the case is like that of Adam and Eve coming to be in the Garden; it is not, as we are supposing, *sheer* accident.) Whereas the act of addition presupposes a "practice"—and it is hard to see how an occupant of that category can gain a foothold in two minutes—breathing and glycolysis pre-suppose a life-form (as of course any so-called practice does). Reflection on some of our ear-lier examples, especially the poly-metamorphic form of butterfly, will I think show that even given two or twenty years in which physical developments in my accidental *Doppelgänger* re-main much as they are with me, still nothing will yet manage to hook my double up with any *determinate form* in the light of which we could ascribe determinate life processes to it.

What is missing, the 'wider context' that would bring these things into focus, I have called a *life-form*. I have also called it a *species*, with some reservations, and would be happy, in an Aristotelian mood, to call it *psuchē*.[11] *But each of these latter expressions carries a baggage of associated imagery—a picture to hold us captive, if you like. I mean: what do I have that* 'he' *lacks*, and by which I am alive? Friends and countrymen? Or a *ghost*? Or perhaps, if we stress the "form" in our preferred expression "life-form", the thing will even be sought in a platonic heaven, or in the mind of God. Here the associated ideas are respectively of things to the right and left of me, or of something "within" me, or of something somehow "above." But all such images should be cast aside. I think our question should not be: What is a life-form, a species, a *psuchē*?, but: How is such a thing described?

11. Aristotle, *De Anima*, II, 1.

~ 4

The Representation of the Life-Form Itself

1. Natural-Historical Judgment

Everyone is familiar with the characteristic discursive mood, as we might call it, of what was formerly called 'natural history'—the supposed content of Aristotle's *Historia animalium*, for example, and of dusty books bearing such titles as *Conifers of the Central Rockies* or *Winged Creatures of Western Pennsylvania*. The voiceovers on public television nature programs are characterized by propositions in the sort of 'mood' I am intending. We will see film footage depicting some particular bobcats, taken perhaps in the spring of 1977; the voiceover will include verbs and other predicates that were verified, as the film shows, in the activities, parts, and environment of the featured, or starring, individual bobcats. But the verbs and predicates we hear will not generally be combined with proper names or demonstrative expressions—words that, as we say, 'make singular reference'. It sounds like this: "When springtime comes, and the snow begins to melt, the female bobcat gives birth to two to four cubs. The mother nurses them for several weeks." (Here perhaps we see and hear violent mountain streams, rioting birds, blossoming alpine flora, and, say, three predictably adorable cubs piled up against a perplexed but stoical mother—not just 'two to four' of them, but exactly three.) ". . . As the heat of summer approaches, the cubs will learn to hunt." (And here the viewer might wit-

63

ness a thankfully inept attempt on a half-fledged California condor.) The filmed individuals themselves are rarely mentioned. Or if they are, it will be for example to give a sort of personal touch to the broadcast: "Ah, this little one seems to have awakened the neighborhood rattle-snake . . ."—that sort of thing.

It is evidently irrelevant to the ends of this sort of employment of film that it might sometimes be a different bobcat family that is filmed later on in the summer. Why should the film-maker wait until next year if the original crop of cubs falls to distemper? There would be no dis-honesty in the substitution, given what is going on, and even though what is going on is documentary production. It would be quite differ-ent, though, if she were attempting to film a biography—a sort of bob-cat version of 7 or 21 or 35 Up; and someone might mistake the nature program for such a thing. The sameness presupposed is not that given by the words "same individual animal". Someone who does not grasp the other sort of sameness of animal will of course not understand the broadcast.

The peculiarity of this sort of employment of verbs and predicates comes out even better in the telegraphic style of a certain sort of field guide. Here we find a Latin binomial name, a common noun, and then some such text as "Four legs. Black fur. Nocturnal. Lives among rocks near rivers and streams. Eats worms and fish. See plate 162." It is im-portant to see that these very predicates can as easily be attached to designations of individuals and to individual variables. Again, someone might mistake the grammar of our field guide for *such* predication, viewing it as something on the order of the FBI's Most Wanted List: "Blond hair. Six feet tall. Lives in cheap hotels. Partial to Italian cui-sine. Armed and dangerous. See photo opposite."[1]

Let us call the thoughts expressed in the field guide and in the na-ture documentary *natural-historical judgments*. We may take as their ca-nonical expression sentences of the form "The S is (or has, or does) F"—"The domestic cat has four legs, two eyes, two ears, and guts in its belly"; "The Texas bluebonnet harbors nitrogen-fixing microbes in

1. The field guide and the FBI list of course aim at supplying materials for *identification*. But the propositions employed in the FBI list record plain facts about the suspect individuals; the further purpose they are meant to serve does not affect the kind of predication involved. Similarly, we should not suppose that the type of predication we find in the field guide or na-ture documentary must limit itself to the attribution of differentiae or 'species-specific' traits.

certain nodes on its roots"; "The yellow finch breeds in spring, attracting its mate with such and such song"; whatever. We are ultimately interested, of course, in the underlying judgments and in the form of fact
they register; but such *sentences* I will call "Aristotelian categoricals".
Our language of course permits the same judgments to be expressed in
a number of ways, for example, by "S's are/have/do F" or "It belongs to
an S to be/have/do F" or "S's characteristically (or typically) are/have/
do F" or "This is (part of) how S's live: they are/have/do F", and a hundred others. The mere form of words, however, is in no case enough to
show that the thought expressed is of our type. It is necessary that a
common noun ("S") and some other predicative expression ("F") be
present or in the offing; the other linking expressions—the definite article, the bare plural—are part of the context that may or may not show
the nexus of signs to be of the sort that interests us. That I am making
voiceovers for a nature documentary is just another part of the context,
tending to force our sort of construction onto my remarks. But background knowledge, my alarmed tone of voice, and the predicate I use in
saying "The domestic cat has three legs" will show that here I am not
making an attempt at natural history, that it is poor Tibbles, the local
house cat, that I am talking about, and that my statement has the more
familiar 'logical form' of "The cat is on the mat."

Natural-historical judgments tend to be formulated in some type of
present tense. If temporal designations enter into their expression, it is
typically a matter of before and after—"in the spring", "in the fall", "in
infancy", "in adolescence"—and not of now and then and next spring
and when I was young and so forth. The temporal indicators thus express a B series, in McTaggart's sense, and not an A series.[2] It is of Elsa,
hic et nunc, that we say: she *bore* three cubs *last* spring. Of her kind we
say: the mature female bears two to four cubs in *the* spring—employing
a form of present tense even if we pass the information on in winter.
The peculiarity of the case shows itself already in this, that the past-
tense proposition about Elsa may be given as providing an *example* of
what is recorded in the intuitively *purely* present-tense general proposition. Of course, we ourselves do have means of throwing these general
propositions into an intelligible past tense, as when we describe life-
forms now extinct—and so we are also able to describe changes in the

---

2. McTaggart, *The Nature of Existence* (Cambridge: Cambridge University Press, 1927).

characteristics natural-historically attributable to particular kinds of living things, and to supply a Darwinian account of these changes. But it is clearly possible to enjoy a capacity for this type of sentence and thought formation, and to apprehend truth through it, and simply lack any past- or future-tense employment of the propositions so formed. By contrast, I think, we could not suppose a language or other conceptual apparatus to admit any description of concrete particulars if it did not contain a past- and perhaps a future-tense employment of these descriptions, in addition to the present. I mean: to know what it is for a person to walk or a raindrop to fall, one must know what it is for the walking or falling to be over; but to know what it is for a form, kind or 'species' of bird to be crested one need not attach any significance to a notion of *its* ceasing to be crested.[3]

It may seem a bit absurd that a form of predication suggestive of field guides, dusty compendia, and nature programs should be supposed to be the ticket for a philosophy of organism. But I think we can see that many of the specifically biological propositions falling under such headings as anatomy, physiology, ethology, biochemistry and so forth are themselves such statements or else, and more commonly, generalizations on the common-noun position in such statements. That is, in a properly *begriffsschriftliche* formulation of these more abstract propositions of terrestrial biology, the verbs and other predicates would be attached to a variable; substitution instances of the corresponding open sentences would be simple Aristotelian categoricals. When Aristotle says that some animals are viviparous, he does not give Helen and Penelope as *examples*; his examples are: *man, the horse, the camel.*[4] His thought may thus be canonically expressed as "For some terrestrial life-forms S, the S is viviparous." And when he says that some animals shed their front teeth, but there is no instance of an animal that loses its molars,[5] he will not give up the sentence when faced with a denture

---

3. Thus I think problems about the re-identification of life-forms across geological expanses of time and through more or less massive alterations in natural-historically attributable traits must fall outside our subject. It is only by supplying a further, perhaps empirically warranted, specification of the bare concept of a life-form and of the form of judgment in which we represent it, that we can get clear answers to such questions.

4. *Historia animalium*, 489b1.

5. Ibid., 501b1.

wearer; denture wearers aren't the 'animals' he was talking about. Similarly—I want to say—when an introductory botany book says that photosynthesis, a process it will spend many pages of chemical formulae describing, is characteristic of flowering plants, among others, the exceptions it mentions will be, for example, *field dodder* and *Indian pipe*, and not this pitiful albino marigold seedling. Our mode of sentence formation must thus, I think, lurk at the bottom of even these abstract pages. It is very easy, in large generalizations about "life" and "organisms", to overlook the possibility that one's propositions have this kind of generality, instances of which will themselves be a kind of generality, and not facts about individual living beings.

It might be suggested that a natural-historical judgment should be able directly to take some higher genus as its immediate subject—a judgment to be canonically formulated as, say, "*The* flowering plant *is* F", or "Flowering plant*s* *are* F", rather than as, say, "For every terrestrial life-form S, if S is a form of flowering plant, then *the* S *is* F" (as I would write it). It is a possible theory. My purposes do not, I think, require that I refute it. But we should remember that it is a merely empirical truth, an artifact of their evolution from earlier forms, that terrestrial life-forms admit of any interesting classification into higher genera. But if the thoughts advanced in the last chapter are sound, then it is *not* a merely empirical fact, given that there are any organisms, that they fall under the particular items we were calling 'life-forms'. The received taxonomical hierarchy is a record either of history or of the similarities that this history explains; but the simple 'classification' of individual organisms in terms of life-form precedes any possible judgment of similarity or of shared historical genesis. It is already implicit in any representation of individual organisms as alive, and thus as, for example, eating or growing, or as having arms or leaves. The real subject of a natural-historical judgment and of an Aristotelian categorical is, I think, inevitably a representation of *the thing that must be there*—that is, something like what was formerly called an *infima species*. But even this description is impure and not properly philosophical: it retains the suggestion of higher 'species', and thus of collateral *infimae species*, which, as I have said, need not be there, and of course were not there when the first life-form came to be, as did once happen.

2. The Irreducibility of This Form of Thought

We have to do with a special nexus of concepts in a judgment, or of general terms in a proposition, however it may be formulated—"The S does F," "S's do F," "This is how things go with an S: it does F." One's first inclination, though, is to attempt to reduce this connection of representations to something more familiar.

So, for example, we might attempt to assimilate "Man sheds his teeth" to "Each man sheds his teeth," or, equivalently, to "For every man x, x sheds his teeth." On such an account the predicate "sheds his teeth" is caught up in the same sort of combination (but with an *individual* variable) as it is in, say, "When little Arthur here sheds his teeth, . . ." The account is of course worthless: 'man' sheds all of 'his' deciduous teeth, but some of us keep a few, and in any case it isn't *shedding* if they are kicked out in a street fight.

Does the sentence then rather amount to something on the order of "*Most* men shed their teeth"? At first sight even Aristotle appears to have made the identification. Something akin to our mode of combination of concepts is explicitly mentioned in his account of accident, for example. He characterizes the propositions so formed as holding *hōs epi to polu*, a phrase typically rendered "for the most part".[6] But, again obviously, although 'the mayfly' breeds shortly before dying, *most* mayflies die long before breeding. And if the description of the 'life-cycle' of the monarch butterfly told us 'what mostly happens', then it would soon be unnecessary to visit that strange Mexican valley in order to wade knee-deep among them. A natural-historical judgment may be true though individuals falling under both the subject and predicate concepts are as rare as one likes, statistically speaking.[7]

Perhaps then the sort of proposition that characterizes natural-historical discourses should be brought under the linguists' rubric: *generic sentence*, and we should follow them in their attempt to supply a

---

6. *Physics*, II, 5, 196b10ff; see also *Posterior Analytics*, A, 30, 87b20. The phrase *hōs epi to polu* is found all over the corpus—see, for example, the discussion of the exactness desired in practical philosophy in *Nicomachean Ethics*, I, 3—but the locution is made an object of reflection in these places.

7. See the remarks on the number of teeth 'man' has in G. E. M. Anscombe, "Modern Moral Philosophy," *Philosophy* 33 (1958): 1–19, reprinted in *Ethics, Religion and Politics* (Minneapolis: University of Minnesota Press, 1981), pp. 26–42.

certain sort of 'semantic' analysis.[8] Here, though, we meet with a different sort of problem. It is not that the suggestion is simply false. If the class of generic sentences is marked off by possession of some such outward form as the unquantified 'bare' plural "S's are F," then there is no question that a natural-historical judgment *can* be expressed in a 'generic' sentence. But is there any reason to think that the class of generic sentences, so understood, is not a ragbag covering many forms of conjunction of subject and predicate—our own type just one among them? We have already seen that a similarly identified class of 'statements with a definite description as subject' would have to constitute a merely surface-grammatical category: it is clear that the words "The domestic cat has four legs" contain a profound syntactical ambiguity, and that the natural reading is not the one Russell attempted to explain.

⁓ IT IS IMPLICIT IN Aristotle's remarks that inferences involving judgments *hōs epi to polu* should mirror those involving universal judgments.[9] And it does seem true that, just as "All A's are F" and "All A's are G" together entail "All A's are both F and G," so also "The S is F" (or "S's are F") and "The S is G" (or "S's are G") together entail "The S is both F and G" (or "S's are both F and G")— if it is our sort of combination that is expressed. The inference would obviously be invalid for any sort of statistical generalization. And it would be too bold to claim that it holds for generic statements or bare plurals generally, if only because the bare plural can presumably express a form of statistical generalization. The validity of such inferences is, I think, one of the reasons why we incline to express natural-historical judgments by means of a definite article—after all, inferences involving proper names and definite descriptions mirror those involving universal generalizations in a number of ways, as was traditionally noticed. A typical page of biochemical exposition exhibits none of the inferential anxiety that would be called for if the propositions it contains and unites all expressed mere statistical generalizations or if they were to admit only the inferences that we can suppose hold generally among what linguists call generic propositions.

8. Standard treatments are Gregory N. Carlson, *Reference to Kinds in English* (New York: Garland, 1980), and Gregory N. Carlson and Francis J. Pelletier, *The Generic Book* (Chicago: University of Chicago Press, 1995).

9. *Posterior Analytics*, 87b23.

A similar recommendation would be that our propositions be taken as Fregean universal propositions after all, but qualified by something one calls a ceteris paribus clause. "The bobcat breeds in spring" will thus, I suppose, amount to something of the form "For all x, if x is a bobcat, and spring is approaching, and . . . x . . . , then x will soon be breeding." How one completes the ellipses will depend on one's understanding of these ceteris paribus clauses. The added condition will either be 'normative' or not; if it is, I will come to it later; if it is not, then the suggestion will be either that conditions are *normal* or *standard* or *ordinary* in some (non-'normative') sense, or else that nothing *intervenes* that might prevent the breeding.

Let us consider the appeal to intervention first. I object: the question "What *counts* as intervention?" is surely to be answered, in any given case, by appeal to the system of natural-historical judgments with the relevant kind as subject. And so we cannot simply take such a category for granted and then employ it in an account of our present form of thinking. If the mother bobcat leaves her young alone, then they will wither and rot; if she nurses them, they will develop thus and so. In which case, though, do we find 'intervention', and in which rather 'what happens, ceteris paribus'? No one will insist that the mother's nursing be viewed as the intervention of something alien, from without, into an otherwise inviolate cub-system set to evolve in its own direction. But to *deny* this proposition is just a more stilted way of expressing the thought that bobcats are not to be compared with caterpillars—they do not strike out alone and set themselves straightaway to munching. No, 'the mother nurses them for several weeks'; I heard about it on a nature documentary.

The same sort of objection may of course be raised against any appeal to 'normal', 'ordinary' or 'standard' conditions. Let us take the simplest sort of judgment to which such an account might reasonably be applied. If I say "Water is a liquid" or "Oxygen is a gas"—and who will not?—I do seem to presuppose what are sensibly called 'normal conditions'. And so, "In normal conditions, water is a liquid" is a more precise and strict formulation of my thought. If, now, I go on to spell these conditions out, I will mention, for example, room temperature. What is 'normal' or 'standard' is here evidently judged by reference to myself. The 'normal conditions' presupposed in such a statement as "Water is a liquid" are not *normal conditions for water*—continuous bits of it will indifferently occupy any of the three states of matter—and to articulate them is not to articulate any truth about water.

Now suppose I say, "Bobcats breed in spring": it is again obvious that this isn't going to happen in any particular case unless certain conditions are satisfied. Perhaps a special hormone must be released in late winter. And perhaps the hormone will not be released if the bobcat is too close to sea level, or if it fails to pass through the shade of a certain sort of tall pine. But, now, to articulate *these* conditions is to advance one's teaching about bobcats. It is not a reflection on the limited significance of one's original teaching. The thought that *certain hormones are released,* or that *they live at such and such altitudes and amid such and such vegetation,* is a thought of the same kind as the thought that *they breed in spring.* The field guide and the nature documentary assign an external environment to the intended life-form, after all, and in the same mood or voice or discursive form they elsewhere employ in describing its bearers' inner structure and operations. These conditions are thus 'presupposed' by the life-form itself; and how the bearer comes to arrive in them will itself be described in natural-historical terms. The conditions in question are thus not something presupposed by the poor observing subject with his low-resolution lens, as they were with "Oxygen is a gas." If Q is simply *true,* then "P on condition that Q" does not supply a more 'precise' or 'strict' formulation of anything that P might 'loosely' formulate—though it may, of course, be an interesting truth in its own right. All of this must, I think, distinguish our natural-historical judgments from the so-called hedged generalities or ceteris paribus laws said to be employed in certain of the 'special sciences'.[10]

The peculiarity of the propositions that interest us might be brought

10. See, for example, the exchange between Stephen Schiffer and Jerry Fodor in *Mind* 100 (1991): 1–34. This particular dispute is in any case over judgments linking event-types with event-types, and not judgments like our own, which link individual-substance-types with all manner of things. It is clear, by the way, that on Fodor's account of his super-abstract category, ceteris paribus statements, the things will emphatically not support the Aristotelian form of inference I mentioned—see especially the diagram on p. 139 of his "Special Sciences," reprinted in *Representations* (Cambridge: MIT Press, 1981). We cannot pass from a conjunction of predications to an application of the conjunctive predicate, any more than we can pass from "Most A's are F" and "Most A's are G" to "Most A's are F and G." The great mass of ensuing discussion of ceteris paribus statements or laws seems to preserve all of these features and thus has little relevance to our present topic.

out if we labor the point that they are consistent with a really vanishing
rate of realization among past, present and future bearers of the life-
form in question—a point implicit in my remark above about the monarch butterfly and about the dandelion in Chapter 3, Section 1. It
might coherently be supposed to characterize some life-form that it re-
leases a thousand or a million eggs, or seeds, each season. The general
natural history of the kind will inter alia state the characteristic developmental 'story' of the egg or seed, saying, for each stage, 'what happens next,' until we come to the mature form. If we can suppose that
the population has for millennia stayed the same, within a few orders
of magnitude, then we are supposing that this imagined story will only
have been realized in something like 1 or 2 in a thousand or a million
cases. Nevertheless, we forge the general connection of concepts, which
must plainly be of a very distinctive kind: I say, pointing to an acorn
and an oak, that such a thing as *this* turns into such a thing as *this*, and
I say it without qualification, and will do so even in the imagined
type of case, however high the numbers go. It is difficult to see how
such a proposition can be supposed to record "what happens ceteris
paribus".

   The same point emerges differently if we notice that by repeated application of our apparently unexciting rule of inference—"S's are F,"
"S's are G," *ergo* "S's are both F and G"—we will presumably always be
able to produce a true statement of our form involving a complex conjunctive predicate that is not true of *any* member of the kind denoted
by its subject, living or dead. I mean: nobody's perfect. (Will anyone
say, by the way, that anything is, ceteris paribus, what it never is?)

   This may seem to cut our propositions entirely free of 'the facts'. But
consider the system of true natural-historical judgments with a given
kind, S, as subject; call it *the natural history of S's*. The individual judgments are to be understood as out-takes from such an ensemble; the
idea of such a judgment is, that is, internally related to the idea of such
a totality; each is a contribution to the description of the "wider context" that came to our attention in the last chapter; the exemplification
of any one of these general propositions in any individual case ("this
one is eating") will rest on the truth of many others. I do not doubt that
many of the features attributed to S itself in this imagined 'history' will
also have to be attributable to many of the individual S's that have existed or will have existed (attributable, that is, in the more familiar
"When little Arthur sheds his teeth . . ." sort of way). To deny it would

in any case make for a bold expression of Platonism. But the affirmation alone tells us nothing about the relation that any *particular* judgment in the 'history' must have to the class of individual S's, past and present, and the facts about them.

The unity of subject and predicate realized in an Aristotelian categorical, "The S is F," and the act of mind expressed in it, are thus not to be compared with those realized and expressed in the English forms "Some S is F," "All S's are F" and "Most S's are F" or indeed "Any S is F in normal circumstances, or ceteris paribus." The latter, we may say, relate directly to features of individuals covered by the subject term; in the proper analysis of such propositions the predicative element will be revealed as attached to an *individual* variable. The attempt to produce a natural history, by contrast, expresses one's *interpretation* or *understanding* of the life-form shared by the members of that class, if you like, and each judgment in it will bring the predicate-concept into direct connection with a representation of that "form". My understanding may of course be shallow or deep, extensive or narrow, mostly true or largely mistaken. It is itself the 'look to a wider context', which we said governs my description of the individual organism *hic et nunc:* what is implicit in the tensed description of an individual organism is made articulate in a natural-historical judgment and is outwardly expressed in an Aristotelian categorical. But in truth the lyrical opposition, 'an understanding of the life-form' *versus* 'a mere survey of the class', is itself just a more abstract re-write of the concrete opposition of natural-historical judgment and, say, statistical or Fregean-universal thinking, or, more generally, a thinking in which the predicative element is attached to a singular representation or an individual variable.

3. Is Natural-Historical Judgment 'Normative' Judgment?

But perhaps I have overlooked a possibility of reduction. Frege himself, in his dispute with Kerry, considers the sentence "The horse is a four-legged animal," clearly intending it to be taken in our natural-historical sense. He says that it "is probably best regarded as expressing a universal judgement, say 'all horses are four-legged animals' or 'all properly constituted horses are four-legged animals'. . . ."[11] The first alternative

---

11. "On Concept and Object," trans. Peter Geach, reprinted in *Collected Papers*, ed. Brian McGuinness (Oxford: Blackwell, 1984), p. 185.

is obviously wrong; the second raises the possibility of what we may call a *normative analysis*.

I should say that I do believe that our natural-historical judgments are closely related to a range of judgments that one would want to call 'normative'. I will object rather to the idea that we can give anything to be called an analysis or elucidation in terms of them; the reverse is closer to the truth. As for sentences of the form "A properly constituted S is F," my own view is that, in them, the words "properly constituted" do not restrict the common noun, S. Rather, the words "A properly constituted ___ is ___" move together and are just another sign that the judgment expressed is a natural-historical judgment.

But Frege wants to construe the original sentence as expressing a 'universal judgment' in his sense. This presupposes that in his substitute sentence the words "properly constituted horse" act as a unit, and designate or express the concept *properly constituted horse*. How is this concept supposed to be explained? If it is a veterinarian's or horse breeder's notion, so to speak, then presumably a horse will fall under it if it meets a certain limited range of conditions. But many of the features we would want to attribute to 'horses' or 'the horse' in a natural-historical judgment will have to fall outside this range; there is no reason to think that all such so-called 'properly constituted horses' will have them.

We might instead try to explain the concept in something like the following terms: a properly constituted horse is a horse that is as a horse should be (or 'ought to be', or 'is supposed to be') *in every respect*. Here, though, we should notice, first, that there is every reason to think that we now have an empty concept, and thus that our proposition would come out true whatever we put in the predicate place. Again: nobody's perfect. Moreover, such an analysis forces us to believe that the quotidian sentences printed in the field guide and voiced over the nature documentary involve an implicit second-order quantification over 'respects', which is intuitively absurd.

But the best objection to this last account is that it ends up attaching the 'normative' expression to the *predicate*, or rather to a variable for which predicates are to be substituted. Why not try that with the original? Let "The horse is a four-legged animal" amount to: "It holds good of every horse that it ought to have four legs." But, now, what are we to make of the sub-sentence "it ought to have four legs"? Here the norm-word falls between a predicative expression and a variable ranging over individuals, which is what Frege really wants. But this norm-word is so far left too abstract to supply us with a complete account of the original proposition. There is, after all, a way of hearing the word "ought" that might have us assent, in certain moods, to something like "It holds good of every cockroach that it ought to be killed." This "ought" evidently pertains to 'human ends and projects' and is thus out of the question. What we want is a so-to-speak intrinsic, or non-relative, oughtness—we want, for example, "It ought, *as far as its merely being a horse goes*, to be four-legged," or "It is supposed, *by its mere horse-nature*, to be four-legged," or "It ought, *considering just what it is*, to be four legged." There are no doubt other ways of bringing off this specification of the "ought". Some may be more elegant, but each must bring the common noun back into the expression for the relation between the individual and the property. Or, if it does not re-introduce the common noun directly, then, as in the lattermost case, it must inevitably employ a pronominal expression—in this case "what it is". But this pronoun is one for which the common noun can be substituted; it is, as it were, a pro-common-noun.

In order to control the shapeless "ought", then, we are forced to join the predicate and the common noun (or its pronominal representative) together *immediately*—though in the presence of a 'normative' expression and an individual variable. But what a given horse is 'supposed by its mere horse-nature to be' must presumably be the same for every horse. The individual variable, and the quantifier that binds it, are thus wheels turning idly in such a formula as "For every x, if x is a horse, then x is supposed by its mere horse-nature to be four-legged." (It is as if one were to replace the proposition "Two and two make four" with "For all times t, two and two make four at t" with a view to rendering the philosophical problems about the former more tractable.) What we are really saying, then, is "Horses are supposed to be four-legged." All we are really *working with* is a common noun, a predicate, and 'something normative'. We are thus no further on than we were with "A properly constituted horse is four-legged."

But, finally, it was only a hope of reducing our kind of generality to a respectable Fregean sort that had us reaching for anything 'normative' in the first place. On reflection, the move was a desperate one, and did violence to the transparently 'factual' or 'positive' character of the teaching of the field guide, the nature documentary and the biochemical treatise. In the end, I think, all we really *are* working with is a predicate and a certain sort of common noun, united in a way distinctive of the representation of life; the appearances are *bene fundata*.

4. Conclusion: Goodness and Life

In natural-historical description, we meet, I think, with a logically special form of appearance of predicative expressions, one to be distinguished from the essentially tensed connection they may have with representations of individuals, including individual variables. We may say that a common noun has the 'grammar' of a *life-form-word* if it is suited to be the subject of such predication—that is, if this is among the powers of combination with other words that go to fix its sense. Or, equivalently, a word is a life-form-word if the capacity to express natural-historical judgments in terms of it is a part of the mastery of its employment. It is here, I think, as it was with Frege's 'concept-words', which may be said to supply the apt predicates for the more familiar form of predication. An expression "F" or "is F" has the 'grammar' of a concept-word if it can enter into the combinations "a is F" and "a is not F" with some singular term; the capacity to form such combinations is evidently a part of the mastery of its employment. This last is not, I think, something we could say of a statistical quantifier, for example. "Ninety-nine percent of ___ are ___" is something we can *add* to a language with the apparatus of common nouns and other predicative expressions; it does not enter into the constitution of this apparatus, though it may help to define some of its more particular terms. The terms united are themselves indifferent to the possibility of this form of combination.

To affirm that the situation is the same with *our* form of combination, taken as a form of thought, is I think to deny that 'when we call something an acorn we look to a wider context than can be seen in the acorn itself.' We may say that a concept is a *life-form-concept* if it provides a possible subject for this form of judgment. A *life-form* or *species* (in the broad sense) is anything that is, or could be, immediately designated by a life-form-concept or a life-form-word. To this sort of 'genus' or *genos*, then, there corresponds *that* formally distinctive sort of generality. An *organism* or *individual living thing*, finally, is whatever falls under a species or 'bears' a life-form. It is whatever might justly be designated by a phrase of the form "this S" for some possible reading of the common noun S as a life-form-word. Or, equivalently, an organism is the object of any possible judgment, *this S is F*, to which some system of natural-historical judgments, *the S is G, H*, etc., might correspond.

If an intellect loses the capacity for the latter sort of 'synthesis' it must also lose the former, and with it, I think, the capacity to experience things as alive. It can no longer 'look to a wider context'.

In saying all of this I of course presuppose that enough has been said to isolate this form of judgment and its expression in speech. Perhaps there are other types of generality that satisfy the various features registered so far. Perhaps my occasional appeal to the notion of a life-form in attempting to impart the idea of such a form of judgment has begged some question and left the essay to fall short of the exalted standard raised by Anscombe's *Intention*. But the answer to the question "When can we say 'Enough said'?" will of course depend on who we are saying it to, and what else there is in our language and thought with which the intended form may be confused. For someone, I suppose, it might be 'enough' to point out a few peculiarities of the nature documentary.

Let it be thought, though, that we have at best isolated some class of what we may call 'non-Fregean generalities'. The dispiriting suggestion will be that the intended natural-historical judgments form a subclass marked off from the others *by content* and not *by form*. It may be helpful then to notice, briefly, that our enterprise can be carried further. For example, we might go on to remark that natural-historical judgments themselves possess certain further possibilities of combination—in particular, of 'teleological' combination with others of their same form. Their linguistic expressions, that is, are fit to enter into certain sorts of 'final clause': for example, "They have blossoms of such and such type in order that such and such insects should be attracted and thereafter spread the pollen about." Here the propositions joined—"They have blossoms of such and such form" and "They attract certain insects, which spread their pollen about"—are of the intended type.[12]

Now, any attempt to employ this further possibility of combination

12. This is the account of the genuine natural-historical judgment adopted by Philippa Foot in *Natural Goodness* (Oxford: Oxford University Press, 2001), pp. 30–32.

as an instrument of 'grammatical' or putatively formal isolation may of course be thought to raise new difficulties: perhaps the whole idea is just a theological survival. But the insistence on an independent, conscious subject who sets up the things thus 'teleologically' expressed presupposes that the relevant 'sense of the question "Why?"' is the one Anscombe and Davidson discussed. It presupposes, that is, that the intended order is the order of intention. But, of course, it is among the marks of *that* sense of the question "Why?" that it attaches to datable descriptions of goings-on—of 'events in a man's history', as Anscombe says.[13] If a student moves behind a pillar and I ask, "What's going on? What's the point? Why?" and am satisfied with the response "He's trying to avoid Professor X; he owes her a term paper", then it is the movements *hic et nunc* and not elsewhere that form the object of my query. But suppose we are dissecting a living frog and—scalpel aimed at the repulsive contractions of the heart—I ask, "What's going on? What's the point? Why?" If I am satisfied with the response, "It's the heart, of course, and by so beating it circulates the blood," then, after all, I think, it was *not* the individual movements here and now that interested me. I was not so much pointing into the individual, as pointing *into its form*. I do not anticipate a different reply at a different lab bench, as I would at a different pillar. The alarming truth I apprehend and query, the 'that' for which I seek the 'because', is to be formulated in a natural-historical judgment.

We are thus, I think, as far as can possibly be imagined from the category of intention or psychical teleology—a fact that is also shown in this, that if the complex thought about, for example, the blossoms is true, then the judgments joined in it are also true. Here, that is, "P in order that Q" straightforwardly entails both P *and* Q. In making out this sort of connection one links a plain fact, not with a possibly unrealized end, but with another plain fact. Natural teleological judgments may thus be said to organize the elements of a natural history; they articulate the relations of dependence among the various elements and aspects and phases of a given kind of life. I said above that the conditions required for some natural-historically attributable phenomenon to arise will themselves be natural-historically attributable to the life-form in question and belong to the natural history of the form. If these

13. G. E. M. Anscombe, *Intention*, 2nd ed. (Cambridge: Harvard University Press, 2000), p. 24.

conditions include a feature of the environment, still the system will contain the judgment that they live in such an environment, and then in turn judgments about how they come to be there—and so we go on, never leaving the system of natural-historical judgments. The teleological connective simply expresses the concept that is converse to this conception of dependence.

And so, I think, even if the Divine Mind *were* to bring a certain life-form into being 'with a view to' securing an abundance of pink fur along the shores of the Monongahela, this 'purpose' would have no effect on the inner natural teleological description of that form of life, for this is its inner causal structure, taken generally. The intimation of the divine that some found in these particular propositions was, I think, always a matter of grammatical illusion arising from the fact that the same predicates can be employed with reference to what is happening here and now, and to 'what happens' in the quasi-atemporal natural history. This distinction is purely formal and intellectual, and cannot be found in experience. The bare description of this sort of order has nothing to do with *natural selection* either; these propositions are in no sense hypotheses about the past. The elements registered in natural-historical judgments and the interconnections registered in a natural history, and specifically in natural teleological judgments, are all alike characterized by that peculiar 'present' that we saw contains both 'spring' and 'fall' in winter, and 'the seventh year of the cicada's life-cycle' even during the second.

This can of worms having briefly been opened, perhaps new doubts will be raised. One may wonder whether even the monstrous phrase "teleologically articulable non-Fregean generality" can isolate our sort of judgment. Don't certain sorts of *general* propositions enter into a final-causal nexus in the description, for example, of techniques, technical processes, *technai*—and also into the description of the artifacts and bits of technology that are among their means and ends? "The point of the lye bath is to harden the leather." "The point of the carburetor is to mix the air and fuel." In each such case we will find a complex of interconnected judgments that might be compared with a natural history. It would be wrong to insist that the teleology relevant here is the one Anscombe and Davidson discussed.[14] For here too the

14. See Sarah Waterlow Broadie, "Nature, Craft and *Phronesis* in Aristotle," *Philosophical Topics* 15, 2 (1987): 35–50; Andrew Hsu, "Artifacts" (unpublished manuscript); and Matthew Hanser, "Intention and Teleology," *Mind* 107 (1998): 381–401.

propositions linked are general and quasi-atemporal, and here too we will find, I think, that "P in order that Q" straightforwardly entails both P and Q.

But the distinction can be marked in other ways. For example, a kind of 'partial idealism', in Professor Anscombe's sense, seems to hold in the technical and artifactual sorts of cases.[15] The *truth* of a proposition of the form "First one does this, then one does this," where it belongs to the general description of a particular technique of, say, bread-baking or aspirin-synthesis, presupposes that someone makes or has made the corresponding judgment, or at least some others belonging to the same system of judgments—though of course it presupposes more than this. An unrecognized technique or craft or artifact-type is after all a merely possible one. Nothing of the sort would hold of a natural-historical judgment expressed in the form "First this happens, then that happens"—which might expound the phases of the embryo-logical development of cranes, or of the synthesis of glucose in red-woods. Natural-historical judgments are in no sense presupposed by what they are about, and unrecognized life-forms are common.

I will end these reflections on the categories of living actuality with a few unguarded remarks on concepts of *good*. I have rejected any account of natural-historical judgment in normative terms, suggesting that the order of explanation must run the other way. If, though, we want to apply 'normative' categories to sub-rational nature, and apart from any relation to 'our interests', then the question inevitably arises, and not so unreasonably: Where does the standard come from? What supplies the measure? The system of natural-historical propositions with a given kind or form as subject supplies such a standard for members of that kind. We may implicitly define a certain very abstract category of 'natural defect' with the following simple-minded principle of inference: *from:* "The S is F," *and:* "This S is not F," *to infer:* "This S is defective in that it is not F."[16] It is in *this* sense that natural-historical judgments are 'normative', and not by each proposition's bearing some

---

15. "The Question of Linguistic Idealism," in *From Parmenides to Wittgenstein* (Minneapolis: University of Minnesota Press, 1981), pp. 112–133.

16. This conception of 'defect' is of course so unnaturally broad that it would take in, say, losing aspects of the individual creature's environment. It is rather the notion of something's being wrong in connection with the organism than the narrower notion of something's being wrong with it.

sort of secret normative infrastructure. The first application of concepts of good, bad, defect and pathology is to the individual, and it consists in a certain sort of reference of the thing to its form or kind and the natural history that pertains to it. Once formed, though, these concepts may of course be employed in general thoughts of various types.

It is true that the judgment of natural defect, so explained, must in a sense reach beyond the 'facts' about an individual. It reaches beyond them, though, to what appear equally to be 'facts'—namely, facts about its kind or species or life-form. What merely 'ought to be' in the individual we may say really 'is' in its form. In another sense, though, the picture of a 'reach beyond' is absurd: *when we call something an acorn we look to a wider context than can be seen in the acorn itself.* A reference to the life-form is *already contained* in the thought of the individual and its vicissitudes. We thus go no farther for critique than we went for interpretation. Consider that we might attempt to explain a conception of, say, oddness, with some such rule as follows: *from:* "Most A's are F," *and:* "This A is not F," *to infer:* "This A is odd in that it is not F." If someone then asks, "But what does 'what most of them do' have to do with what *it* does?" the answer will have to be "Not much, really." But if, in the other case, someone asks, "What bearing does 'what they do' have on what *it* does or is doing?" the answer will have to be "Everything." For, again, every thought of an individual organism as alive is mediated by thought of the life-form it bears. A true judgment of natural defect thus supplies an 'immanent critique' of its subject.

But in truth the abstract category of natural defect is an artificial one. One tends to employ more concrete concepts: sickness, need, lack, deformity—or, still more concretely: lameness, blindness, color-blindness, etiolation, and so forth. Such concepts may be said to express *forms* of natural defect. Whether and when any of them is applicable to a given individual organism will of course depend on the character of its life-form, on the particular content of its form's 'natural history'. They are all, as we might say, 'life-form-relative.'

A certain type of contemporary Aristotelianism in practical philosophy has attempted to defend the ancient notion that, as we may now put it, *irrationality and vice are forms of natural defect;* in Philippa Foot's *Natural Goodness,* for example, we have an unusually striking exposition of the idea. The sort of life in which such concepts gain a foothold is a life caught up in categories of thought and action and passion, of custom and 'culture', and of much else besides. All of these matters raise philosophical problems of their own. It is clear that the relation between *the stupidity of an individual human action*, say, and the character of its agent's life-form is something far more complex and mediated than is the relation, for example, of *the etiolation of a given geranium* to the character of *its* form. The real problem is to grasp this complexity and the distinctions that are introduced with the categories of intellect and will. But no special difficulty arises from a moralist's appeal to the life-form, named "human", that all of us share: we make such appeal already in everything we think of ourselves and one another.

~ PART TWO

Naive Action Theory

～ 5

Introductory

1. Naive and Sophisticated Explanation of Action

It doesn't really befit a philosopher to make such a statement, I don't suppose, but nevertheless I will hazard the following bold empirical hypothesis: the explanation of action as it appears most frequently in human thought and speech is *the explanation of one action in terms of another:*

"Why are you pulling that cord?" says one
  —"I'm starting the engine," says the other;

"Why are you cutting those wires?" says one
  —"I'm repairing a short-circuit," says the other;

"Why are you crossing Fifth Avenue?" says one
  —"I'm walking to school," says the other;

"Why are you breaking those eggs?" says one
  —"I'm making an omelet," says the other.[1]

The question "Why?" that is deployed in these exchanges evidently bears the "special sense" Elizabeth Anscombe has linked to the con-

---

1. The immediately following paragraphs elucidate some of the terms and concepts central to Part Two; its central claims are outlined in the following section.

cepts of intention and of a reason for action; it is the sort of question
"Why?" that asks for what Donald Davidson later called a "rationalization".[2] The special character of what is given, in each response, as formulating a reason—a description, namely, of the agent as actually *doing*
something, and, moreover, as doing something of which the act queried might be said to be a part, phase or "moment"—marks each of our
exchanges as an instance of what I will call *naive action explanation* or,
more generally, *naive rationalization*.[3]

Naive explanation of action is opposed to a distinct, *sophisticated*

---

2. G. E. M. Anscombe, *Intention*, 2nd ed. (Cambridge, Mass.: Harvard University Press,
2000), especially pp. 9–11; Donald Davidson, "Actions, Reasons and Causes," *Journal of Philosophy* 60 (1963): 685–699, reprinted in *Essays on Actions and Events* (Oxford: Oxford University Press, 1980), pp. 3–20.

3. It should perhaps be emphasized that throughout this essay we will have to do only with
what are typically called "explanatory" reasons, and never directly with reasons in the sense of
"justifying" reasons—or (I suppose equivalently), that we treat the notion of *a reason why a
person did something*, not that of *a reason why he or she ought to have done it*. This is not to suggest
that a complete account of the former sort of reason could fail to involve discussion of the latter, but only to allow that we will not here reach a complete account of the former, our topic.

In the Davidsonian usage adopted here, a "rationalization" is of course understood to formulate an "explanatory" reason; the point of this rather artificial usage is to avoid complicated
circumlocution involving reference, for example, to "a certain sense of the question 'Why?'"
The phrase "explanation of action" must also be understood in this sense, as covering only explanations 'by reasons' or 'in the order of reasons'—so that, for example, overtly neurological
accounts of action are ruled out. "Rationalization", as I use it, is wider than "explanation of
action", for it covers reasons-explanations of other things—for example, explanations of intention, of wanting in a certain sense, and of attempt.

I should perhaps also remark that in company with the whole action-theoretical tradition, I
presuppose a more or less realistic, or anti-pragmatic, theory of specifically *practical* explanation, that is, of rationalization considered as a phenomenon of speech and thought. The ultimate aim of action theory is a philosophical understanding of a particular etiological nexus, or
relation of dependence, that joins certain "things in the world"—together, of course, with an
understanding of these things themselves, for example, actions and wantings. The assumption is that such a nexus or order is revealed in certain forms of speech and thought, even if
often incompletely or in somewhat confusing ways. In brief defense of this 'realism' we may
note, first, the peculiar fatuity that appears to threaten any attempt to explain away practical
explanation *pragmatically*, and, second, that the capacity to represent these phenomena seems
to enter into the constitution of the order that is represented—here, that is, the 'order and
connection of ideas' is in a sense a *part* of the order and connection of things.

Whether the intended nexus is *causal* in any particular pre-conceived sense is of course a
separate question; I will not enter into the matter explicitly. Certainly, I think, the so-called
'belief component' of such explanation should be viewed as a cause, and it contains what is
most properly called her reason, i.e., the consideration on which she acts. But our interest
here is in the other 'component', the wanting, and the other things that can take its position. I
employ the word "etiological"—thinking of Aristotle's four *aitia*—where I might have said
"causal", in order to express my agnosticism in respect to this formerly much vexed question.

form—a form that, if it is less common in life, is all the same much more common in the pages of philosophy. This is the explanation of action in terms of desire, or, as we might rather call it, the explanation of action in terms of wanting, or of what the agent wants. Here are a few examples, lifted at random from Professor Davidson's essay "Actions, Reasons and Causes"[4]:

"Why are you flipping that switch?"
  —"I *want* to turn on the light";

"Why are you biting your thumb at me?"
  —"I *want* to insult you";

"Why are you turning left?"
  —"I *want* to get to Katmandu."

The philosophers' emphasis on the question "Why?" lends a certain colloquial realism to the discussion of reasons for action, of course, but it imports into the discussion all the further complexities that attend the interrogative form. The self-same etiological content, whether it be naive or sophisticated, can always be expressed apart from any such interrogative context. The agent can simply volunteer such a "sophisticated" rationalization as this one:

"I am gathering kindling because I *want* to build a fire,"

or (perhaps a little later) this one:

"I am building a fire because I *want* to burn the evidence of my crime."

Similarly, an agent might volunteer such "naive" rationalizations as these (here perhaps more or less simultaneously):

"I am mixing mortar because I am laying bricks," and

"I am laying bricks because I am building a monument to the great works of Frege."

4. Donald Davidson, *Essays on Action and Events* (Oxford: Oxford University Press, 1981), pp. 4–6.

Where naive and sophisticated articulations of peoples' reasons are uniformly assertoric in this sort of way, they are alike in employing the all-purpose explanatory connective "because". But the content of either form of account can be reformulated in terms of a so-called final or purpose clause (with, of course, the loss of whatever information distinguishes them). Our sophisticated and naive pairs transpose, respectively, into these finalized formulae:

"I am gathering these sticks in order to build a fire," and

"I am building a fire in order to burn the evidence,"

and these:

"I am mixing concrete in order to lay bricks," and

"I am laying bricks in order to build a monument."

A final or purposive rendering of a rationalization permits us to attach an undeclined verb of action directly to the explanatory connective "in order to", omitting even the second reference to the agent. With a non-final rendering, things are different: whether it is employed in meteorology, medicine or financial reporting, or in the rational explanation of action, the word "because" must be flanked by complete propositions, to each of which the writer commits herself. However we understand it, that is, *P because Q* will entail both *P* and *Q*. In adopting a non-final form of expression of an action explanation we are thus forced to decide how to fit the second verb of action into a complete sentence, a truth. Are we going to join subject and verb directly and without varnish—saying of our egg-breaker, for example, that he *is* making an omelet; or indirectly, by the interpolation of a new verb, saying merely that he *wants* to make an omelet?[5] This is the choice of naiveté or sophistication.

To sum up, then, we are faced with three linguistically given forms of rationalization: I'm doing A because I'm doing B; I'm doing A because

5. See the parallel remarks in Anscombe, *Intention*, pp. 39–40.

I want to do B; and, finally: I'm doing A in order to do B—which last form tends to swallow the other two up.[6]

2. Preliminary Formulation of Central Claims

The notion of rationalization with which I am operating is restricted to such as *can* be given a final-clausal or purposive or "instrumental" or "teleological" formulation; it is the notion, as I will sometimes say, of *straightforward rationalization.*[7] The focus of the present discussion will, however, be on the non-final form of expression of straightforward rationalization—the sort that uses the word "because" or an equivalent. Though a blinkered understanding of this mode of connection of representations arguably lies at the bottom of much received opinion in ethical theory and in the philosophy of practical rationality, the aims of the present essay are in the first instance metaphysical or action-

6. Since they will appear throughout this essay, I should perhaps remark that the schematic letters "A", "B", "C", etc., do not contain the whole variable element: typical substitution instances of "He wants to do A" would be, for example, "He wants to walk across the street" and "He wants to make an omelet," which dispense with the verb "to do". As the function of the copula "to be" is to receive distinctions of tense, the point of introducing a "pro-verb" like "to do", in the present context, is to have something that will receive distinctions of both tense *and aspect.*

7. Thus, in the sense in which the term is used in this essay, "I killed him because he killed my brother" and "I turned onto Negley Avenue because Highland Park Avenue was closed" do not express rationalizations directly. Corresponding genuinely straightforward rationalizations might be, for example, "I killed him because I wanted to avenge the death of my brother" and "I turned onto Negley Avenue because I was going to the dentist"; these transpose into the purposive forms ". . . in order to avenge the death of my brother" and ". . . in order to go to the dentist", respectively.

What is posited as an "end" in what I am calling a straightforward rationalization is always something that can be thought of as completely realized or effected or "done" at some point. Given such completion, if later actions are subordinate to pursuit of an end formulated in the same terms, then it is a new end—*another* act of omelet making, for example, or another trip to Katmandu. Rationalizations that associate action with what might be called generic ends are thus not straightforward in this sense, and fall outside our present enquiry. Such rationalizations are frequently formulated in English by the use of "for the sake of"—for example, "he did it for the sake of health" (or science, or our freedom, or his own happiness, etc.). The radical distinction between such "ends" and those represented by, say, ". . . in order to get the good guys in" or ". . . in order to make an omelet" is emphasized by Anscombe in *Intention*, p. 63; in "Authority in Morals," in *Ethics, Religion and Politics* (Minneapolis: University of Minnesota Press, 1981), pp. 43–50, especially pp. 48–49; and in "Practical Inference," in *Virtues and Reasons*, ed. R. Hursthouse, G. Lawrence and W. Quinn (Oxford: Clarendon, 1995), pp. 1–34, especially pp. 28–34.

theoretical. Our enquiry is into the nexus of things that is made articulate in rationalization, and also into the nature of intentional action. Anscombe, as everyone knows, taught that these enquiries are the same: intentional action, as she put it, is "that to which a certain sense of the question 'Why?' has application."[8] And Davidson, as everyone also knows, taught that *any analysis of the rationalization-connection must account for its non-final form of expression.*[9] My aim is to trace out the consequences of taking seriously the idea, implicit in the ubiquitous practice of naive rationalization, that intentional action can figure in the order of things equally as grounded and as ground, as rationalized and as (non-finally) rationalizing. If naive rationalization *is* taken seriously, our conceptions of intentional action and of rationalization alike must, I will argue, be appreciably altered.

But is naive action explanation to be taken seriously? It may be ubiquitous, but is it anything more than a dispensable manner of speaking? Arguments crowd in, after all, to the effect that the explanatory content of naive action explanation, its underlying etiological basis, must be something that is more directly or more appropriately expressed in some sophisticated form. Our agent is building a house, indeed, but *that's* not why he's laying these bricks, not *really;* the ground, in nature, of the brick-laying, must be rather something like this, that she *wants* to build a house. Such thoughts are the mark of what I will call a sophisticated philosophy of action, which finds in every genuine straightforward rationalization a movement from inner to outer, from mind to world, from spirit to nature, from "desire" to "action". One of my principal theses will thus have to be this, that a sophisticated position cannot be defended, that the linguistic appearances ought to be saved, and that the role played by wanting, in the one sort of case, really is taken up, in the other, by what we might call the progress of the deed itself.

That such a position seems strange, in spite of the ubiquity and

---

8. Anscombe, *Intention,* p. 9.

9. "Central to the relation between a reason and an action it explains is the idea that the agent performed the action *because* he had the reason" (Davidson, "Actions, Reasons and Causes," p. 9). This does not entail that finality or purposiveness are somehow expelled from Davidson's doctrine as it is expounded, amid revisions, in the first six papers in *Essays on Actions and Events.* The selection of apt belief-desire pairs is evidently controlled by the intelligibility of a purposive rendering of the rationalization; and we are surely supposed to advert to this form in characterizing a causal relation as non-deviant or rationalization-supporting. His doctrine is not a rejection of practical teleology, but a theory of it.

seeming transparency of naive rationalization, is in part a consequence of received conceptions of intentional action itself, above all, of the tendency of students of practical philosophy to view individual human actions as discrete or atomic or pointlike or eye-blink-like units that might as well be instantaneous for all that it matters to the theory. Part of the present effort, then, is to break up such conceptions. A person might, after all, spend a few years building a house, a few months raising an acre of cantaloupe, a few hours baking a loaf of bread, a few minutes playing a hand of poker—or a few seconds assassinating a political opponent. Any of these will make an apt illustration of the concept of intentional action, none more apt than any other.[10] If we reach for the last and shortest of these as our preferred illustration, as the one that makes everything especially clear—and proceed to dwell, for example, on its supposed identity with an apparently unanalyzable *moving of a finger*, rather than its equally attractive and likely resolution into *reaching for*, *raising*, *aiming* and *firing* a gun, to say nothing of *checking to see if the victim is done for* and *repeating as necessary*—it is, I will suggest, because we are moved by considerations alien to the philosophy of action, however legitimate they may be from the point of view of, say, a physiologist investigating "voluntary" as opposed to "reflex" movement. The nature of intentional action, or of the kind of being-subject-of-an-event that characterizes a rational agent and a person, resides in the peculiar "synthesis" that unites the various parts and phases of something like house building, for example, mixing mortar, laying bricks, hammering nails, etc. This synthesis is rendered explicit in naive rationalization, which brings them successively to the one formula "I'm building a house." But the synthesis can be exhibited, I will suggest, even in the moving of a finger.

The recognition of naive rationalization is impeded not just by a narrow conception of intentional action, but also, I think, by a wrong conception of the sorts of practical-psychical state that can be given as straightforwardly rationalizing—for example, *wanting* and *intention*. An attempt will be made in the later sections of this essay to unite naive

---

10. Notice also that the periods mentioned might be superimposed in a description of the activity of a single person. Having set a few more bricks this morning, and irrigated the melons this afternoon, I might pick off a passing peasant organizer as I sit on the veranda, waiting for the bread to rise and for my friend to place his bet. Such phenomena will take on increasing significance as our argument develops.

and sophisticated rationalization as co-equal forms of expression of a single etiological nexus. This will turn on a re-conceptualization of these practical-psychological phenomena and, in particular, on the isolation of a *genus* under which *intending to do A, wanting to do A* fall together with *doing A intentionally* (in one of its modes of appearance). To grasp this genus, it will be necessary to intrude into the general metaphysics of events, processes or happenings—or rather, into the part of this metaphysics that belongs to the analysis of what Wilfrid Sellars called the "Manifest Image."[11] The general form of straightforward rationalization, I will suggest, can only be understood properly if it is brought into connection with certain frequently suppressed features of natural or pre-scientific temporal awareness and conception.[12] The resulting theory involves a considerable alteration in the categorical standing of wanting and intending and other such "acts of will"— among other things, a complete break with the apparently uncontroversial idea that they are properly called *states*.

The argument will conclude with a speculative reversal of the idea of a sophisticated philosophy of action. I will attempt to defend the conjecture that naive action explanation is no mere co-equal of sophisticated action explanation, but is in an important sense *prior* to it. It is, I want to suggest, only because we are to start with the kind of thing of which you can say something like "She's doing A because she's doing B" that we can be or become the sort of which you might say "She's doing A because she wants to do B." It is possible to imagine a form of life and thought in which the latter, sophisticated form is simply unknown. Among such agents, all of the work of straightforward rationalization is effected by means of the rationalization connective combined only with the categories of ordinary event consciousness. The more "sophisticated" forms of straightforward rationalization can then be depicted as arising from this rustic state of things in a series of stages akin to that described in, say, Sellars's "Myth of Jones."[13] If barter is the

11. "Philosophy and the Scientific Image of Man," in *Science, Perception and Reality* (New York: Humanities Press, 1963), pp. 1–40. Sellars calls this sort of philosophy "philosophia perennis"; I suppose that ethics and the philosophy of rationality, as well as their servant, the philosophy of action, all necessarily fall under it.

12. Chief among the features I mean are those that, when they manage to find independent expression in the forms of human speech, are ranged by linguists under a heading of "aspect", and distinguished by them from "tense".

13. *Empiricism and the Philosophy of Mind* (Cambridge, Mass.: Harvard University Press, 1997), pp. 90–117.

naive and unsophisticated form of exchange, then naive action explanation is the barter form of rationalization.

3. Remark on the Intellectual Aspect of Our Material

I should perhaps remark, before continuing, on something that may already have been noticed: in my preliminary characterization of the concepts of naive and sophisticated explanation of action I said nothing about what might be called the intellectual aspect of rationalization. This is the aspect that is registered, in the received jargon, in terms of the 'belief component' of a rationalizing 'belief-desire pair'. Where naive explanation of action is possible, we could, I think, speak with equal justice of the 'belief component' of a belief-*action* pair. No one can be said to break an egg "because he's making an omelet", after all, if he is unaware of any possible connection between these things. It is just for this reason, though, that most of this discussion will proscind from the matters of belief, practical thought, practical calculation and so forth. My principal topic is the *distinction* between naive and sophisticated rationalization; if a link with the powers exercised in belief is something they have in common, then we can reasonably divide through by it.

From the point of view of this work as a whole, however, the so-called belief component is all-important. For it contains the consideration upon which the agent acts in doing A, that is, the thing that is most properly or narrowly called the 'reason' or *ratio* or *logos* upon which her doing of A is founded. In a proper and canonical representation, this reason or consideration will always be a thought precisely *about doing A*. The action is founded on something the agent sees in it; there's something about it, as she thinks, that moves her to act. (Not all explanation of action that fits with Anscombe's sense of the question "Why?" will be like this; if I say that someone is eating because he is hungry, I do not thereby put the *eating* down to something the agent sees in it, or to an idea he has about it.)

Thus, for example, the bearer of fidelity and justice—our topic in Part Three of this work—will often do something, A, on the basis of the consideration that *she promised Y that she would do A*. In the 'straightforward' sort of case that is the topic of this part, the relevant 'thought about doing A' is *instrumental*, to use the familiar jargon. In particular, it will link the idea of doing A up with the idea of doing B, where doing B is the larger objective that is mentioned in the various sub-types of straightforward rationalization we have been considering. The thought in question might take a number of forms: for example, the agent may think that by *doing A she will thereby do B*, or *might thereby do B*; or she might think that *doing A is the first stage of doing B* or the *second* or *third*; or she might think that *doing A will make things apt for doing B*, or *might make them apt*, or *might help make them apt*; and so on. In any event her thought must have the form *... to do A ... to do B. ...*

The dependence of an action on a consideration, or on a reason, narrowly construed, is presumably always a sort of causal dependence; but the contrast between the thought-dependence found in our present sort of case and in something like genuine fidelity to promises suggests that the thought-dependence of human action can take radically different forms. As Aristotle would say, it is not just any chance thought that can operate as the consideration upon which just any chance action is founded: if it is an action of doing A, it must be a thought about doing A, as we said above; but not just any *such* thought will do either. What sort of thought about doing A it might be will depend on what operates in the background and makes the dependence of action on thought to be of the 'right kind' to be called a dependence of action on a reason or consideration. In the case we are considering here in Part Two, it is the fact that the agent *wants* to do B—or even, as I think, the fact that the agent *is doing* B—that joins *the thought that ... to do A ... to do B ...* and *the agent's doing A* together as cause and effect of the right kind.

It is not like this in the case of the hero of fidelity, whose action, under the description contained in the promise, also exhibits a dependence on thought-about-action. Her consideration is not instrumental, it is of the form *... to do A ...* simply, or in the case at hand, more specifically *I promised X that I would do A*. The dependence of faithful action on thought is again made to be 'of the right kind' by the presence of something else, which we will later identify with the virtue of fidelity, or of justice simply. Its category is very remote from that now under consideration.

One gets a sense of the categorial transposition or slippage when one reflects on the obvious point that the same thought might operate in a straightforward explanation of action. It might be that some other agent, not the hero of fidelity, wants simply *to do something he promised Y he'd do*—for example, in order to fake out Y for later bilking, or to impress a girl here present who is an admirer of Y and also of justice. The consideration on which such a character's doing A is founded might be the same as we find in our hero's case, *but it will enter into the account in accordance with different analysis,* in Frege's sense. In representing the consideration or reason upon which his action is founded, we would do better to write something like "My doing A is a case of my doing something I promised Y I'd do" rather than "I promised Y I'd do A," though these are the same thought presented in different shapes. The long-winded formulation merely brings out the instrumental form, . . . *to do A* . . . *to do B* . . . , which is the crucial one in his case—it puts "to do something I promised Y I'd do" in the "to do B" position, and "is a case of" in place of the ellipses.

Similarly, in the parallel 'theoretical' case, someone who knows (or believes) that *Cato killed Cato* may come to know (or believe) that *either Cato killed Cato or Caesar killed Cato,* by or-introduction; or he may come to know that *someone killed Cato,* by existential generalization; or he may come to know that *someone killed himself,* again by existential generalization. In all three cases the premise is the same, but the inference, or the dependence of cognition on cognition, turns on a different analysis of it. In the first inference, the proposition is treated as an unanalyzed whole, *Cato killed Cato;* in the second, it might better be expressed as *it holds of Cato, that he killed Cato;* and in the third as *it holds of Cato, that he killed himself.* But, again, these are just different ways of formulating the same thought.

In sum, then: any thought that might engender another thought after the fashion of existential generalization might also engender another after the fashion of or-introduction, but in accordance with another analysis; and so also any thought about doing A that might engender a doing of A non-instrumentally might also engender a doing of A instrumentally, but, again, in accordance with another analysis. For the thought *F(to do A)* can always be reformulated as *to do A is to do something F.* Moreover, any thought of the form . . . *to do A* . . . *to do B* . . . is also of the form *F(to do A),* and might enter into a non-straightforward account of action, though the cases will tend to be a bit recherché.

If this is right, then the distinction between instrumental and non-instrumental considerations pertains neither to their content nor their form, but to the specific form of dependence of the action on the consideration, which turns on the presence of something else.[14] Here we consider one such form, and in Part Three another. If Aristotle or Kant

---

14. In "Actions, Reasons and Causes," Davidson famously argues that 'reasons are causes' starting from the fact that the wanting to do B and the thought that . . . to do A . . . to do B

is right, there must be still others. What is distinctive of the form of thought-dependence under discussion here, as will I think be seen, is that it is internally related to the idea of action in ways the other things are not. Action is typically a process that runs through phases, and the case where the resolution into phases turns on the agent's thought must be typical or possible. The sort of dependence on thought that is characteristic of those phases, which are themselves actions in that sort of case, is the type at issue here.[15]

. . . , and, on the other hand, the wanting to do B* and the thought that . . . to do A . . . to do B* . . . , can all co-exist with the action of doing A. It might be that only the second thought, the thought that . . . to do A . . . to do B* . . . , states the agent's reason for doing A. How then to distinguish this consideration from the other thought, except by its causal relation to the action? This seems reasonable enough, but it should be noticed that the argument has here been stated, and the conclusion drawn—reasons, that is considerations, are causes—without declaring that the wantings are causes. No doubt in some sense they are, but in fact Davidson gets this result only by summing consideration and wanting under the title of the 'primary reason' earlier in the paper, then proving that this primary reason contains the cause. This doesn't tell us what in this aggregate does contain the cause in question.

If the agent in question is a bearer of fidelity and, on the one hand, wants to do B and thinks that . . . to do A . . . to do B . . . , but, on the other hand, thinks that she promised Y that she'd do A, then it might be that she does A 'because she promised', and not in hope of doing B. That is, only the second thought contains her reason or operates as the cause in the way that thoughts can in practice. If Davidson's argument is taken in this way, as affirming the doctrine that reasons in the strict sense, that is considerations, are causes, then there will be no cause to assimilate the wanting to do B and fidelity as two cases of an imaginary super-category 'desire'. These things are very remote from each other logically speaking, and the senses in which they are causes must be separately explained. To put them together is like putting *Begriff* and *Gegenstand* together as, say, 'entities'.

I should note further that there is no evidence that Anscombe would reject the doctrine I have outlined in this note. It has been thought by those unfamiliar with the evidence that she is among the targets of Davidson's paper, which mentions Ryle, Melden, Winch and Kenny as offenders. Some of her jargon—for example, the concept "mental cause", which is more or less explicitly introduced as an unanalyzable unit, and the associated opposition between *thoughts as reasons* and *thoughts as (mere) 'causes'* (such as we find in some cases of the badly so-called 'mental [mere] causality')—has aided and abetted in this. Though she claims early on (p. 10) that "the topic of causality is in a state of too great confusion" to be employed by her in any crucial elucidatory way, still the whole purpose of the book is clearly to argue for the proposition that at last appears on p. 87, viz. "practical knowledge is the cause of what it understands," that is, that the agent's self-knowledge in respect of action is productive, not reflective, of what is known. This is not the particular 'causalist' doctrine Davidson was propounding, since for one thing the element of self-consciousness or self-knowledge—which is I think Anscombe's ultimate interest—is undeveloped by him; but it is very far from any horror of finding causality in the sphere of the mind.

15. This is I think a better formulation of the purpose of Anscombe's *Intention*, secs. 20 and 21, which might be put by saying that the capacity to act for reasons must inter alia be the capacity to act for instrumental reasons, or, as she puts it, 'some chains must begin' (24).

～ 6

Types of Practical Explanation

1. The Table of Forms of Rationalization

My principal end, as I have said, is to argue that naive action explanation is an independent and legitimate type, as much revealing of the true "causes" of action, in its place, as is the philosophers' preferred form, the one I have called sophisticated. But even if it is true that any strict and philosophical formulation of someone's reason for action must be sophisticated, still it is clear that what is supposed to explain *action* in such a case—namely, the agent's wanting something—might equally well be given in explanation of an agent's *wanting* something. Where desire or wanting is thus explained by another wanting it is thereby shown to be what Thomas Nagel called a "motivated desire"— as indeed the want or desire that explains it might already have been. I might want to do A *because I want to do B*, but want to do B *because I want to do C*—in which case, of course, I want to do A because I want to do C—and so forth.[1] Such psychical rationalizations of the psychical are of course straightforward: they admit purposive reformulation in such exchanges as "Why do you want to do A?"—"In order to do C."

But notice that, just as, at least in vulgar speech, the unvarnished formula of an *action* can be used—naively—to explain another action, so also can an unvarnished formula of action be used, in that same vulgar

---

1. See G. E. M. Anscombe, *Intention*, 2nd ed. (Cambridge, Mass.: Harvard University Press, 2000), pp, 26–27.

speech, to explain someone's *wanting* to do something. That is, I might want to do A because I *am doing* B. Such rationalizations also, of course, admit purposive reformulation.

Consider, for example, the following bit of banal domestic patter, a serial deployment of non-purposive forms:

> "Why are you stepping up onto that stool?"
> —"Because I want to get the flour down."
>
> "And why do you want to get the flour down?"
> —"Because I'm preparing chicken and dumplings."
>
> "And why, I ask, are you preparing chicken and dumplings?"
> —"Because I want to make something nice for Aunt Clara: she's coming down from Altoona to see us, you know."

Here, if we cleave to appearances, an *action* (of stepping) is explained by a *want* (for getting flour), which is then explained by an *action* (of preparing chicken and dumplings), which is in turn explained by a *want* (for making something nice). Thus, whether mediately or immediately, all four types of rationalizing connection are exhibited: want by action, action by want, action by action, and want by want.

Moreover, just as, in vulgar speech, the formula of a want can rationalize either a want or an action, so also can it rationalize an *intention*. I might, that is, intend or plan or mean to do A because I want to do B.

But, once again, it is the same with an unvarnished action description. Indeed, we find a nice illustration of the fact in an example of Davidson's, an example calculated to show that there can be what he calls "pure intending"—intending detached in a certain way from action. "I am not writing it now," I might say, "but I intend to write the letter 'c'; in fact I plan on writing it as soon as I finish writing the letter 'a'"—"And why is that?" you might ask—"Because I'm writing the word 'action,'" I could reply.[2]

---

2. We might draw a distinction between *independent* and *dependent* intention, parallel to that which Davidson draws between *pure* and *impure* intention. The distinctions pertain to the relation of the intention to actions in progress. My intention to do B is impure, in Davidson's sense, so long as there is some truth of the form "I'm doing A with the intention of doing B" or ". . . because I intend to do B"; otherwise it is, at the moment, pure. My intention to do B is in our sense *dependent*, on the other hand, if there is some truth of the form "I in-

Indeed, in suitable circumstances, propositions of any of the following forms—*I want to do B, I intend (or mean or plan) to do B, I'm trying to do B, I'm doing B*—can be given in straightforward rationalization of what is expressed by any of the four sorts of proposition, *I want to do A, I intend to do A, I'm trying to do A, I'm doing A.* Altogether, then, we have sixteen possibilities, as in the following table:

	I'm doing B	*I'm trying to do B*	*I intend to do B*	*I want to do B*
I'm doing A	I'm doing A because I'm doing B	I'm doing A because I'm trying to do B	I'm doing A because I intend to do B	I'm doing A because I want to do B
I'm trying to do A	I'm trying to do A because I'm doing B	I'm trying to do A because I'm trying to do B	I'm trying to do A because I intend to do B	I'm trying to do A because I want to do B
I intend to do A	I intend to do A because I'm doing B	I intend to do A because I'm trying to do B	I intend to do A because I intend to do B	I intend to do A because I want to do B
I want to do A	I want to do A because I'm doing B	I want to do A because I'm trying to do B	I want to do A because I intend to do B	I want to do A because I want to do B

The table suggests a clarification of terminology: all of the proposition-types exhibited are forms of (straightforward) *rationalization;* those exhibited in the top row are forms of *action explanation;* those found in the leftmost column are forms of *naive* rationalization; the others (but especially those exhibited in the rightmost column) are forms of *sophisticated* rationalization. Our starting point, *naive action explanation*, appears in the upper left.[3]

---

tend to do B because I'm doing C"; otherwise it is independent. When I am writing the letter "a" in "action", my intention to write the letter "c" is pure but dependent, for I am already doing that for the sake of which I intend to write the letter "c". When I buy eggs because I intend to make an omelet, my intention is impure but my action is independent, for I am intuitively not yet making an omelet.

We can speak of pure and impure, dependent and independent wanting as well. Note that *even actions can be so classified:* as we saw above, it may be true to say that I am baking bread though it is in the oven and, at the moment (as we say), I am playing cards or napping; such bread-baking is, for the moment, Davidsonian "pure" action. Any act that naively rationalizes another is impure, and any act it rationalizes is dependent.

3. I am thinking of these "propositions" indifferently as forms of speech and of thought. My principal conjecture, of course, is that to the sixteen of them there correspond sixteen distinct forms of (rational) etiological connection among elements of an agent's life.

The attention of Davidson, like that of the rather different type of philosopher who finds it in himself happily to employ the expressions "folk psychology" and "belief-desire psychology", is almost entirely absorbed in the contents of the upper right-hand corner—a single species in our expanding botanical garden, a single point in what we have so far developed into a space of sixteen. By a "psychology", in this literature, one after all understands a theory that issues in explanations of action, or else explanations of 'behavior', if that is something different. But it is clear that any psychology or other sort of teaching that admits the sophisticated action explanations schematized in the upper right can have no quarrel with any of the other forms registered in the rightmost column. Where 'wants' can explain action, such wants must exist; and where 'wants' exist, why shouldn't they sometimes be explained or rationalized—even if only by other *wants?* And if wants are potentially rationalized, why shouldn't intentions and attempts also be? There is nevertheless something sound in the fixation of the philosopher's attention on the want—*action* form, the head of the right-hand column; it expresses the converse intuition that, where wants can explain *wants,* in our present rationalizing sort of way, and where wants can explain our intentions and attempts, they must also potentially explain *action* in the same sort of way. All forms of rationalization must tend toward the rationalization of action, even if, in many particular cases, nothing ends up getting done.

The question before us is whether some such reasoning can move us not only upward and downward but also to the left, that is, to a serious acceptance of naive rationalization.

2. The Elements Joined in Our Table

To the sixteen points of our space, there correspond four final or purposive forms of rationalization, one for each row:

I'm doing A *in order to do B,*

I'm trying to do A *in order to do B,*

I intend to do A *in order to do B,* and

I want to do A *in order to do B.*

Given the truth of any one of these propositions, the question how many of the four associated *non-final* forms of rationalization are appropriate or felicitous or true will depend on a variety of circumstances. On certain crude but natural assumptions, though, entailments will run rightward from one column of our table to the next, and also downward from row to row. These are the same natural assumptions as also suggest that the simple unconjoined proposition "She wants to do A" is entailed by "She intends to do A," that "She intends to do A" is entailed by "She is trying to do A," and further, as Brian O'Shaughnessy and Jennifer Hornsby have argued, that "She is trying to do A" (like "She intends to do A") is entailed by "She is doing A *intentionally*."[4] That "She is trying to do A" isn't entailed by "She is doing A" *simpliciter* is obvious; but it is clear that where they instance forms on our table, "She's doing A because P" and "P because she's doing A" both entail the detached proposition "She's doing A intentionally." On our assumption about trying, then, "She's doing A because P" and its converse would also both entail "She's trying to do A." It is a short step to the thought that "She's doing A because P" and its converse, respectively, entail "She's trying to do A because P" and *its* converse. This would complete our sequence of entailments.

This view of the entailment relations among our simple unconjoined propositions follows the teaching of Davidson's "Intending", once it is expanded to take account of trying or attempt, which he does not discuss.[5] If the view of the entailments just propounded is defensible, each simple proposition must be interpreted as saying a bit more than its immediate successor. If, for example, I say that I intend to do A, I don't suggest that I am actually *doing* anything that might bear on doing A—as I seem to do when I say that I am trying to do A. And if I say that I want to do A, I don't suggest, as I seem to do if I say I'm doing A intentionally, or am trying to do it, or intend to do it, that I have hit upon any determinate scheme for potentially realizing the doing of A, cer-

4. See especially Brian O'Shaughnessy, *The Will: A Dual Aspect Theory*, vol. II (Cambridge: Cambridge University Press, 1980), pp. 39–55, 75–126; and Jennifer Hornsby, *Actions* (London: Routledge, 1980), ch. 3.

5. Certainly any genuine *attempt* to do A would involve a Davidsonian "all-out judgment" in favor of doing A, and thus an intention to do it; I don't, however, mean to commit myself to any detail of Davidson's theory, but only to attach the same pre-analytic sense to my expressions.

tain or uncertain—apart from the ever-ready "scheme" of reflecting practically on the matter.

Of course, each of the proposed entailments among our simple unconjoined propositions has been rejected, implicitly or explicitly, somewhere in the literature. There is clearly limitless scope for intuition about particular cases, and thus for controversy about entailments among the simple propositions—and thus also for controversy about the entailments among the complex etiological combinations of them that are exhibited on our table. On the other hand, though, there is also limitless scope for the introduction of novel practical-psychological verbs. Some of these might exhibit more complex entailment relations with the others. My claim is that where rejection of the entailments I have mentioned does not spring from a familiar sort of misreading of conversational implicatures, it springs from the association of a different content with some of our practical-psychical verbs—that is, from an unobjectionable attempt to extend the table.

Let us briefly review some of the literature. It will help if we adopt abbreviations for the four simple unconjoined forms of proposition I have mentioned—"I'm doing A intentionally," "I'm trying to do A," "I intend to do A" and "I want to do A"—as AI, T, I and W, respectively. Ludwig Wittgenstein notoriously rejected AI→T and perhaps also AI→W; it is natural to accuse him of overreading conversational implicatures as entailments, and I will ignore his view.[6] Michael Bratman has familiarly rejected AI→I, which he calls "The Simple View," and perhaps also T→I (if his "endeavoring" can be read, when applied to *present* activity, as "trying"). My "intending" appears to be equivalent to Bratman's "endeavoring" (taken in its complete scope); his "intending" is equivalent to mine combined with some sort of inner "commitment" to perform.[7] David Velleman, developing remarks of H. P. Grice and Gilbert Harman, argues, against Davidson, that agents intend only what they believe they will successfully perform.[8] This doc-

6. *Philosophical Investigations*, trans. G. E. M. Anscombe, 3rd ed. (New York: Macmillan, 1958), para. 116 and 621.

7. See *Intentions, Plans and Practical Reason* (Cambridge, Mass.: Harvard University Press, 1987), chs. 8 and 9, pp. 111–138.

8. See Velleman, *Practical Reflections* (Princeton, N.J.: Princeton University Press, 1989), pp. 109–143; Grice, "Intention and Uncertainty," *Proceedings of the British Academy* 57 (1971): 263–279; and Harman, "Practical Reasoning," *Review of Metaphysics* 29 (1976): 431–463.

trine, which might also be found in Anscombe,[9] certainly involves a rejection of T→I. My "intending" (and Davidson's) might perhaps be represented in the systems of Grice, Harman and Velleman as "intending to try"; the *pre-analytic* notion of intending that they share might be represented in my language as intending combined with confidence in success.

It seems, then, that the concepts that figure in my table are, or can be, represented in all of these systems, and that, once constituted, they would exhibit the entailment relations I have propounded. Moreover, the concepts those writers introduce, in different ways, under the heading of "intention" can be *added* to mine. The expanded hundred flowers table, with its twenty-five or thirty-six points, would of course exhibit a less lovely structure of consequences.[10]

But however the question of these entailments is to be managed, the suggestion of our table and any improved supertable appears to be this, *that all such matters are details.* It seems, that is, that the construction of a symmetrical table of this sort ought to draw our attention from the particular psychical states mentioned in it, taken in isolation, toward the general form of combination that is exhibited throughout the table. The nature of all of the states under discussion evidently resides partly in their fitness to enter into this peculiar sort of articulation; if it is not understood, then none of the particular states is understood; but once it is understood, we have every reason to think that the disputes of the learned about the distinctions among the particular states that might thus be joined will seem tiresome and scholastic.

3. The Kind of Wanting or Orexis That Enters into Our Table

Though the point has frequently been made, it is worth emphasizing our claim that *wanting to do A* is entailed by *intending to do A*. The claim

9. See Anscombe, *Intention*, pp. 90–94.

10. Any theory that attempts to encode some notion of futurity into the possible contents of intention and wanting will of course have to reject AI→I and AI→W, unless it also holds that whatever is done intentionally was *antecedently* intended or wanted. John Searle suggests that the word "intend" covers two profoundly diverse mental states: one, "future intention", does encode futurity and invalidates AI→I; the other, "intention in action", validates it. Thus, though he attacks authors who reject AI→I, his doctrine seems to provide all that is needed for a sympathetic exposition of their views. See his *Intentionality* (Cambridge: Cambridge University Press, 1983), pp. 79–111.

is often rejected, even if only implicitly, but it is in fact the most certain of these entailments, if the words are taken in their most typical conventional senses. Consider that if someone says that he or she is doing A with the intention of doing B, it is always legitimate to ask "And why do you want to do B?" Of course, the question might get no answer beyond "I just thought I would" or "No particular reason," but these do not amount to a rejection of the question. The intuition that intending to do something does not presuppose wanting to do it is fueled by the same peculiarities of the word "want" as make it possible to say, for example: "But I don't want to do what I *want* to do—I want to do what I *ought* to do." This sentence brings out fairly clearly that the English word "want" bears what can unfortunately only be called two different senses.[11] The phenomenon most paradigmatically covered by the emphasized use is of course *appetite*, though it covers other things as well; such a use is, I think, comparatively rare, unless perhaps in the mouths of children, and it generally appears, as it does here, with a special emphasis. The concept expressed by the two unemphasized uses would formerly have been expressed, in philosophy, by the verb "to will"; but certain empiricist and psychological excesses seem, now, to have put that expression on the Index. The unemphasized wanting is the wanting that is presupposed in intention, the wanting that can rationalize and be rationalized alike, the wanting that is most typically discussed in ordinary life—and, I think, the only wanting that interests us in the philosophy of action.[12]

11. It is a quotation from really existing pre-philosophical life—a student's response to the advice "Do whatever you want"; I take it that what is essentially the same thought, or a thought categorially very close to it, could be expressed by the words "I don't intend to do what I *want* to do, I intend (plan, mean) to do what I ought to do"—on condition that the agent supposed he knew what he ought and *wanted* to do, or supposed he could readily find this out. Similarly, once he has got down to business, he could say, "I'm not trying to do what I *want* to do, I'm trying to do what I ought to do."

12. As Anscombe writes in *Intention:* "The wanting that interests us, however, is neither wishing nor hoping nor the feeling of desire, and cannot be said to exist in a man who does nothing toward getting what he wants," and a little later: "The other senses of wanting we have noticed have no place in a study of action and intention" (pp. 67–68 and 70). Sec. 36 of *Intention* would have been unnecessary if Anscombe had had use of a word that possessed unambiguously the force of Aquinas's *velle;* the distinctions of *Summa Theologia*, Ia, IIae, 8–17 are certainly operating in the background of the passage. (Nevertheless, again, I do not mean to accept the whole of her teaching on the matter.)

I take it that much of the interest that has attached to the concept of intention springs precisely from the fact that the English verb "intend", unlike the verb "want", unambiguously represents what would formerly have been called an "act" of the power of "will". No one could confuse an intention to do something with a passion or an operation of sense-appetite. But, on any view of it, the notion of intention is too narrow to capture all that one wants thus to distinguish from passion, appetite and so forth. An ambiguity in our language thus cramps the philosophy that is pursued by means of it. I take this to be the point of Grice's lecture, mentioned above. He is not interested in the analysis of intention for its own sake, but rather aims to dispose of it as an object unworthy of a philosopher's attention.

Though he rightly detaches wanting in our present sense from the "prick of desire", I do not understand Thomas Nagel's claim that such wanting is somehow a mere "consequence" of intentional pursuit of a goal, and its attribution "trivial". See *The Possibility of Altruism* (Princeton, N.J.: Princeton University Press, 1970), ch. 5, pp. 29–30. I agree of course that it is a consequence: "I'm doing A in order to do B" entails "I'm doing A because I want to do B," which entails "I want to do B." But surely this wanting can exist, as intention also can, though the agent is, for example, shot down before the moment to act has arrived; and, again like intention, it can continue to exist, one and the same, through an alteration in envisaged subordinate means. Similar objections can be raised against Anscombe's remark, just quoted, that such wanting "cannot be said to exist in a man who does nothing toward getting what he wants," if it is interpreted straightforwardly. Nagel's remarks seem to me to come perilously close, as Anscombe's do not, to claiming that this wanting cannot provide a genuine explanation or account of action or intention or attempt. If it is a triviality, an epiphenomenon, a projection or a fiction, then, I suspect, intentional action must also be so.

Wanting in the present sense might perhaps be explained, rather indirectly, as the weakest unitary concept that can generate both a row and a column in a table of forms of rationalization. Methodological scruples aside, I would prefer a sort of conceptual ostension or, if you like, of eidetic intuition: consider someone who wants to do A because she wants, or is trying, to do B (she wants to buy another ton of concrete because she is trying to build a dam across the Ohio), where the "because" is that of straightforward rationalization; fix on the connection you yourself thereby pose between the agent and the would-be doing of A—the thing that you are laying at the door of her wanting, or trying, to do B. *That* is wanting in the present sense. It can of course exist whether or not anything else in the way of wanting or acting is (yet) to be put down to it, and whether or not it is to be put down to any *other* wanting of the same sort. (Thus we ought not speak of "motivated desire", as Nagel does, but at best of "wanting of the type that can be rationalized"; that every case of such wanting is "motivated" or rationalized by something else is a contentious further claim *about* such wanting—as contentious as the corresponding claim about intentional action—and would preclude "No particular reason" and "I just thought I would" as responses to the question "Why?")

~ 7

Naive Explanation of Action

1. How Much Scope Is There for Naive Explanation of Action?

Every verb phrase with which Anscombe and Davidson illustrate the concept "description of action" expresses a kind of thing, a kind of *event*, as they teach, that is intuitively continuous and divisible, that takes time, and that can be interrupted; the phrases themselves thus typically admit the "continuous tenses" or the progressive. Their illustrations may be said to express the intuition that, where instantaneous 'actions' can be said to exist, it is as secondary or dependent phenomena that can with justice be left aside until the primary categories are elucidated; in this, I propose to follow them.[1] Now, some of the temporally extended intentional actions that interest us are, as we see in our examples of naive action explanation, intuitively resoluble into a heterogeneous collection of sub-actions that are themselves clearly intentional—organs, as it were, of the whole. Such is the relation of egg-breaking and egg-mixing to omelet-making, of brick-laying and door-framing to house-building, and of writing the letters "a" and "c" to

---

1. Examples of non-durative action might be found in certain so-called acts of mind, in 'ingressions' or beginnings-to-act and in certain so-called achievements in Ryle's sense, such as winning and finding. See Gilbert Ryle, *The Concept of Mind* (New York: Barnes & Noble, 1949), ch. 5.

writing the word "action". Here the notion, obscurely expressed in naive rationalization, that the part or 'organ' is to be explained in terms of
the whole, and understood through it, will exercise an irresistible attraction on the undisciplined philosophical imagination.[2]

But, of course, the resolution of a deed into heterogeneous organ-
like parts, and of these parts into further such parts, will come to a
limit, no matter how the intended notion of articulation of heterogeneous parts is rightly to be explained. The suspicion I want to raise, in
the present section, is that such resolution is not necessary, and that
wherever a completed individual action is intentional under a description of the sort Anscombe and Davidson have contemplated it will be
possible to find a true naive rationalization in which that description
appears *in the explanans*. Even actions that, like arm-raising, do not divide in this way need not, after all, be viewed as pointlike. To show this
properly, one would need a clear view of the intended class of descriptions, an apt division of cases and perhaps a true theory of vagueness. I
will illustrate the claim with a provisional discussion of continuous acts of
moving or of *moving something*—giving a turn to a crank, say, or pulling
a curtain open, or drawing a bow, or pushing a stone, or raising a hand.

Let it be, then, that I have pushed a stone along a certain path from α
to ω, and that this is a completed intentional action of mine. It must
also, of course, be that I have pushed the stone from α to β, if β is a
place about halfway along the path from α to ω. And as I began to push
off from α it would have been as much *true* for me to say, "I am pushing
it to β" as "I am pushing it to ω." How, though, can we deny the further
claim that I was pushing the stone to β, the midpoint, *intentionally*—just
as, by hypothesis, I was pushing it to ω intentionally, and along that
path? A proof that I must have done it intentionally will perhaps require the further premises that the whole trajectory is given to me in
sensory intuition as I begin to push, and that the expression "β" as it appears in the formula "I'm pushing it to β" makes what is called "direct

---

2. Though the typical case of naive action explanation is indeed one in which the act mentioned in the *explanandum* will intuitively be a 'part' of the act mentioned in the *explanans*, or
of its completion, the point needs to be handled with some care. The motion of a molecule
that is trapped in someone's rising limb is not, in our present sense, a *part* of the agent's intentional raising of her hand. Though it could hardly be more familiar, it is clear that the relevant notion of part is a special one and is not independent of the connection expressed in rationalizations generally.

reference".[3] But given all that, it is hard to see why we shouldn't say not *just* that I was pushing the stone to β *intentionally*, but also that I was pushing, and pushed, the stone to β *because* I was pushing it to ω. Why not? The push from α to β might not be "salient", of course, so it might be a bit odd, conversationally, to point it out. But if it were as much of my operation as you could see, the rest having been occluded by a curtain, you might legitimately attach the question "Why?" to that description, and I, in turn, might legitimately offer a naive rationalization using the other. But, now, every bodily movement that is intentional under what might be called a "bodily movement description" takes a limb from one kinesthetically given position to another: why, then, shouldn't we isolate some such initial segment in every such case?

The line of thought most likely to be opposed to this one rests on the notion that if an action is intentional under a given description, then this very description, or the concept that is expressed by it, must have been deployed by the agent in some occurrent thought—that is, in some prior act of reflection or calculation. But this seems to be a prejudice. After all, as Aristotle (for example) teaches, skill or craft or *technē* often drives out deliberation.[4] What is done in accordance with skill in doing B, or in exercise of a practical capacity to do B, is not, as such, determined by deliberation or reflection—unless by a peculiarity of the skill itself (which might involve measurement and calculation, say, as laying carpeting does). But the absence of reflection does not make the action thus skillfully performed, making a pot of coffee, as it might be, or raising a hand, into a sort of unanalyzable whole; egg-breaking certainly does not lose its character as an intentional action after the agent's thirty-fourth omelet. Why should we suppose that acquisition of the type of skill that interests us, skill in moving a limb or object along this or that type of path, must deprive movement along sub-paths of their status as intentional? A more serious objection to my conjecture—that acts of moving and of

---

3. Not every trajectory that is intentionally traversed can be said thus to have been directly given: if I am walking from Kingman to Barstow along Rt. 66, then the intended trajectory is evidently apprehended only in thought. In thinking of this whole, which extends for some miles, I need not think of any of its parts, nor need they be objects of my cognition in any other way. Yet, I will suppose, the actual intentional movement along any such trajectory will involve intentional movement along any number of potentially overlapping trajectories that *are* in some sense directly given, and thus given together with their parts. Since the movement along the larger trajectory can be viewed as a naive ground of the movement along the shorter, intuitively apprehended trajectory, our problem reduces to the contemplation of the latter.

4. See, for example, *Nicomachean Ethics*, 1112a34–b12.

moving things intentionally always have parts of the same character—might spring from consideration of very short trajectories. One might argue that the process of taking initial segments of trajectories moved across, outlined above, must come to an end. If I am doing A because I am doing B, or, more generally, if I am doing A intentionally, then perhaps I needn't have *thought* of doing A, or *proposed* it to myself, or *decided*, or undertaken a *commitment*, to do A; nevertheless, one thinks, *doing A* must figure somehow as a content of my thought or cognition. In particular, if I move along a certain path intentionally, or move something along it, I must somehow apprehend the path itself. Call this weak and under-formulated proposition "the implicit cognition requirement." Now, it is natural to say that there are lower limits to the lengths of paths that I can apprehend by sense or imagination.[5] This will prompt the suggestion that, even if there is no *minimum movibile*, in the sense of a minimum distance I might be said, truly, to have moved or to have moved something, still there must be some *minimum movibile intentionaliter*—a minimum distance I might be said, truly, to have moved something intentionally. As the apprehended trajectories approach this minimum, it will become impossible to find any initial segment that is intentionally traversed. And so we will have actions without naively explicable parts, and my conjecture will be in ruins.

On this skeptical view, actions of moving (or of moving something) across one of these sub-minimal paths will have something like the status of the muscular contractions involved in straightforwardly intentional movements; though I can be said to *do* such things, the actions will be, as Anscombe puts it, "pre-intentional."[6] Suppose that I have moved

5. But see Kant's remarks on the intuition of extensive magnitudes, *Critique of Pure Reason*, trans. N. Kemp Smith (New York: St. Martin's, 1965), pp. 198–199, A162–3/B203.

6. G. E. M. Anscombe, *Intention*, 2nd ed. (Cambridge, Mass.: Harvard University Press, 2000), p. 28. We will have to speak not of "actions" but of "movements" if we follow Davidson in speaking of an action only where we can find a description under which the thing is intentional. But, in any event, Davidson's remarks about *walking across the room* and *tripping* seem implicitly to commit him to the truth of the present conjecture. See "Agency" in *Essays on Actions and Events* (Oxford: Oxford University Press, 1980), p. 47. Mention of this great paper, in the present context, invites the remark that its account of the concept of agency fails to take proper account of actions with parts. Surely it will be "agency" in the sense Davidson means to capture if the agent sinks the *Bismarck*, or ruins her finances, by doing A, B and C, each of them intentionally. But the events falling under the descriptions A, B and C need not fall *severally* under the description "a sinking of the *Bismarck*" or "a ruining of her finances", as the case may be; none by itself, we may suppose, adds up to *that*. And so it might be that nothing done intentionally falls under that description, and thus that something "done", in the emphatic sense Davidson means to elucidate, isn't done intentionally under any description.

something intentionally from one place to another along a certain path, where this path is definitely above the alleged minimum, so that there is some other, nearer, place along the path to which I have also moved the thing intentionally. Let us fix, now, on the class containing all descriptions of me as moving the thing *from* the starting place *to* any of the particular places along the projected path. Each of these will be a description of a "thing I've done"—in some cases intentionally, and in others, on this view, "pre-intentionally".[7] Notice, then, that the soundness of this skeptical counter-argument hangs on both of the following: first, that a nested class of descriptions of this sort admits this kind of complete division, that is, that the question "Was there a maximum pre-intentionally moved in this case, or rather a minimum intentionally moved?" can have a determinate answer; and second, that the answer is sometimes this: "The latter."

At this point the thought of affecting the manner of Quine and declaring ourselves to be deep among the "don't cares" at the crucial point, the limit—and thereby licensed to adopt the microscopical attunement of the senses of "intentional" and "pre-intentional" that would make our handsome simplifying conjecture true—seems to become irresistible. There is no *minimum sensibile*, we can insist, but rather only a *maximum insensibile*; likewise with any supposed minimum intentionally movable. It is like dividing a line into two segments at a point; I must decide which segment gets the point of division and which is left 'open' in that direction. If such a maneuver is judged too artificial, let us note a few other routes available to a friend of our conjecture, leaving the decision among them to the reader's pleasure: (1) First, of course, there is the quasi-Kantian[8] high road of insisting that the intuitive apprehension of trajectories involved in continuous intentional action always involves an intuitive apprehension of all of the parts of all of them, no matter how small—and thus that even a strong form of our "cognition requirement" can pose no problem for my conjecture. (2) It would,

---

7. It should be observed that these are by no means "different descriptions of the same", but attach, in every case, to *distinct* events; an action and a proper part of it, if it has any, are always distinct events. An act and its part might of course fall together under some one description, as someone else's action might also fall under that same description. But generally a description of an act and a description of its part will not be two descriptions of the *same* act. It is interesting that the examples through which Anscombe attempts to illustrate the idea of "many descriptions of the same" do not actually illustrate it: it is the rare act of moving an arm that can be classified as a replenishment of a house water supply.

8. See n. 5 above.

however, be more in keeping with the inspiration of our imagined skeptic, if, while maintaining a strong form of the cognition requirement, we were to argue that the effect of the alleged limits of human cognition is to introduce a certain vagueness into the objects apprehended practically—that is, into the proposed trajectories and the associated descriptions of action. Such an appeal to the idea of vagueness carries with it a number of theoretical difficulties, but supposing them handled, the same vagueness would no doubt then be found to infect the division of our nested classes of descriptions into "pre-intentional" and intentional. In that case, my conjecture—viz., "Acts of moving something somewhere intentionally always have an initial segment that is also an act of moving something somewhere intentionally"—could again be sustained, if only it were given the sort of construction that an adequate theory of vagueness might supply for such sentence as "No one is made bald by the loss of a single hair."[9] (3) But it is most natural, I think, to object that the cognition requirement is still too strong, even when it is shorn of the supposed need for an "occurrent" thought of each and every path intentionally traversed. The relation to our capacities of sense and conception that is necessary to secure the intentionalness of the actions falling under such nested descriptions ought to be realized if only (a) all of the descriptions involve some such conceptual complex as: *moving it from here to ( )*, (b) this conceptual complex is appropriately in play, and (c) the substituends arise from an analysis of the intuitively given path and are not *outré* definite descriptions. The nested descriptions are homogeneous in a certain respect, a respect that *is* apprehended, and the corresponding actions are homoiomerous; if some of them *aren't* alien to the agent's mind in the intentionalness-destroying way that a description in terms of muscular contractions is likely to be, why should any of them be? A free appeal to coarse folk-geometrical facts should not, after all, put us outside the sphere of the intentional, if the human will is the will of an intrinsically spatial sort of being.

Let us move forward, then, and grant provisionally that my conjecture is true, and also that the object of the philosophy of action is legitimately restricted, in the first instance, to a category of intentional ac-

---

9. That an adequate theory of vagueness will have to find means to legitimate such statements is emphasized by Crispin Wright, "The Coherence of Vague Predicates," *Synthese* 30 (1975): 325–365, and by Jamie Tappenden, "The Liar and the Sorites Paradox," *Journal of Philosophy* 90 (1993): 551–557.

tion that excludes acts of mind, startings-to-act and other such non-durative actions-by-courtesy—to intentional action proper, as we call it. We might then provisionally attempt to isolate that category with the following formula: X's doing A is an intentional action (proper) under that description just in case the agent can be said, truly, to have done something else *because he or she was doing A*. The intended sense of "because" is, as usual, the one deployed in rationalization.[10] If we may be permitted free appeal to the notion of a *part*, then our thought might also be expressed, a bit more metaphysically, as follows: an event, the building of a house, for example, is an intentional action just in case it is the "cause" of its own parts—where, again, the intended notion of "cause" is not pre-conceived, but is that captured by the "because" of rationalization, whatever it may be. Given that anything that has parts is constituted by them, we might go on to infer, with a special metaphysical abandon, that it is among the marks of intentional action that such a thing is "cause of itself" in a certain sort of way—and thus also "cause and effect of itself, though in different senses".[11]

If my conjecture is right, and if naive rationalization is to be taken at face value, then it is not so much by its being caught up in a rationalizing order, or in a "space of reasons", that behavior becomes intentional action; rather, the rationalizing order, that peculiar etiological structure, is inscribed *within* every intentional action proper. In any given case, of course, this order might extend beyond the deed—to another deed, to an intention, or to any other sort of act of will. Any intentional action (proper) figures in a space of reasons as a region, not as a point; or, equivalently, each of them, whether hand-raising or house-building, is itself such a space.[12]

10. The proposed definition is a sort of reverse of the one formulated in Anscombe's *Intention:* "Intentional actions are ones to which a certain sense of the question 'Why?' has application" (p. 11), that is, actions admitting a certain sort of account or explanation or ground. We say rather that an intentional action is *itself* a certain sort of account or ground—an *explanans*, not an *explanandum* (though perhaps it is that too). Such an account as I have proposed would evade some of the difficulties Anscombe must resolve: for example, those involving "backward-looking motive" and "motive in general", and also the possibility of such null accounts as "No particular reason" and "I just thought I would" (see ibid., pp. 11–23).

11. Kant, *Critique of Judgment*, trans. W. Pluhar (Indianapolis: Hackett, 1987), pp. 248–255 (*Ak.* 369–377).

12. Though I have put the questions of practical thought and so-called justifying reasons outside the scope of the present essay, it should be noticed that, *prima facie*, intentional action can as much govern practical calculation and the affirmation of practical modalities as wanting or intending can. I can say, for example, that I have to do A because I'm doing B, or that I

2. Excursus: Hume's Argument for Final Ends Queried

Notice that, if a suitable elaboration of the argument of the last section is sound, it will hold generally that if I am intentionally pushing a stone from α to some place ω, then I am intentionally pushing it to any other place β that you might care to name, so long as β falls somewhere short of ω and along my intended trajectory. And it will also hold that I am pushing it to β *because* I'm pushing it to ω. These claims, joined with a few folk-geometrical truisms, have some further interesting consequences.

For example, why shouldn't I be able to isolate a position γ, a place about halfway from β to ω; and a position δ about halfway between γ and ω; and so forth?

$$\alpha\text{-----------------------------}\beta\text{--------------}\gamma\text{--------}\delta\text{---}\varepsilon\text{--}\zeta\ldots\omega$$

As I push off from α, it will be true to say that I am pushing the stone to *each* of these places. That's clear. But, again, it seems that we must also allow that I am doing each of these things *intentionally*, and moreover that I am doing *each* "because" I'm doing the next one. And so, even though the imagined series of isolated positions has an obvious geometrical limit in ω, it seems that an interlocutor and I might together forge a potentially infinite sequence of perfectly legitimate questions and answers, "Why?"

Of course, I might put an end to this torture at any one of the interpolated points, saying, "Well, I'm pushing it to ϕ, you know, because I'm pushing it to ω." But this doesn't show that any of the intervening "because"-statements that I have thus left unframed would not have been perfectly legitimate and true. And anyway I never said *why* I was pushing the stone to ω; it might be that I was pushing it to some place a bit further on—$\omega + 1$, as it were.

Notice that we can as well say that I *wanted* to push the stone as far

---

can't do A because I'm doing B (or, more colloquially: "I can't do A; I'm doing B"). Intentional action is thus a sort of zone of practical modality. Similarly, I can say, for example, that I'm trying to figure out how to do A because I'm doing B. Much practical thought will inevitably figure in the building of a house, and this 'syllogizing', like the subordinate deeds with which it 'concludes', can itself be viewed as naively explicable in terms of it, though perhaps not exactly as a part of it. Notice further that it is possible to reflect practically on the question how to do something, even as, and because, one is doing precisely it. Having broken a few eggs, for example, I am making an omelet, even if, in sudden self-doubt, I now reach for a cookbook.

as γ, δ, etc., as that I was intentionally pushing it to any of them. Dialogue of the following sort can always be inserted into such a case:

"Do you want to push it as far as ε?"
—"Yes."

—"Well, then, I'd better bring down the drawbridge at δ."

If this is right, then Hume's famous argument that a sequence of "instrumental" wantings can't "go on forever" is defective.[13] The proximate conclusion implicitly drawn by Hume, that everything rationalized by anything is rationalized by something that isn't rationalized by anything else, *might* nevertheless be right; the propositions "Every sequence not contained in any greater sequence has a last member" and "Some (or all) sequences not contained in any greater sequence have sub-sequences that have no last member" are of course simply independent.

I do not doubt that we need some such notions as "final end", "ungrounded desire" and "desirability characterization"; but arguments like Hume's give us no insight into the matter. Insofar as it is possible to mark off action theory as an independent fraction of philosophy, distinct, for example, from ethics, it is, I think, by this formula: the status of a rationalizing element as "ultimate" is of no interest to it. It is like criminal law in this respect, and like Wolff's "universal practical philosophy", as Kant professes to understand it.[14] Any network of relations that can figure in it (e.g., of action with wanting, of wanting with attempt, of wanting with intention and in turn with action, and so forth) might be subordinate to a larger network of the same type. Similarly, any configuration of circles and lines in a diagram in Euclid might appear later on in a more complex diagram. Reflection on the present material could not lead us to infer the existence of any such thing as, say, appetite or pleasure (hunger, for example, or pleasure in consum-

13. *An Enquiry Concerning the Principles of Morals*, app. I, sec. V. The similar argument on the first page of Aristotle's *Nicomachean Ethics* (1094a16–20) should, I suspect, be distinguished from Hume's. Aristotle seems to be thinking of the stages in practical calculation moving down from a given end, rather than of stages in explanation moving outward from a given deed; hence the thought that if the series is without limit, then "desire" is "in vain".

14. *Groundwork of the Metaphysics of Morals*, trans. M. Gregor, in *Practical Philosophy* (Cambridge: Cambridge University Press, 1996), pp. 46 (*Ak.* 430–431).

ing chocolate); nor could we, on the strength of it, pose or resolve the question, how such a thing as pleasure or appetite might explain or ground or give reason for an *action* (or an attempt, an intention or a wanting, or indeed any "state of mind" that might figure in symmetrical tables like ours). It is the same, I think, with the concept of emotion; and it is the same with the concepts of a principle, a value, a virtue, a "moral reason" or any concept peculiar to ethical theory. The questions, how *any* of these things might figure in the determination of action; whether every action (and thus every intention, attempt and wanting) exhibits such a determination, mediately or immediately; whether these determinants can reasonably be viewed as constituting any one genus, so that conclusions can be drawn about them by any but a piecemeal treatment—they all transcend the action-theoretical material. One might as well try reaching transfinite numbers by counting or, I suppose, a Prime Mover by a cosmological argument.[15]

3. Sophisticated Philosophies of Action

Let us return, though, to main course of our argument, and to the question of the credentials of our naive explanations of action. In the spirit of ever more ruthless simplification, let us restrict our attention to the following subspace of our original table:

	NAIVE *I'm doing B*	SOPHISTICATED *I want to do B*
I'm doing A	I'm doing A because I'm doing B	I'm doing A because I want to do B
I want to do A	I want to do A because I'm doing B	I want to do A because I want to do B

15. Michael Smith, "The Humean Theory of Motivation," *Mind* 96 (1987): 36–61, argues that every straightforwardly rationalized action springs from, or is genuinely 'motivated' by, a state with a mind-to-world 'direction of fit', that is, a fit opposite that exhibited in, for example, belief. In our sub-Thomistical language, the conclusion of his main argument is that every straightforwardly rationalized act of will arises from a prior act of will, in other words, that "I did A in order to do B" entails "I did A because I wanted to do B," where the latter expresses a genuine etiological connection. The trouble, if this transcription is right, is that the claim has nothing to do with the Humean theory of motivation. Hume's teaching, expressed

It is the mark of a *sophisticated philosophy of action*, as I will call it, that its proponent is happy to recognize the propositions registered in the right-hand column as legitimate and distinct, but supposes that each of the rationalizations on the *left* finds its real explanatory or etiological content expressed in its nearest neighbor in that right-hand column. To this, the genuine account, these left-hand pieces of linguistic artifice simply add the non-explanatory, purely "descriptive" information that the agent is actually getting what he or she wants.[16] That it so often pleases us, in speech, to omit the verb "to want" is to be explained away, in accordance, presumably, with pragmatic principles.

Before we haul out this artillery, we must first address the question of motive. Our tables, after all, suggest that a system is at work in our practices of rationalization, and this, it seems, must place a certain burden of proof on any sophisticated theory of action. It is, after all, a bold reductive hypothesis. So what is to be said for sophistication? Here is an argument: often an agent is herself tempted to give a naive account of her action, but in a legitimate third-person account of the facts of her case, a corresponding sophisticated rationalization will nevertheless have to take its place. The agent may be wrong, the world may secretly be uncooperative, it may be that the agent isn't actually doing B—replenishing the house water supply, as it might be—but only thinks that she is. The *general* rules governing all uses of the word "because", we said, require the truth of the propositions linked by it; *P because Q*, that is, entails both P and Q. And we may grant, for the pur-

---

in the same language, is plainly this, that every act of will (i.e., every intentional action, attempt, intention and wanting) is founded, mediately or immediately, on a *passion*, understood as including appetite. It is clearly impossible to defend this doctrine without an analysis of concepts like passion, appetite and pleasure.

16. The reduction cannot be *quite* so simple as this. Though I have allowed that "She's doing A because she's doing B" entails "She's doing A because she wants to do B," as it of course entails "She's doing B," nevertheless it is clear that the mere conjunction of the latter propositions does not entail the former as it is actually employed. We can show this by constructing a naive equivalent of a so-called deviant causal chain. It might after all be that though our agent wants or wills or intends to do B, she is only actually *doing* it by some sort of accident. She is replenishing the house water supply, indeed, but not by moving the pump handle—the fractured old pipes are delivering *that* water to the rhododendrons; it is rather that she is leaning on the switch for the new, electrical system. In such a case, "I'm replenishing the house water supply," though true, seems to fail as a response to, say, "Why are you moving the pump handle?" A naive rationalization must thus add to its alleged sophisticated core some information more than that the agent is getting what he or she wants.

poses of this argument, that the special rules governing the employment of this connective in *rationalization* in particular include something in the way of a "cognition requirement": a requirement, namely, that the agent has some grasp of the rationalizing connection, even if only inarticulately, and thus also of its terms.[17] If, then, the *explanans*, or the reason, must be something the agent grasps, and if there is nothing to distinguish the cognition of the average successful agent from that of a possible parallel unsuccessful agent, then it might seem that the truth that gives the ground of the action must express something that is present and grasped in either case, the successful one and the unsuccessful one. And what can this be but the agents' *wanting* to do the thing? So the *wanting* must be the true account, the real reason, and so forth.

The first thing to notice about such an argument is the structure it evidently shares with the epistemologists' "argument from illusion". The formation of the perceptual judgment that, say, *this is a dagger* doesn't strike us as so different in the case where I am victimized by a dagger-hallucination, and in the case where a dagger is there and we would ordinarily say that I see it. And once again we have the apparent truism that I, as judger, must apprehend the connection between my judgment and whatever appearance I take to be its ground. So (one wants to argue) the real ground of judgment must reside in what is common to the two cases—the 'highest common factor', if you like—namely, the *as-of-a-dagger* sensum (or whatever it is) that I get in either case. The judgment that this is a dagger, then, can never really be founded on the fact that I see one, for this would entail a dagger's actual presence.

I mention the epistemological analogy only with a view to raising suspicion. The "argument from illusion" seems suspicious to me; but perhaps the reader knows better. Fortunately we can steer clear of these deep waters: the particulars of our own *practical* case provide destructive materials of their own. Our case is different because of the complete symmetry, in rationalization, between possible *explanantia* and possible *explananda*, or between possible grounds and possible groundeds, a symmetry exhibited in the appealing squareness of our tables. For suppose that I *must* indeed grasp the rationalizing connection,

17. Notice that here the "cognition requirement" is directed to the *form* of the elements linked in rationalization, as *doing* or *wanting* to do something, and not to their contents, as doing (or wanting to do) A or B or C, as it was in the last section.

but *may* be in a state of illusion about my doing B. And suppose that this shows that it must be *the wanting to do B* that properly speaking does the rationalizing—since it's the thing that I can't be wrong about, the thing that must be there. If it shows this, then it also shows that all that ever really gets *explained* is itself wanting. For the same possibility of error and failure also afflicts my would-be doing of A.

The epistemological analogy evades this sort of difficulty for the simple reason that if I think I am judging that *this is a dagger*, then I must really be judging that; there is no scope for illusion in respect of the existence of the thing potentially grounded, as there is in the practical case.

This sort of reason for thinking that only wants rationalize anything is thus equally a reason for thinking that only wants are rationalized by anything. But if there are only reasons for wanting, then there are no reasons for acting; and if there are no reasons for acting, then, arguably, there is no such thing as acting at all; and if there is no such thing as *doing* something in the emphatic sense that we call acting, then, in the end, there is no such thing as wanting to do anything either.

4. Sophistication and Simplicity

These absurd results did not follow from sophistication itself, of course, but from a certain basically skeptical rationale for affirming it. But other arguments for sophistication are possible. Mightn't something be made of the idea of simplicity, for example? If what we understand by a "rationalization connection" is merely a form of linguistic transaction, then there is no problem; the more forms the merrier, one might think. But if instead we understand by a "rationalization connection" a nexus of things that is captured and expressed by such forms of human speech—and such a thing is of course our real quarry—then, on the face of it, to admit naive etiologies as genuine and independent is to multiply causes without necessity. For all sides will agree that wherever naive action explanation is legitimate, a sophisticated action explanation is also available, though the reverse is not the case.

Some ways of developing this line of thought will lead, I think, to absurd results of the sort we found above; but in place of an attempt to canvas all of them, I propose to accept its main premise—and employ it instead in the interpretation of the phenomena. The idea that we win any significant theoretical or metaphysical simplification with the elimination of our naive etiologies presupposes that what is given as rationalizing in such a case, for example, *that I'm making an omelet,* is something profoundly different from what is given as rationalizing in the other columns, for example, *that I want to get to Katmandu.* This seems, on the face of it, obvious: after all, to put the matter crudely, the sophisticated sorts of *explanans* would traditionally have been classified as states of the soul; naive *explanantia* seem by contrast to be events "in the world". They are absolutely unlike. This is what we find so hard to fit with the other, equally forceful appearance, that a single generic explanatory relation, or nexus of things, is at issue in every entry on our tables—a suggestion invited by the symmetry of the tables and of their uniform transposition, row by row, into final or purposive forms. The program of the next several sections is to disarm any such appeal to simplicity by breaking up the appearance of deep metaphysical diversity among the elements linked in rationalization—that is, among trying, intending and wanting, on the one hand, and doing, or acting intentionally, on the other.

～ 8

Action and Time

1. The Primitive Objects of Attempt, Intention and Wanting

Let us consider, for the moment, just the former trio—the specifically psychical, or psychological, sorts of *explanans*. Here we must be struck, first, by the fact that the objects of attempt, intention and wanting are typically not formulated with a complete proposition; these states are not, at first sight anyway, what are called "propositional attitudes". If you ask what I want, then, in the most primitive sort of case, the answer will be: *to get the vanilla down*, or *to turn on the light*; if you ask what I intend, the answer will be: *to write the letter "c"*, or *to kill his brother*. It is still more obvious that in the standard sort of case, what I try is again: *to do something*. Such facts have often been noticed; they have even been emphasized, especially by Annette Baier.[1]

Of course, once an apparatus of representation has come to sup-

---

1. Professor Baier's remarks are restricted to intention. See "Act and Intent," *Journal of Philosophy* 67 (1970): 648–658; and "The Intentionality of Intention," *Review of Metaphysics* 30 (1977): 389–414. The point is also made in Anselm Mueller, "Radical Subjectivity," *Ratio* 19 (1979): 115–132. H.-N. Casteneda repeatedly attacked the notion that the object of intention is given by a proposition, but he also rejects the thought that it is completely expressed by the like of "to wash the clothes". Casteneda insists that a correlate of the first person must somehow appear in his "practitions". ("Practitions", the contents of intentions in his system, may roughly be characterized as the correlates, in the realm of sense, of self-addressed imperatives.) Baier's remarks against Roderick Chisholm in "Act and Intent" thus also apply to Casteneda's doctrine (see p. 658: "I think Chisholm's ever-present agent has over-advertised," and the following remarks). Casteneda's criticism of Baier in *Thinking and Doing* (Dordrecht:

ply general means for expressing these psychical states—that is to say, once it has come to contain *verbs* fitted to receive these special non-propositional complements—these same general expressions might then be refitted to receive propositional complements, or their like, as well. But then, they might also be refitted to take plain common nouns as complements—"a horse", for example, or "a saucer of mud"; or else mass nouns like "milk" and "turpentine"; or even singular terms like "the Mayor" and "Mary-Beth Ellen". This is how things stand in English, for example, which allows that we can try the Mayor, or try turpentine, and that we can intend Mary-Beth Ellen (as a spouse), or intend for the children to go to college, and, finally, that we can want milk, or a saucer of mud, or for everyone to stop shouting.[2]

Given the gross categorial diversity of the "objects" superficially given as possible, Fregean scruples will force a choice on us: we must say either that none of these apparently category-indifferent psychological verbs is really univocal across the several cases, or else that

---

Reidel, 1975), pp. 151–154, thus seems to miss her point. George Wilson discusses Baier's teaching in *The Intentionality of Human Action*, rev. ed. (Stanford, Calif.: Stanford University Press, 1989), pp. 111–117.

The thought that the objects of intention and wanting are uniformly propositional pervades the literature on the philosophy of content, but difficulties about the first person have occasionally threatened orthodoxy. See, for example, Gareth Evans's subtle attempt, in *The Varieties of Reference* (Oxford: Oxford University Press, 1982), pp. 258–261, to dismantle Anscombe's puzzles about the first person, which was later clarified and extended by Ian Rumfitt, "Frege's Theory of Predication," *Philosophical Review* 103 (1995): 599–637. Evans and Rumfitt presuppose that "She intends to engage-in-an-act-of-self-reference"—i.e., "She intends $\lambda x(x$ refers to $x)$," as Evans puts it—is not to be explained as "She intends that *she herself* engage-in-an-act-of-self-reference"—i.e., as "She intends that *she herself* fall under $\lambda x(x$ refers to $x)$." This last plainly *is* to be explained as equivalent to "She intends that *she herself* refer to *herself*." If the object of intention were always a proposition, then it would evidently contain a first–person component (the indirect reflexive, "she herself") in all of these cases; this is what the authors are attempting to avoid. So, in conclusion, they too presuppose that the object of intention is something less than a complete proposition. (See further below, n. 10.) A much broader anti-propositional doctrine is found in David Lewis, "Attitudes *De Dicto* and *De Se*," *Philosophical Review* 88 (1979): 513–543, and a similar but somewhat less radical view is taken in Anscombe's essay "The First Person," in *Metaphysics and Philosophy of Mind* (Minneapolis: University of Minnesota Press, 1981). pp. 21–36. Where Lewis holds that all belief takes a property as object, and self-attributes it, Anscombe holds that some cases of *believing, knowing* and *telling someone* do take a complete proposition; the first-person or self-attributive forms of them take something less than a complete proposition as object. These matters are independent of the question of the object of intention and wanting, and in any case the 'sub-propositional' object I will propose is subtly different from that taken by 'beliefs about oneself' in Lewis and Anscombe (see n. 10 below).

2. The really difficult feat is to manage an ostensibly propositional object of attempt.

some of the complements are systematically under-expressed in actually existing speech. In a proper *Begriffsschrift*, as we know, *every* verb that takes an object will be "standardized", as David Lewis puts it, to receive complements expressing items that occupy some one logical category.[3] Our Baierian common sense may thus be put as follows: a "standardized", *begriffsschriftliche* expression of the sense primitively attached to any of these particular psychological verbs—"tries", "intends" and "wants"—will be fitted to take as complement just the sort of verb phrase exhibited above: "walk to school", "make an omelet", etc. Where propositions employing these verbs cannot be forced into such a form—as "She intends for X to be F" might perhaps be turned into "She intends *to make X F*" or "She intends *to arrange for X to be F*"—then they simply must express some other "psychological state". The Baierian thought is not that there is no propositional sense of intending or wanting, but that there is a prior and irreducibly non-propositional one.

2. Aspect and Event-Form

But, now, cleaving to this intuition, in the hope of justifying it by its consequences, let us ask what sort of category *is* occupied by the items captured by the verb phrases that make for apt bottom-level complements of the words "want", "intend" and "try". The next thing to notice, I think, is that such items are not to be compared with those expressed by such phrases as "is taller than Henry" or "is red" or "believes in God". The apt complements do not, that is, designate states or properties, as we put it in philosophy (much less Fregean "concepts").[4] Of course, we must again allow that psychological verbs with the senses primitively attached to "try", "intend" and "want" can be refitted in one way or another to receive such state- or property-expressing complements; and English again supplies us with an illustration. The bits of speech that formulate the basic objects of attempt, intention and want-

---

3. Lewis, "Attitudes *De Dicto* and *De Se*," pp. 513–515.

4. The distinction between a state and a Fregean 'concept' can be provisionally expressed as follows: "N.N. believes in God" and "M.M. believes in God" refer to different people but to the same Fregean *Begriff*; "N.N. *believed* in God" and "N.N. *believes* in God" refer to the same person and to the same *state*, but they share no reference any single Fregean 'concept' or *Begriff*. See, for example, "Function and Concept," in *Translations from the Philosophical Writings of Gottlob Frege*, ed. P. Geach and M. Black, 3rd ed. (Oxford: Blackwell, 1980), pp. 26–41.

ing rather designate what Ryle, Kenny and Vendler—in a tradition that seems now to survive only among the linguists—have variously called accomplishments and performances. I will call the intended items simply "event- or process-forms", and their linguistic and conceptual expressions "event- or process-descriptions".[5]

The question of the difference between a state-expressing predicate and what I am calling an event- or process-description may be approached as follows. There is only one way to join a stative expression immediately to a singular term in order to form a proposition of the sort that can then be subjected to tense and to logical operations. With "Louise" and "to be taller than Henry" as raw materials, all I can say is that Louise *is* or *isn't* or *was* or *wasn't* taller than Henry, and the like. The *logoi* that figure as standard complements of verbs like "intend", "try" and "want" can, by contrast, generally be joined to subject expressions in two *different* ways, even in advance of any subjection to tense and logical operations. The instruments contrived by human languages to effect the relevant distinction are classified by linguists as markers of "perfective" and "imperfective" *aspect*, and distinguished by them from markers of *tense*.[6]

The so-called aspectual distinction among modes of predication is

5. The Ryle-Kenny-Vendler tradition was somewhat distorted by an emphasis on phenomena peculiar to rational life. The result was that the notion of an accomplishment or performance could not be said to capture anything on the order of a logical category—no more than does the parallel notion of 'what is done' on one or more occasions. The genuine *category* occupied by *walk to school* and *make an omelet*—things many of us have done—is also occupied by *dissolve*, *fall to pieces* and *burst into bloom*. So I speak more colorlessly of a process- or event-form.

The present criticism is one of many made by A. Mourelatos in "Events, States and Processes," *Linguistics and Philosophy* 2 (1978): 415–434. This paper contains the best exposition of the Ryle-Kenny-Vendler line of thought, along with copious references, and links their distinctions explicitly, as linguists have, and as I will, with the idea of 'aspect'. It should be read in conjunction with a later essay, "Aristotle's '*Kinesis/Energeia*' Distinction," *Canadian Journal of Philosophy* 23 (1993): 385–398, which rectifies some features of the earlier.

6. What follows is a crude account of the idea of aspect, or rather of some of what is traditionally put under that heading. I include it for the obvious reason that my argument presupposes a certain angle on the material, but also because the material has failed somehow to enter into the received armature of philosophy, even of the philosophy of action, in spite of a number of attempts to draw attention to it.

The works on the topic that I have found most helpful are the recognized classic, *Aspect*, by Bernard Comrie (Cambridge: Cambridge University Press, 1976), essentially a work of comparative linguistics, and the great work *The Logic of Aspect*, by Anthony Galton (Cambridge: Cambridge University Press, 1984). The latter, as its title suggests, is a work of pure philosophy untainted by any specifically linguistic motives. Though I depart from Galton's account easiest to apprehend if we attend to the possible formulations of what are intuitively *past* states of affairs involving our event- or process-forms. The English past progressive, for example, imports imperfective aspect into a proposition; the English perfect and the simple past alike import perfective aspect, in application to such verb phrases as these. Thus we can say either that I *was walking* to school, or else that I *walked*, or *have walked*, to school. Though contemporary action theory is bent on assimilating these propositions and the states of affairs expressed by them, the thoughts they express are of course quite unlike. That I walked to school presumably entails that I was, at some point, walking to school. But that I was, at some time, walking to school does not entail that I ever walked to school; I might have been gunned down or kidnapped by aliens, or, again, it might be that I am still walking there. The former possibility, that the truth of what is expressed by the progressive and imperfective "I was walking to school" might *never* be followed by the truth of what is expressed by the corresponding perfective "I walked to school," belongs, I think, to the essence of what we might call ordinary, natural or pre-scientific event-consciousness, and will be of paramount importance in what follows. Though the expressions are somewhat dangerous, it helps intuition, a bit, if we say that what is registered as complete or whole or as "perfected" in "I walked to school" or "I have walked to school," is represented as incomplete or partial or as "imperfect" in "I was walking to school."[7]

---

in a number of ways, I believe that any reader of his book will be convinced that the topic is essentially a logical and metaphysical one, and only indirectly the object of linguistic or grammatical inquiry.

7. Though the English perfect ("I have walked to school") and the English simple past ("I walked to school") are both employed in simple event reports with perfective content, this is in fact a peculiarity of English, which has what is called an experiential perfect. ("Experience" is here to be understood as it is in a worker's résumé.) Generally, perfects presuppose something in the way of "present relevance," which makes for a complete distraction in the present context. (See Comrie, *Aspect*, pp. 52–53 and 58–59; though his book treats of perfects, yet Comrie insists, apparently paradoxically, that they are linked to perfective aspect only *per accidens*, and would be expelled from a proper treatise of his subject.) Traces of the ancient "relevance" requirement survive in modern English—and not only in the obvious fact that the auxiliary verb "to have" is put into the present tense. For example, the sentence "I have arrived in Rome" is poor material for postcards once I have left for Paris, though it is legitimate in other contexts; and one can only say of someone now living, but not of Caesar, that he or she "has crossed the Rubicon".

The facts that (1) ancient Greek did not exhibit a merely experiential perfect—a "been

Perfective aspect cannot be combined with the present tense. If I insist on knitting together the first person and an event- or process-description like "walk to school", meaning thereby to produce a report on current events, all I can manage is the progressive, and thus imperfective, proposition "I'm walking to school." It is where my thoughts turn to the past that I can manage a different sort of stitch. We may express the point metaphysically as follows: to such a past state of affairs as this: *I was walking to school*, there corresponds such a possible present state of things as this: *I am walking to school;* but to such a past state of affairs as this: *I walked to school*, nothing present corresponds.

Our own language does of course permit a present-tense sentence "I walk to school," distinct from "I'm walking to school"—a sentence that is, on the face of it, linked to the simple past sentence "I walked to school" as "I am hungry" is linked to "I was hungry." But it doesn't have the content that went missing in my metaphysical formula; the English sentence "I walk to school" can only be read habitually.[8] "I walked to school" can be used to express a past habitual thought, but English is blessed with an unambiguous expression of this thought, namely, "I used to walk to school." The topic of habituality (as we might call it) is of great significance for practical philosophy, as we will

---

there, done that" perfect, as we might put it—and that (2) English is barely conscious of any other, together make it impossible properly to translate the passages in which Aristotle attempts to explain his concept of *energeia*. (His thought, put crudely, was that an expression, for example, a verb for sight, denotes a kind of *energeia* just in case the admissibility of the Greek present entails the admissibility of the Greek perfect.) The confusion this difficulty has brought into the scholarly discussion—in which it has been suggested, for example, that *walking* is an *energeia*, though *walking to school* is not—is convincingly analyzed by Daniel Graham in "States and Performances: Aristotle's Test," *Philosophical Quarterly* 30 (1980): 117–130; see also the recanting essay by Mourelatos, "Events, States and Processes." The concept Aristotle opposes to this one, namely, *kinēsis*, is, I hope, equivalent to the present "event- or process-form". The contrast properly employed in its elucidation is not, however, that between the present and perfect tenses, as he supposes, but that between perfective and imperfective aspect, and it appears properly only in the past tense.

8. I mean the free-standing sentence. I leave out, as pretty clearly devoid of philosophical significance, the use of sentences of this shape in certain types of narrative ("So, she says to me, 'That's crazy' and I say to her . . ."), in newspaper headlines ("Hitler invades Poland"), in live radio sports announcing and in the titles of paintings and chapters of books. Their appearance as antecedents of conditionals and in "temporal adverbials" and the like (e.g., "If you walk to school, then . . ." or "When Hell freezes over, . . .") is a more serious matter, but these are very dark, and presumably involve some notion of futurity.

see in Part Three, but it falls outside the scope of the present essay, and of theory of action as it is generally understood.[9]

It is clear that the basic aspectual distinctions have nothing specially to do with human action: thinking of the past, we can judge either that *the tree was falling over* or that *the tree fell over*; but, again, thinking of the present, all we can manage is that *the tree is falling over*. Notice again that the first of these is consistent with the negation of either of the others, and also with the conjunction of these negations. "Everything at ground zero was vaporized more or less instantly," we might be told, "and so, in particular, everything that happened to be falling over at ground zero was vaporized more or less instantly; so nothing that was falling over there ever fell over." The use of the progressive in the articulation of ordinary event-consciousness seems somehow to span the present, reaching into the future (as *falling over* typically includes, say, *striking the ground*); but the "reach beyond" the present that characterizes such thought does not expose it to simple disproof on the strength of what happens next.

Of course different human languages express our three-fold distinction among propositions, and the underlying two-fold distinction among modes of predication, in quite different ways; some leave the matter entirely to context. Where the distinctions are explicit, the instruments chosen to express them will inevitably find other uses in connection with verb phrases not of our type, or else instruments forged for another purpose will find a secondary employment in expressing them. These facts tend, as Frege would say, greatly to enrich, or 'fatten', treatments of the present topic undertaken from a specifically linguistic point of view. But it is clear that the central business, the aspectual distinction among modes of predication, is not a matter of linguistic subtlety. We may say that it is apprehended by an act of logical insight; certainly it will figure in the true *Begriffsschrift*, once it is extended to cover, for example, practical thought. A similar insight is evidently involved in a grasp of the distinction our opposition induces among predicable expressions—the distinction, that is, between phrases

---

9. Taking habituality into account, as a form of possible states of affairs, we may re-express our "metaphysical formula" as follows: to the possible past state of affairs *I was walking to school*, there corresponds the present *I am walking to school*; to the past state of affairs *I used to walk to school*, there corresponds the present *I walk to school* (or: *these days I walk to school*); but to *I walked to school*, unless it is the same as one of these, nothing present corresponds.

that generate a triad of sentences of the sort we have noticed, and those that don't. Similarly, that it should admit corresponding modes of combination with a singular representation is part of what makes the *conceptual* complex expressed by the phrase "walk to school" into the sort of conceptual complex it is. And, likewise, that it should admit three corresponding modes of '*inesse*', or of being-in-a-subject, is part of what makes *walk to school* (which is something many people have done) and *fall over* (which is something many people and many trees have done) into the sort of element of being that each of *them* is—namely, as I put it, an event- or process-form. Something to be called an aspectual distinction of modes of "predication" can, that is, be found in trios of statements, trios of judgments or thoughts, and also in trios of states of affairs (if states of affairs are something other than Fregean thoughts); associated categories can be supposed to subsume the items thus "predicated" at the levels of speech, thought and being.[10]

Once this feature of things has been apprehended reflectively, it becomes a bit easier to make trouble for the mechanical application of the notion of a "propositional attitude" to all of the states of mind that are of interest to us in practical philosophy—to see, that is, why the objects of typical attempts, intentions and wantings should resist formulation in a proposition. Suppose that I am walking to school intentionally. It follows, we have supposed, that I *want* to walk to school—that's why I'm taking this step, for example. What, on a propositional construction, will the object of this wanting be? Presumably this: *that I walk to school*. And when philosophers do manage to fill in the blank in the omnipresent "I want that p," we inevitably find just this sort of substitution. The trouble, of course, is that the requisite proposition doesn't

10. Thus to continue the series begun in n. 4: "The tree fell over" and "The monument fell over" refer in common to a single Fregean "concept" or *Begriff*, and to a single event- or process-form, but to no one object. "The tree is falling over," "The tree was falling over" and "The tree fell over" refer in common to a single object and a single event- or process-form, and to no one Fregean concept. (Nor, I think, do any of these sentences refer to a state, properly speaking.)

This is why I reject the attempt of Evans and Rumfitt to bypass Anscombe's puzzles about the first person (see above, n. 1): their use of apparatuses akin to Church's lambda notation presupposes that the feature of a proposition that expresses an event- or process-form is reached by the simple elimination of one or more appearances of a singular term; they thus assimilate the notion to that of a Fregean concept. The same elementary error besets almost all uses of Church's lambda notation in linguistics, especially in the discussion of generics. It is not noticed that the open sentence that follows "λx" must already have tense and aspect.

exist; the bit of English we use here, in an attempt to reach the fugitive thought-content, in fact expresses a habitual sense, which is nothing like what we had in mind. In order to make a *proposition* out of these materials ("I" and "walk to school") we have to employ aspectual glue, and tense as well. Experimentation with the other possibilities that suggest themselves will, I suspect, show that every way of doing this yields either the wrong sense, generally a much more sophisticated sense, or else no sense at all.[11]

3. Aspect and Naive Rationalization

We can now see that where we have hitherto spoken of "the explanation of action"—namely, in cases where the *explanandum* is given with an unvarnished description of action, as I have put it—two importantly distinct cases have been assimilated. This distinction did not appear in our tables, though, because the propositions registered in them were all in the present tense, which demands imperfective aspect.

If, now, we attempt to shift a typical action explanation into the past, we immediately find that we can say that I *was doing* A because I want*ed* to do B (or intended to do B, or was doing or trying to do B); but we also find that we can say that I *did* A because I want*ed* to do B (or intended to do B, or was doing or trying to do B). We have, for example, both "I was turning left because I wanted to get to Katmandu" and "I turned left because I wanted to get to Katmandu." The two rationalizations are internally related to each other—the latter, again, entails the former—but they are nonetheless obviously different. Whatever else may happen, it seems that we need to add a new row to our tables, once we throw them into the past tense. The top row splits into two, and we

---

11. Thus, for example, "I want that I am walking to school" suggests that I am indifferent to my actually making it there—as I might intend to *be doing* my homework when my parents come in, but not intend to *do* it. "I want that I (have) walked to school," if the content clause is *true*, seems to express satisfaction in a job well done, and, if it is false, an idle wish. "I want that I *will* have walked to school" has a defect opposite that of "I want that I am walking to school," in that it seems to express an indifference to my own agency; this can be seen more clearly if we substitute an event- or process-form that can be realized either intentionally or unintentionally, as in, say, "I want that I will have slid across the ice." Insofar as any of these sentences can be heard as bearing the sense of "I want to walk to school" (or "I want to slide across the ice"), it is, I think, by the hearer's training herself to delete the subject, tense and aspectual "glue".

retain our downward and rightward entailments. Our abbreviated table would come to look like this:

	NAIVE *I was doing B*	SOPHISTICATED *I wanted to do B*
I did A	I did A because I was doing B	I did A because I wanted to do B
I was doing A	I was doing A because I was doing B	I was doing A because I wanted to do B
I wanted to do A	I wanted to do A because I was doing B	I wanted to do A because I wanted to do B

But the more important point is this: in our naive rationalizations—those in which the *explanans* is given with what I have hitherto called an "unvarnished" description of action—the *only* acceptable form, past or present, is the progressive. We can of course say that I wanted to do A because I *was doing* B; but unless we shift to some other kind of account, we cannot say that I wanted to do A because I *did* B (or *had done* B). If we are to find a rationalizing reading of, say, "I wanted to cross the street because I *walked* to school (or *had walked* to school)," we must interpret it as we would "I wanted to skip town because I *killed* my brother," or even "I wanted to kill Henry because *he* killed my brother." Any of these would have to give indirect expression to the underlying straightforward rationalization. None *by itself* entails anything that might be expressed in a purposive or final-clausal form.

Thus we do not need to add a new left column to a purely past-tense version of our table, as we *did* need to add a new top row. To frame a naive rationalization is to associate the thing "grounded" with an intrinsically imperfective state of affairs as "ground"—that is, with a state of affairs that can only be grasped through an imperfective judgment, or expressed in forms of speech that admit an imperfective interpretation.[12]

12. It is of interest, in this connection, that we frequently give a *present* state of things, whether it be my being doing something or my trying or intending or wanting to do it, in rational explanation of a *past* state of things expressible in any of these same forms—and that, by

Of course, this introduces an asymmetry into the past-tense version of our table; what appears as potentially rationalized in it does not always appear as a potential "reason". Mightn't grounds for rejecting a new left column be turned, once again, into grounds for rejecting our new top row? This was my formula for defusing our practical "argument from illusion". But we have no reason to expect this. Though it needs careful interpretation, the following is clearly a general requirement applying to any form of explanation, or any "interpretation of 'because'", or any category of etiology: *if* it can be deployed in connection with imperfectively expressible states of affairs—events-in-progress, if you like—it can also be deployed in connection with perfectively expressed states of affairs, or completed events; the reverse is also true. Whatever it takes as ground, whether potencies, dispositions, structures, the will of God, fate, or antecedent events, no form of explanation or etiology could be used to account for facts of the form *X was doing A*, or *E was happening*, unless it could also account for facts of the form *Y did B* or *F happened:* no more than a language could capture and express either sort of fact, but be blind to the other.

4. The Red Thread Uniting the Forms of Straightforward Rationalization

We are now in a position to make an impossibly crude first attempt at an account of the unity of the different forms of rationalization.

When I was speaking above of the special psychological verbs that appear in our table of rationalization forms—"want", "intend" and "try"—I declared that, in their primary employment, these verbs can take as complements only such phrases as express event- or process-

---

contrast, we generally do *not* straightforwardly rationalize a present state of things in terms of something past. Thus, for example, I can say, in straightforward rationalization, that I *did* A because I *want* to do B, for example, "I turned left a minute ago because I want to get to Katmandu"—but not, without an audible change of key, that I *am doing* A because I *wanted* to do B, for example, "I am now turning left because I wanted, a minute ago, to get to Katmandu." The sign of this, once again, is that the former, but not the latter, admits a straightforward transposition into a purposive or final-clausal form. Past states of affairs admit the same sorts of rational bearing on present *explananda* that perfective states of affairs, or completed events, admit in connection with past and present *explananda* alike; as indirect rationalizations they fall outside our present sphere of concern. Thus, though we must admit a mixed tense table in which past *explananda* are joined with present *explanantia*, we do not need a mixed tense table joining past *explanantia* with present *explananda*.

forms. This is to say that we can only join a subject and a verb phrase by means of one of our practical-psychical verbs if the subject and verb phrase thus joined exhibit the basic aspectual duality in their own "un-varnished" combination. It is, that is, only because the representations "she" and "walk to school" can be joined perfectively, as in "she walked to school," or imperfectively, as in "she was walking to school," that they can be joined by "wants", "intends" or "tries"—as in "she intended to walk to school."

Let us now pose the question why this should be. The formulations just reached invite the following hypothesis: the function of such practical-psychical verbs is precisely to express certain forms of imperfective judgment. In judging that, say, Martha *wanted* or *intended* or *was trying* to walk across the street, we join a representation of Martha and the general conception: *walk across the street.* The thoughts thus formed all stand opposed in a special way to the thought that Martha *walked* across the street, that is, that she made it. In other words, the three practical-psychical thoughts stand opposed to that *perfective* judgment in just the way in which the thought that Martha *was walking* across the street also does. The four potentially rationalizing judgments differ in important ways, but formally their relation to the perfective judgment is in each case the same: what is represented as coiled up or incomplete or partial in them, is represented as unfurled or finished or whole in the other. Twisting Brentano's vocabulary, we can say that "try", "intend" and "want" express modes of "imperfective inexistence" (of an event- or process-form)—but modes of imperfective inexistence that, unlike that expressed by the simple progressive, find application only in connection with rational life and its like.

If the distinction between imperfective and perfective modes of "inexistence" of an event- or process-form can be said to be "founded deep in the nature of things," in Frege's sense,[13] then "try", "intend" and want" merely express some of the ways in which a bearer of will or rational agency can be fitted into a particular dimension of this meta-physical structure; "is . . . ing," which figures within and without the rationalization connection, expresses another. Though it acts as a para-

---

13. "Function and Concept," p. 41. The phrase is intended to apply to such distinctions as that between function and object and concept and object. It is, by the way, astounding to me how many of our philosophers of intentionality and 'content' understand the "in" in Brentano's "inexistence" to be privative; the word means "being in" and follows the Aristotelian usage found in, for example, the *Categories*.

digm, progressive judgment, as we have it, is in the present view only one form of one pole of the corresponding *conceptual* opposition, mastery of which is presupposed in ordinary event-consciousness and the intellectual apprehension of event- or process-forms.[14]

The unity that pervades our table of forms of straightforward *rationalization* resides on the present view in this, that the sort of rationalization registered in it is in general a form of explanation by the imperfective, or by the "incomplete"—though a specifically self-conscious and reason-involving one. In particular, the type of explanation of *action* at stake in action theory, whether naive or sophisticated, is uniformly a matter of locating the action explained in what might be called a developing process; it is just that this progress, development or "imperfection" must be understood to exhibit various types or grades. If I break a few eggs in order to make an omelet, then the event- or process-form *make an omelet* is in the works or under development in the narrowest and most paradigmatic sense; its imperfection can be expressed in the progressive; naive rationalization is available. If, on the other hand, I *buy* a few eggs in order to make an omelet, then the mode of imperfection is likely to be denied progressive expression; a sophisticated rationalization must take its place. As Anscombe says: "I do not think the distinction is quite sharp. Is there anything to choose between 'She's making tea' and 'She's putting on the kettle in order to make tea,' i.e. 'She [wants] to make tea'? Obviously not."[15] We are not willing to call egg-purchase a part of omelet-making, but in the imagined case the unity that joins egg-purchase to omelet-making, thus narrowly construed, is the unity that joins the acts we are willing to call parts of omelet-making to one another, and makes an intentional action out of them. This unity spans, or reaches beyond, any of them; it is captured in an imperfective judgment, paradigmatically a progressive judgment.

Of course, this particular etiological relation of happenings to an

14. It should be noticed that the verb "to try", a rogue in other respects as well, exhibits, in its own use, both perfective and imperfective possibilities. This is because, as is often remarked, an attempt to do something frequently consists in the *doing* of something else. The notion of completion or "perfection" thus acquires a second significance in connection with attempt: one sort would ordinarily be called "completion", and the other "success".

15. Anscombe, *Intention*, 2nd ed. (Cambridge, Mass.: Harvard University Press, 2000), p. 40, replacing "She is going to make tea" with "She wants to make tea." On this distinction, see sec. 6 below.

imperfectively present over-arching process—the relation that constitutes the unity of such happenings with one another in an intentional
action, though it can also extend beyond it—cannot be supposed possible except where the agent's thoughts have come potentially to subserve it. It is plain that our formula "explanation by the imperfective"
can stand only as the isolation of a genus, and that the specific difference of straightforward rationalization will emerge properly only with
its intellectual aspect. This last, though, is a matter I have put outside
the scope of the present investigation.[16] For our present purposes, then,
the important question is that of the genus itself. It is necessary, above
all, to dispel the air of paradox that might be supposed to attach to the
idea that progressive judgment, as we have it—the sort found in the
thoughts *it's falling over* or *she's raising a crop of cantaloupe*—is in fact, as I
put it above, only a *special* case of one pole of the opposition through
which we come to apprehend events and event- or process-forms, and
that the representation of trying, intending and wanting can thus be
seen as others. I will argue in the next two sections that resistance to
this thought must be founded on an exaggerated view of progressive
judgment and, more generally, on a failure to appreciate *how* different
it is from perfective judgment.

However it is further developed, it is an obvious consequence of this
doctrine that we should beware of searching for illumination in the
thought of intention and wanting as *states*—and thus also, for example,
in the thought of rationalization as involving a sort of causality appropriate to states. Intention and wanting are states only in the thinnest
possible sense, the sense in which a thing's falling under any predicate,
or at least any tensible predicate, might be characterized as its "being in
a state". Though the distinction between "The tree is falling over" and
"The tree was falling over" is one of tense, yet we resist thinking of

16. See ch. 5, sec. 3 above. In further defense of this we may now note that it is presumably only because its exercises can be supposed somehow to subserve this sort of process and
its articulation into narrower subordinate processes that a capacity can be characterized as a
capacity for *thought* at all. If this is right, then the questions (1) how thought figures in rationalization, and (2) what thought is, can in any case not be handled independently.

Alternate forms of "explanation by the imperfective" might be found in connection with
the operations of sub-rational animals, of course, and even, but in another way, in the operations of plants and of the parts of plants and animals alike. The philosophers' emphasis on teleological explanation, which is really a limiting case of this sort of account, inclines us to
overlook it. These points are made, though perhaps not ideally clearly, in Part One.

these propositions as representations of states in any emphatic sense, for the simple reason that they are internally related to a third, "The tree fell over," in which their content is, as I put it, uncoiled; this places our thoughts in a radically different categorical space, the space of *kinēsis*, if you like, and not of *stasis*. But "He was doing A intentionally," "He is doing A intentionally" and "He did A intentionally" evidently constitute a triad of just that type (though its elements fit it especially to the representation of rational life), and so also, on the present conception, do "He intended to do A," "He intends to do A" and "He did A intentionally".

5. Event-Forms, Event-Types and Individual Events

Whatever sort of being is expressed by the phrase "fall over", it has a sort of real presence, one thinks, if a tree is falling over; and whatever *walk to school* may be, it acquires a corresponding reality if someone is intentionally walking to school; no such presence or reality is required if an agent merely intends, or wants, to walk to school. Our proposed assimilation of these things must thus, one supposes, be groundless, and governed only by a vague intuition of incompleteness. A number of constructions can be placed on the notion that the genuine imperfective aspect expressed by the progressive must involve some further reality, concreteness or determinacy; one sort will be discussed in the present section, another in the next.

First we treat a spare and logical construction of the thought. Let us remember that we have a proper event- or process-description only where we have a real opposition of perfective and imperfective aspect. Given such an expression, it is, I want to argue, only the truth of standard perfective uses—in English, the simple past and the perfect, as they work out in application to these phrases—that can be said generally to *entail* the existence of a corresponding individual event. So, though the truth of, say, "I baked a loaf of bread" or "I have baked a loaf of bread" entails the existence of an act of baking a loaf of bread with myself as agent, yet, I want to say, the truth of "I am baking a loaf of bread" does not. The situation with the supposed event, or act, of bread-baking is just as it is with the would-be loaf itself: if it is true to say that I have baked a loaf, then it is true to say that there is a loaf that I have baked. We might give it, or each of them, if there are several, a name. But the truth of "I am baking a loaf" does not entail anything of the sort.

Notice that these remarks about loaves have nothing to do the impossibility of referring to future contingents, whether for lack of knowledge or determinacy or causal contact. Even if we imagine ourselves speaking "tenselessly", or, equivalently, as looking backward from an ideal moment placed after all of the actual moments of history, we might still have both "At some point, he was baking a loaf of bread" and "There was at no point a loaf of bread such that he was at any point baking *it*." Our problems are thus completely independent of the familiar difficulties about time and the future.

The matter might be clarified if we consider the relation that event- or process-descriptions in our sense—a sort of verb phrase, really—bear to the corresponding noun phrases that are also often called by such a name, for example, descriptions of the forms "an act of doing A" and "an event of Ving," or "X's doing of A" and "Y's Ving". The content of simple action statements, as of other event statements, might uniformly be expressed with indefinite descriptions of the latter "nominal" sort. Indeed, it is often suggested that the English progressive "X is Ving" has such a formulation buried in its history: it abbreviates an older "X is *in a* Ving", comparable to the French "X *est en train de* V." If, however, we are to express everything necessary to the constitution of discourse about events and actions by means of such indefinite descriptions, then the abstract auxiliary verb we use to unite particular subjects with them will have itself to admit the three-fold distinction we have elsewhere found in the employment of our own more concrete verb phrases—the concrete verb phrases that are to be swallowed up in our newly nominalized indefinite descriptions. In this respect, the alleged older English "is in" falls short as an auxiliary: the copula admits only distinctions of tense—this is its peculiar function—and so "is in" can express only an imperfective connection. If we can be permitted to narrow our focus to the sphere of action, we will, however, find appropriate auxiliaries in the verbs "do" and "perform". We can say all of these:

"I performed *an act of baking a loaf of bread*"

"I was performing *an act of baking a loaf of bread*"

"I am performing *an act of baking a loaf of bread*"

—propositions that bear, respectively, the contents of these:

"I baked *a loaf of bread*"

"I was baking *a loaf of bread*"

"I am baking *a loaf of bread.*"

Here the formerly latent symmetry is revealed; if we cleave to the level of discourse at which the concept of an individual action (as of an individual event) is generated, then the italicized phrases in these propositions must move, logically, in parallel. To reformulate our points: just as "I baked a loaf of bread" entails "There is or was a loaf of bread, x, such that I baked x," so also "I performed an act of baking a loaf of bread" must entail something on the order of "There is or was an act of baking a loaf of bread, a, such that I performed a"; and similarly, just as "I was baking a loaf of bread" does *not* entail anything on the order of "There is or was a loaf of bread, x, such that I was baking x," so also "I was performing an act of baking a loaf of bread" should not be supposed to entail anything on the order of "There is or was an act of baking a loaf of bread, a, such that I was performing a"—and likewise for their present-tense versions.[17] Notice that, as usual, the point has nothing to do with action: a tree may have been falling over at some point, or a house collapsing, though no event in either thing's history can be characterized as *its fall*, or *its collapse*; and a tree may have been forming leaves, though, thanks to a great meteor or to an ax, no leaves ever

17. Here we might advert to the obvious etymological connection between the English words "event" and "act", and the fourth parts of the Latin verbs *"evenire"* and *"agere"*. "X *eventum est*" and "Y *actum est*" can be taken to mean, respectively, "X has happened (or come to pass)" and "Y has been done"; they are the true originals of the propositions "X is an event" and "Y is an act."

The schedule of inferences propounded above appears, at first sight, to put the present doctrine at odds with that of Davidson's paper "The Logical Form of Action-Sentences," in *Essays on Actions and Events* (Oxford: Oxford University Press, 1980), pp. 105–149. It is interesting, though, that *every sentence Davidson analyzes there is in the simple past*; the theme of the paper is "He did it," not "He's doing it." Hence, strangely, I have not rejected anything Davidson actually says. I will not comment on the matter, except to remark on the almost eerie contrast we find, in respect of aspect, between the illustrative propositions given in the first six essays of Davidson's work and those provided in Anscombe's *Intention*. Davidson's are typically in the third person and past; Anscombe's are in the first or second person of the present progressive.

formed. The progressive may thus be said to trap the phrase it governs in an 'intensional context'.[18]

The intuition that in "I am doing A," in particular, we have essentially to do with something real, particular and individual, in the shape of *an act of doing A*, as we don't in, say, "I intend to do A," and that some such idea is involved in the constitution of ordinary action- and event-consciousness, is thus, I think, a mistake—a mistake arising from a failure to perceive the distance between imperfective and perfective employments of event- or process-descriptions.[19] If this is right, we can also dispense with any difficulties arising from the supposition that wanting and intending are in some sense *general*, though actions are particulars.[20] "I am doing A" is no more, or less, "general" that "I intend to do A" is; the transition to a genuine particular arises only with "I did A."[21]

---

18. Notice, however, that since perfective and imperfective aspect evidently stand or fall together, and enter, as possibilities, into the constitution of the sort of thing that can be joined to a subject in *either* way, it is impossible to adopt toward the present sort of "intensionality" the attitude that Michael Dummett finds in Frege's treatment of belief-contexts. We cannot pretend to carve off the "extensional" part of a system of event-representation, that is, its purely perfective fragment, and subject it to analysis, while reserving the "intensional", here imperfective, part for a later treatment founded on the results of the former. The idea of an indirect, opaque, oblique or intensional context thus seems to make a poor fit with the present material. See, for example, Michael Dummett, *Frege: Philosophy of Language*, 2nd ed. (Cambridge, Mass.: Harvard University Press, 1981), pp. 402–404.

19. Terrence Parsons, in "The Progressive in English," *Linguistics and Philosophy* 12 (1989): 213–241, attempts to supply a formally straightforward extension of Davidson's doctrine, mentioned above (n. 17), to imperfective propositions, and brings out a number of peculiarities that must attend any such account. (Parsons does not object to them.) Even if it is intelligible, though, an ontology of, say, individual unformed loaves, of memorials to Rogers Albritton for which even the blueprints could never be finalized, of particular impeded fallings-over of trees, and of individual acts of crossing of the country that ended tragically in Joplin, Missouri, is evidently a rather esoteric attainment; it cannot, I think, be supposed to figure in the fundamental constitution of the forms of judgment that interest us.

20. See, for example, Davidson's "Intending" in *Essays on Actions and Events*, p. 97.

21. The doctrine of the present section is closely parallel to one attributed to Aristotle in G. E. L. Owen's "Particular and General," *Proceedings of the Aristotelian Society* 79 (1978): 1–21. Owen means, among other things, to make Aristotle's familiar claims that "Substance is form" and "No substance is a universal" consistent with the equally familiar fact that Aristotle takes whatever is signified by the word "horse" as a paradigm of form. If *horse*, *Equus caballus*, isn't something universal or general, what is? The way out, in Owen's account, is to see that nothing on the order of the Fregean concept *horse* or the universal *horse* (if that is something different) can exhaust the reference of the word. This, he suggests, is shown by the compatibility of "A horse is coming to be" and "There is no particular horse x, such that x is coming

6. Naive Agency as a Form of Thought and Life: The Primacy of Naive Rationalization

Can we describe a mode of speech, thought and life that constitutes its bearers as rational agents potentially recognizing one another as such, but that dispenses entirely with psychical forms of rationalization? Where do we go wrong if we suppose a use of "is . . . ing" in which it covers all of the cases covered by *our* "is . . . ing", "intends to . . .", "is trying to . . ." *and* "wants to . . ." together—or anyway as much of their field as is necessary to constitute the machinery of rationalization? We may of course allow that the practical thought and agency of such "naive agents" is restricted in ways ours isn't. The question is whether connectives could nevertheless attract, among them, the senses of the rationalizing "because" and "in order to" and whether these senses would figure in the judgments they frame—or whether instead the whole apparatus must fall to pieces for failure to make the obvious distinctions. A brief reflection on this thought experiment will, I think, help clarify the sense of our doctrine that all of the rationalizing terms given to us express forms of imperfective presence, and that the progressive, as it figures in the context of rationalization, is their model.

Our present-tense table of forms of rationalization, with its four or sixteen entries, would reduce, among these naive reasoners, to a single point:

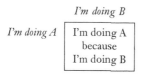

---

to be." (Owen argues that such an opposition is operating implicitly at a number of points in *Metaphysics* Z.) *Horse* can thus figure where no horse does, or better, *horse* enters into some states of affairs in an irreducibly non-predicative way. So *horse*, as a form, does something more than divide things into what is and isn't a horse, and thus more than a universal or a Fregean *Begriff* or any other "general" item does.

My own thought is structurally the same: *build a house, fall over* and *burn down* do something more than classify individual events, I want to say; this shows itself in the way they figure in specifically imperfective states of affairs. This is why I do not say that *fall over* (for example) is an event-type, but rather that it is an event-form; "what was done" by someone is not a universal or a kind, though it might be that many have done it.

Our past-tense table, with its six or twenty entries, would retain just these two:

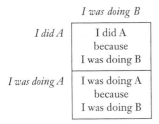

Each table would, that is, collapse into its upper left. If it is reckoned too bold to employ the progressive in describing the thoughts of these people—on the ground that it must cover much more, here, than it does among us—suppose it to be replaced by some artificial alternative, so that the reduced present-tense table becomes, say:

	I am IMP to do B
I am IMP to do A	I am IMP to do A because I am IMP to do B

The essential features of the opposition with which our naive agents operate are these: (a) the ostensibly perfective form, "I *did* A," has exactly the same range in their usage as it does in ours; (b) their "is . . . ing" (or "is IMP to . . ."), like our "is . . . ing", applies both within and without the context of rationalization, and is as much used to describe the vicissitudes of leaves and planets as intentional action; and (c) its employment outside of the context of rationalization is, in essentials, the same as ours (a divergence in the representation of intuitively future events is discussed below).

If the construction is intelligible, then, in spite of the obvious divergence from our own forms of thought and speech, we can surely suppose that the opposition of "X was doing A" (or "X was IMP to do A") and "X did A," as *they* have it, is an opposition of imperfective and perfective aspect, and that the capacity exercised in the two forms of judgment thereby expressed is adequate to the apprehension of event- or process-forms and thus for a genuine form of event-consciousness. If, then, we can see our own use of the progressive as arising by restriction from such a use of "X is doing A" (or "X is IMP to do A"), as practical-psychical verbs come to take up some of its scope, then we can say that whereas *they* apprehend the imperfective mode of presence of an event- or process-form directly and abstractly, *we* apprehend it in a number of forms or guises.

Consider, then, the objection that our naive agents must wind up with intuitively incompatible self-descriptions. One of *us*, armed with our sophisticated apparatus, might say, for example, that she is writing the word "action", and writing the letter "a", but that she merely intends to write each of "c", "t", "i", "o" and "n", and isn't actually writing any of them. Won't one of our imagined naive agents have to say, in the same situation, that she is writing "a" and "action", as we would, and also, on account of her naiveté, that she "is writing" the letters "c", "t", "i", "o", "n"—but nevertheless also, as we would, that she *isn't* writing any of the latter? This incoherence can only be expelled if we deny that such an agent can exhibit any form of action as complex as writing the word "action", which would surely destroy her claim to rational agency.

But of course our naive agent will not express her position by saying that she isn't writing the letter "n", simply: she will say that she isn't writing it *now*, or isn't writing it *yet*. Where one of us sophisticates might say, for example, that he intends to do A *tomorrow*, she will say, "I'm doing A tomorrow." Notice, though, that this is something that we sophisticates can *also* be heard to say, and even give as rationalizing present actions (as naive agents do) and also present wants, intentions and attempts (as naive agents can't). "I'm sharpening the shovel because I want to turn the soil a bit," I might say, "and I want to turn the soil a bit because I'm planting the tomatoes tomorrow." The use of temporal designators in "I'm doing A tomorrow (or *in a minute*, or *on Tuesday*, or *when Hector arrives*)" is subordinate to the imperfective aspect that is here reckoned as strictly present; it is no different from the use of temporal designators in "I *want* to do A tomorrow," and any contradiction to which it tends is the 'contradiction' present in "I want to do A, but I don't want to do it *now*."

Here we begin to see, I think, that the actually existing employment of the progressive completely outstrips the expectations we are likely to form reflecting on it abstractly, and with a certain philosophical atti-

tude. The peculiarities we might claim to find in the speech of our naive agents are already found in our own speech. The just-mentioned
'anticipatory' use of the progressive (as it might be called) is just one
example, and might easily be discounted. Another, more prevalent sort
of case has already been mentioned: we happily affirm, of someone
who is napping, that she is organizing the peasantry; of someone who
is sitting reading the paper, that she is baking a loaf of bread; and of
someone who is playing a hand of poker, that she is building a house.
If confusion arises, we once again concede that our agents aren't baking or building or organizing *at the moment* or *right now*, but rather
reading, playing poker or napping. We must grant the same power to
our naive agents. The distinction between what a person is doing simply and what she is doing 'now' is not absolute:[22] on closer inspection,
our bread-baker might not be reading either, not *just exactly now*, but
rather shooing an irritating fly; and our house-builder might not be en-
gaged in play *at this very instant*, but pouring a cup of coffee, await-
ing the next deal. Nevertheless, the agents are respectively reading and
playing *simpliciter*, as they are baking and building *simpliciter*; the office
of such expressions as "now", "at the moment" and "at this very instant" is very different from that of a marker of present tense. Note
that, as usual, these phenomena have nothing especially to do with
human action: "The sycamore I planted ten years ago, it's growing
well, it's overtaking the house"—this is something I might say in Janu-
ary, when things are pretty much reduced to the sluggish swaying of
molecules.

The above-mentioned 'anticipatory' uses of the progressive are really no different from these uses 'in hiatus', as we may call them. They
all show that it is a mistake to look, at each moment at which a progressive proposition is true, for something in which the progress might
be supposed to consist; indeed, it is often in the nature of an event- or
process-form that there should be times at which nothing of the sort
can be found, as any piece of music is likely to contain silences.[23]

We find more of this in the thoughts of our naive agents than we do in

---

22. Thus I reject Anthony Galton's attempt to define a single "broad" and a single "narrow" sense of the progressive. See *The Logic of Aspect*, pp. 129–149.

23. Of course, if anything ever gets *done*, or gets completed, there will be things in which
the doing of it can be said to have consisted at different moments, and these will be its sub-
events or sub-deeds.

our thoughts about ourselves, of course; and we find more of it in our thoughts about ourselves as agents than in our thoughts about other things and about ourselves as anything other than agents; but if there is nothing incoherent in what we do, then there is nothing incoherent in doing more of it. Why shouldn't it extend so far as to cover the materials necessary for the constitution of reasoned practice and its representation?

Let the thought then stand as a conjecture. Can we imagine the seamless development of a sophisticated, or (partly) overtly psychical, system of practical concepts out of a system like this one? The progression will be clearer if we interpolate another prior stage, one not limited to the practical domain.

Let us suppose an advance in which our naive agents come to enjoy a locution akin to the English "X is going to V" (which is, of course, not to be confused with the progressive of the concrete verb "to go to L", which expresses local motion). Though actual uses of the sign "going to V" often escape the symbol to which an apt *Begriffsschrift* would restrict it, so that it can be said in some cases to express simple futurity, I will argue that it is, in its primary and most interesting use, an instrument for the expression of imperfective aspect—it expresses, as we might put it, the "prospective imperfective", and no tense at all. In evidence of this consider, first, that we can say of someone that *she's doing A because she's going to do B*, but not, in straightforward rationalization, that *she's doing A because she will do B*. Of course, this evidence is not independent of our theory, and might be reckoned a mere subtlety of idiom. A more telling difference from the future tense, properly so called, emerges in the complication of such thoughts with the past tense. That it *was* that it *would be* that p entails that it is, was, or else will be that p; in traditional tense-logical symbols: $PFp \rightarrow Pp \lor p \lor Fp$ (or rather: $CPFpAAPppFp$). This formula will hold even if we suppose an "indeterminate" future.[24] By contrast, the thought that I

Though I expect that anyone who accepts either will accept the other, the present point should be distinguished from that of the last section. There the question was whether the progress of an event- or process-form B, at a given moment, requires the existence, at that moment, of an individual act of *doing B*. Here the question is whether the progress of such a form requires the progress of any narrower event- or process-form A, in which the progress might be supposed, at the moment, to consist.

24. The formula fails in so-called relativistic tense logics, but in a way that complicates dis-

was going to walk across the street is perfectly consistent with the thought that I never was, never will be, nor am now walking across it. It is as it was with simple progressivity. Considered as judged atemporally, or from an ideal moment succeeding all of history, the thought that I *was doing* A and that I *was going to do* A are alike consistent with the thought that I never *did* A; but the thought that it *was* that I *would do* A is not so consistent. "Going to" thus appears to be, in the first instance at least, and in application to our sorts of verb phrase, an instrument for the expression of aspect, and in particular a form of *imperfective* aspect. The perfective opposed to "She was going to do A," in this sense, is "She did A" and not, as superficial grammar would suggest, "She went to do A" (which means something like "She went away to do A" or "She left to do A," and involves the idea of local motion).[25]

Now, once a locution akin to our "going to" exists, it is possible to reconfigure the imagined naive uses of sentences like the narrow "He's

---

cussion without, I think, affecting our point. Consider again the device of posting an ideal moment definitely after all others, and surveying world history from above; PFp→Pp will then hold.

25. The distinction between "X is going to V" and "X will V" is a favorite illustration of Michael Dummett's. He regards each as an interpretation of the future tense, distinguished from the other not by the conditions under which it is itself asserted, but by the contribution it makes to more complex sentences, for example, past-tense sentences. The former he calls the "future as expressing present tendencies", and the latter "the genuine future". This is already, in the present view, an unwarranted assimilation: the one form is a sort of aspect, the other a tense. The only connection between them, I think, is that in suitable circumstances "X is going to V" can itself be a ground for asserting "X will V"—a rather trivial way of procuring identical "assertion conditions". See *Truth and Other Enigmas* (Cambridge, Mass.: Harvard University Press, 1978), pp. 152–153, 161, 336, 340; and *Frege: Philosophy of Language*, p. 450.

Peter Geach, turning the tables on Dummett, argues that "X is going to V" (understood as admitting "X was going to V but never did") is itself the genuine future "tense", and that anything else is a fiction invented by philosophers. But surely a future tense, distinct from this, can be forged (as Dummett notes in different terms), and is forged when present facts are habitually brought into certain particular connections, realized case by case, with past affirmations of a suitable form; the appropriate connections are most clearly exhibited in the practices associated with betting and promising. They are without parallel in the employment of our "prospective imperfective" (that is, Geach's alleged future tense), which presupposes much looser such connections, as the divergent logical links discussed above show. The cogency of Geach's description might, however, be taken as demonstrating the possibility of dispensing with such practices and with such a form of thought, and it invites the conjecture that "prospective aspect" is the primary phenomenon, and the future tense a secondary development that must be understood in terms of it. See *Providence and Evil* (Cambridge: Cambridge University Press, 1977), ch. 3, pp. 40–66.

doing A now," the anticipatory "He's doing A in a minute" and the abstract "He's doing A," which in their original employment is entailed by either of the others. It becomes possible and attractive to attach the sense formerly associated with "He's doing A now" to "He's doing A" *simpliciter*—and then also, in order to block the inevitable inference from "He's doing A in a minute" to "He's doing A," which has now become invalid, to rewrite the former as "He's going to do A in a minute." This we might call the first stage in the process of sophistication. Note that it brings their use of the progressive, outside the context of rationalization, into line with ours.[26] An ideal of "presence" is imposed on the progressive, but it is a presence of the sort expressed by "now" and "at the moment", not that expressed by the present tense—for even "It's going to . . . in a minute" is in a genuinely present *tense*, for them as for us. Once the step is taken, the underlying metaphysical connection between such fact-structures as that *he's doing A* and *he's going to do A* (as they would *now* be expressed) is rendered occult, and it might take a bit of philosophy to retrieve it, under the name (as I am supposing) of imperfective aspect.[27]

Similarly, if a genuine future tense has formed, or some minimal probabilistic locutions have been introduced, it becomes possible to restrict the sense of "She is going to do A," and to further contract that of "She is doing A." We can, for example, *add* the requirement that the assertion of either commits the speaker to "She will (in the end) have done A" or, in another scenario, to "She is likely (in the end) to have done A." Here the assertion of either imperfective proposition is controlled by the expectation, simple or probabilistic, of future completion or success.[28] Other, similar restrictions can be imagined.

Here, a different kind of reality-constraint is imposed on the legitimate affirmation of the progressive (and, with it, of the prospective imperfective). Unless new locutions are formed, though, expressive capacity will be lost. It is clear, in particular, that the rationalization-

26. Within this context, they will still say, "He's doing A" in cases where we will insist on "He's trying to do A."

27. Here I omit discussion of uses in hiatus, as I called them. If we suppose that the new use of "She's doing A" is incompatible with these, then information will be lost. We must suppose a new form, say, "She's *in a hiatus in* doing A," which will express the facts about our napping organizer and our frozen sycamore.

28. See Anscombe, *Intention*, pp. 39–40.

connection, the elements of which were expressed at the previous stage by means of "is . . . ing" and "is going to . . .", and at the earlier stage by "is . . . ing" alone, can be recognized as holding by one who harbors neither of the superadded expectations. The movement that narrows the conditions for the assertion of the progressive and prospective forms of verbs (that is, of event- or process-descriptions) must thus be one that introduces new forms for them, fitted to the enterprise of rationalization. These might take the shape of such practical-psychical auxiliaries as "tries", "intends" and "wants", but could equally appear in the shape of, say, verb endings that 'grammaticalize' these offices (in the linguists' restricted sense). These new modes of employment of process- or event-descriptions, if they are more than one in number, could then attract peculiar constraints of their own, and exhibit among themselves distinctions of the sort made out in the last paragraph between "is . . . ing" and "is going to. . . ."[29] Whatever in the way of first-person authority was formerly attached to "is . . . ing" and "is going to . . ." in the context of rationalization would necessarily be reserved for these overtly psychical constructions, which are fitted especially to that context; such authority, however it is to be understood and limited, cannot, after all, be supposed to extend to the future.

Here the process of sophistication is complete. The imperfective enfolding or compression of an event- or process-form, which was expressed directly at the earliest stage of development, among our naive agents, has now been sorted into a variety of forms, some of them overtly psychical and practical, some not. Their unity has been submerged or rendered occult. The conditions for the possibility of a sophisticated philosophy of action, and a subtle philosophical treatment of the various practical-psychical attitudes, are in place.

Of course, the use of psychical verbs, as *we* have them, as also of the progressive and the prospective imperfective, does not in fact completely realize either of the two stages of the advance of sophistication I have outlined. The obscure criteria of 'presence' and 'reality' that they impose act on us rather as a sort of regulative ideal. The effects of this ideal are, however, quite adequate to provide materials and inspiration for what I have called a sophisticated theory of action.

29. For example, "I intend to do A" could be constrained by the agent's belief that he will successfully complete the act, as Grice, Harman and Velleman suppose that it is (see ch. 6, n. 8).

I conclude with the following analogical representation of the doctrine I have attempted to propound. Our two forms of rationalization,
naive and sophisticated, are to be compared with the different forms of
exchange distinguished in, say, Aristotle, Marx and von Mises—these
are the forms of exchange marked out (in different ways) by the expressions "barter", "money" and "credit". In claiming to find a certain order of priority among these things, this line of thought was not, or was
not *just*, advancing a historical hypothesis. In a so-called credit economy, after all—one in which *purchase* and *payment* are distinguished
conceptually and practically—the simple act of *buying* something, in
which purchase and payment are not distinguished, is still possible and
intelligible. In a simple money economy, in which the acts of *selling*
and *buying* have been distinguished conceptually and practically, a pair
of us might yet engage in a simple act of *barter*, or of immediate exchange—an act in which the roles of *buyer* and *seller* are not distinguished. Credit and money presuppose barter in the sense that they
presuppose a structuring of life that makes barter possible and intelligible, while the reverse is not the case. We can, after all, speak of a system
of exchange by simple barter, in which such acts provide the only possible illustration of the concept of exchange. A treatment of the concept
of exchange that disallows this, or that insists that every act of barter be
construed as, say, the simultaneous purchase, payment, extension of
credit and cancellation of debts on the part of *each* of two agents, is
clearly absurd. My hope is to have shown that the theory of action falls
into just this sort of absurdity in neglecting what I have called naive rationalization and the sort of connection of ground and grounded that is
expressed in it.

~ PART THREE

Practical Generality

~ 9

Two Tendencies in Practical Philosophy

1. Introductory

This essay is an inquiry into the workings of two concepts, *practical disposition* and *social practice*, as they enter, or might enter, into moral philosophy. Or rather, it is a fragment of such an inquiry. Its point of departure is a pair of familiar tendencies in moral philosophy, the tendencies we meet with in what might be called *dispositional accounts of the rationality of morality* and *practice versions of utilitarianism*. Of course, the concepts of a practice and a disposition enter into other types of moral theory, some of them perhaps intuitively more attractive than either of these. But the deployment of our concepts in these two lines of thought is, I think, uniquely clear and intelligible. A study of their workings here can therefore be expected to supply a general elucidation of the two concepts as they are properly understood in practical philosophy and thus potentially in quite different types of normative theory.

The concepts *practice* and *disposition* appear at first sight to be quite diverse: one looks to be a concept proper to social theory, the other perhaps to psychology. A comparative treatment will, I hope, tend to burn off this dross of associated ideas and reveal an underlying kinship at least in their specifically practical-philosophical use. But further, recognition of this kinship will in turn put us into contact with a more extensive class of practical concepts and with it a larger logical, metaphysical and normative topic, namely, *the role of a certain kind of generality in practice and practical thought.* This same field of inquiry, the problem of generality, is crossed wherever a philosopher speaks of *virtue* or *character*; of moral or other practical *principles*; of *maxims*; of *forms of practical reasoning* or of such *reasons* as bear an intrinsically general content; or, finally, of practical *conceptions*, whether they be conceptions of justice, rationality or happiness, or of one's "self" or one's practical "identity". A certain conceptual darkness and obscurity overtake any text that deploys one or another of these phrases, an obscurity we do not find where it speaks, for example, of *action, intention* or *desire*. The obscurity arises, I believe, from a common source in all of these cases, the peculiar "generality", as I am provisionally calling it, of the things meant. This is a feature we already find in the items captured in the concepts *disposition* and *practice* as they figure in the comparatively clear light of our two tendencies. A more remote aim of this study is thus to make sense of this larger logical and metaphysical problematic.

As a central representative of the tendency toward dispositional accounts of the rationality of morality, I will consider a number of David Gauthier's works, but especially *Morals by Agreement.*[1] I will also refer to Philippa Foot's "Moral Beliefs," which exhibits, though in a much less developed way, the structural feature of Gauthier's account I want to discuss.[2] In connection with difficulties about practices and utilitarianism, the text I will mostly consider is John Rawls's early essay "Two Concepts of Rules." This work is at first sight merely a defense of the utilitarian idea against certain familiar objections, by means of some consideration about practices and rules. But Rawls's real aim was of course to redeploy these latter considerations in a more complex, and decidedly non-utilitarian, theoretical environment. (We will in fact find that this aim is not quite realized.) His attitude toward the theory

1. *Morals by Agreement* (Oxford: Oxford University Press, 1986). The other works mentioned are "Reason and Maximization" and "The Unity of Reason" in David Gauthier, *Moral Dealing* (Ithaca, New York: Cornell University Press, 1990), pp. 209–233 and 110–126; "Assure and Threaten," *Ethics* 104 (1994): 690–721; and "Rationality and the Rational Aim," in Jonathan Dancy, *Reading Parfit* (Oxford: Blackwell, 1997), pp. 24–41.

2. "Moral Beliefs," in *Virtues and Vices* (Berkeley: University of California Press, 1977), pp. 110–131, especially pp. 125–130.

It tends to be forgotten that the original rationale for Professor Foot's introduction of the category of virtue, that is, of a certain sort of "disposition", was to account for the rationality of morality. The latter topic has remained her central theoretical interest, but it must be stressed that *only the last eight paragraphs of "Moral Beliefs" will be at issue here*, and that these are paragraphs Professor Foot has long since rejected, for different reasons at different times, while always retaining the critique of non-cognitivism propounded in the bulk of the essay.

under construction in "Two Concepts" is thus a model of the attitude I am taking toward both types of theory.[3]

Following the example of Gauthier and Rawls alike, the substantive focus of this part will be on a particular moral phenomenon, namely, promising and the obligation of promises. But its more special focus is on what I will call the *act of fidelity* and its normative and evaluative standing. An agent X's doing A for another agent Y is an act of fidelity where we can affirm, in a certain familiar sense, that *X did A for Y because she promised Y she would*—that is, 'precisely because' or 'just because' she promised this. We distinguish such acts of promise-keeping from those in which, as we say, an 'ulterior motive' is at work. The Prichardian conception of a promise as potentially exhausting the agent's ground in the keeping of it is an intuitive conception, one fitted to the everyday enterprise of action explanation. It need not, I think, be supposed to impede the more articulate and philosophical analysis of the act of fidelity that our authors are attempting to supply.

The order of discussion here runs as follows. After an initial characterization of the two tendencies, I attempt a preliminary articulation of the genus to which their respective 'mediating elements', *practice* and *disposition*, belong. They are, I suggest, at the same time 'general' and 'actual' in senses I attempt to specify. The two tendencies are then compared with so-called 'two-level' normative theories and some of their peculiarities addressed. The fundamental difficulty for either tendency is to find a justification of its central claim—a 'transfer' or 'transparency' principle as I call it—that is consistent with the special status that the principle must be assigned within the theory. The aim of finding a suitable justification of this claim places further constraints on the apt interpretation of the concepts *practice* and *disposition* that are implicit in our theories. I suggest that it is because neither Rawls nor Gauthier articulates a suitably narrow and properly practical-philosophical interpretation of his central concept that neither manages a proper defense

---

3. "Two Concepts of Rules," in John Rawls, *Collected Papers* (Cambridge, Mass.: Harvard University Press, 1999), pp. 20–46. I will also refer occasionally to "Justice as Fairness," ibid., pp. 47–72, and to *A Theory of Justice* (Cambridge, Mass.: Harvard University Press, 1971).

Rawls's early essay is much more important to his later work than is usually recognized. His later works all preserve and complicate its central doctrine about the need to distinguish *the justification of a practice*—and, more generally, the justification of a 'principle' and a practical 'conception', in the senses attached to these terms in his later works—from *the justification of an action as falling under a practice*. The former sort of justification is of course subjected to a non-utilitarian standard in all of the works in which Rawls speaks entirely in his own person.

of his central principle. I then make my own provisional attempt to impart a suitably narrow and practical-philosophical interpretation of the concept of a practice—one that might realize Rawls's ambitions—and suggest a possible parallel treatment of the object of Gauthier's intention. I conclude by developing certain metaphysical aspects of the phenomena, once they are thus properly understood.

2. Preliminary Exposition of the Two Tendencies: The Problem and the Proposed Solution

Particular doctrines manifesting either of our tendencies might cover the whole of morality, but since we are restricting our attention to the part of justice that pertains to the keeping of promises, we may say that Rawls is interested in the *moral goodness,* as he puts it, of acts of fidelity, whereas Gauthier and Foot are interested in their *individual rationality.*[4] *How might these doctrines be compared?*

First, they may be seen as framed in response to structurally similar problems, certain perceived *tight corners,* as we might call them, that promising tends to generate. For Rawls, presupposing a background allegiance to utilitarianism, the difficulty is the familiar Humean one that by breaking a promise we are sometimes able to do people more good than we would by keeping it; the question thus arises how it can be any good, morally speaking, to act on the strength of a promise in such circumstances. For Gauthier and for Foot, the problem is the more ancient one that, like any requirement of justice, promise-keeping will sometimes cross our *interests,* even if we take into account the irritating noise of complaint, the threat of never being trusted again, and the like. The question is how there can be any sense in fidelity in those circumstances, or how such a thing can be rational.

It is natural to see the difficulty as arising in either case from the uncritical acceptance of a consequentialist or maximizing understanding of morality or rationality. It is true that such ideas are in the background in these works; this is part of what makes them so clear and thus

---

4. Note that this means that our point of entry into this material is through an idea of 'subjective' goodness in one form or other, rather than through a corresponding notion of 'objective' rightness. We are in the first instance asking "Did the agent act well (or rationally) in doing A, given that she did it precisely because she promised she would?" and only secondarily "Is the agent morally required to do A (or does she have most reason to do A), given that she promised she would?"

such useful theoretical models, as Rawls saw. But in truth neither conception of a tight corner depends on any very determinate 'teleological' idea. The essential thing is simply this, that the goods and evils to be pursued and avoided in the tight-corner context are such as would make the faithful person's conduct either morally blameworthy or imprudent if it were performed by a similarly situated person, but one who had not made a promise. The promise, the 'dead hand of the past', is supposed to overturn that calculation and to do this without introducing any new prospect of good. How are we to make this fit with *any* form of the idea that sound deliberation is a matter of having one's sights on some kind of good?[5]

As the problems faced by the two tendencies exhibit something of a common shape, so also do their respective responses to it. On neither account is the individual act of fidelity held to acquire the relevant characteristic, *moral goodness* or *rationality*, from the agent's setting his sights on some benefit or excellence or merit that might reside in the *individual* action itself or in the series of *individual* events it is likely to entrain. Gauthier's and Foot's suggestion is not, for example, that the faithful agent has cottoned on to some subtle, easily missed and peculiarly moral delight to be found in individual acts of promise-keeping or any slice of the noble that might tip the scales in favor of fidelity. And Rawls does not recommend, say, a 'goal rights' consequentialism, nor more generally does he attempt to assign a special intrinsic value, whether 'agent neutral' or 'agent relative', to the mere fact of a properly discharged promise—a 'value' the faithful agent might then be understood as apprehending and seeking to realize. On neither account does the faithful agent anticipate the appearance of anything in the order of individual events that might outweigh the more readily recognizable benefits of tight-corner infidelity.

Rather, on Foot's account, the difficulty philosophers have felt about

---

5. Of course, any theory of the obligation of promises will allow that one is often *justified* in leaving off keeping one's word, and hence not guilty of infidelity, when it develops that to do the thing would be dangerous or somehow especially counter-productive for oneself, or when the needs of persons other than the promisee are sufficiently alarming. Neither type of circumstance would fall under my description "tight-corner situation"—neither the type that interests Gauthier and Foot, nor the type that interests Rawls. But it is clear that any reasonable account of the obligation of promises must allow for genuine tight corners as well: it must allow that even where the obligation stands, the faithful person is sometimes left doing what would simply be stupid or wrong for a similarly situated person who had not given her word.

the rationality of fidelity and justice in general arises from the fact that "they consider in isolation particular just acts."[6] Their attention ought to pass from the typical individual act of fidelity to something that runs through them all, something that each of them *manifests* or *instances* or *expresses*, namely, a certain putative *virtue*. This, in our present case, is fidelity itself: a particular practical disposition, a *hexis* or *habitus*, a familiar practical 'trait'. Blindness to this category of practical reality is the source of the apparent difficulty about the tight corner, for the friend of fidelity can adduce nothing in its favor from the materials present in these situations considered severally or individually. But if we are granted this category, and compare the various forms of faithless vice with fidelity—each as a disposition that operates within and without the tight corner—then, Foot argues, a link to the agent's *interest* or *profit* might perhaps be found. Indeed, she argues that if no such link can be found, then fidelity, and justice in general, must lose its claim to the title of a genuine virtue.[7]

On Gauthier's account, the philosophers' difficulty about the tight corner arises from a wrong conception of the relation between individual action and the maximization of good that the rational agent allegedly pursues. A passage in "The Unity of Reason" links his thought especially clearly to our concerns. The illusion arises, he there suggests, from a temptation to pass from the correct characterization of the rational agent as one who "chooses in such a way as to maximize" to the seemingly equivalent, but wrong, characterization of her as one who "chooses [simply] to maximize".[8]

If these descriptions are heard as applying to an *individual choice*, and thus to an individual action, they are indeed equivalent: if I maximized in the particular choice I made at t, then I chose, at t, in such a way as to maximize. Gauthier's thought is that if his first characterization is to

6. "Moral Beliefs," p. 129.

7. A high-minded moralism was and is ready to oppose this constraint together with the apparently empirical claim that fidelity considered as a *hexis* meets it. But this moralism inevitably overlooks the *specifically moral* considerations that motivate these ideas: Foot's thought, later retracted, was clearly that the rejection of any such link is a confession that fidelity works to the disadvantage of its bearer. It is thus also the confession that to bring someone up into such 'virtue', to counsel its acts, is to injure her. How could that be any more respectable, morally speaking, than binding her feet? Gauthier's motivations are similar, as we see especially in the later chapters of *Morals by Agreement*, and he too has had to contend with this thoughtless and peculiarly amoral moralism.

8. "The Unity of Reason," p. 122.

capture the idea of rational agency, it must be heard in another logical register, as expressing a formally different type of judgment. In that case, it will be possible to distinguish it from the second characterization similarly heard. In this other, de-individualized register, our two characterizations might be put into the past tense with the words "one who *used to choose* in such way as to maximize" and "one who *used to choose* to maximize". In the opposed individualized or 'tokenized' register, by contrast, they could only be put into the past tense with the words "one who *chose* (or *has chosen*) in such a way as to maximize" and "one who *chose* (or *has chosen*) to maximize".[9]

In the language of *Morals by Agreement*, an agent who falls under the second characterization, properly heard, is said to exhibit a certain practical *disposition*, namely, the disposition to "straightforward maximization", an item potentially exhibited or instanced or exemplified in many individual actions. In other works, Gauthier speaks not of the agent's "disposition" but rather of her "conception of rationality" or of the "deliberative procedure" she "employs". But nothing should be made to hang on Gauthier's choice of words, any more than on nice features of his grammar. It is necessary rather to lay hold of the function of these phrases and grammatical forms in Gauthier's argument, which is in each case fundamentally the same.[10]

GAUTHIER'S CHIEF EFFORT is of course to show that only agents who have rejected the straightforward maximizer's disposition in favor of another, which he calls "constrained maximization", can satisfy his first characterization, "one who chooses in such a way as to maximize". Constrained maximization, which is basically Gauthierian justice, is the practical disposition that *itself* maximizes, as we see by reflecting on its effect on the choices of certain other agents. Only *its* bearers, then, are ideally rational. The superior disposition is supposed to be exhibited inter alia in what I am calling acts of fidelity or else in a slightly restricted class of them.

9. I use the past tense to express the point because it is difficult to hear the English present in this sort of case as bearing anything but habitual or 'frequentative' meaning—the natural sort to employ in the description of a disposition. Historical uses of the present fit the bill: in place of the caption "Washington crosses the Delaware" a textbook illustration might bear the words "Washington chooses to maximize" or, equivalently, "Washington chooses in such a way as to maximize." All of these formulae might describe the same choice.

10. The expression "conception of rationality" predominates in "Reason and Maximization"; its place is taken by "disposition" in *Morals by Agreement*, and then by "deliberative pro-

In sum, then, the philosopher's suspicion of irrationality in one who has kept her promise in a tight corner derives, on Gauthier's analysis, from an incapacity to switch conceptual registers and see past the *individual choice* and the consideration on which it is founded to the rational *disposition* that is displayed in their connection—a disposition that might also be displayed in any number of other individual acts of fidelity.

For Rawls, on the other hand, the appearance that has to be overcome is that certain ends appropriate to morality itself are crossed in some acts of fidelity. And once again the trouble is said to arise from the fixation of the philosopher's attention on the individual action and the particular situation on which it bears. But in this instance the trouble arises more precisely from a failure to recognize the so-called *practice* that the individual action is said to instance or embody, and the associated failure to distinguish between "the justification of a practice" and "the justification of an action falling under it". This so-called practice is again something instanced in many individual actions, but in this case in many individual actions of many people. In describing a practice that prevails among some class of agents we say "what they do", in some sense, and not what any or many or most or all of them "are doing", "have done" or "will do". The thing characterized thus falls outside the order of individual events into which individual actions are fitted.

The item thus multiply realized, in our case *the practice of making and keeping promises*, is again allegedly suited to realize certain larger ends (ends which, for the duration of the paper, Rawls takes over from utilitarianism). If, for example, we compare the practice as we have it with a variant that would permit default in tight corners, the latter will appear less beneficial, indeed destructive of the point of 'giving one's word'. Like the individual promises that precede them, individual acts of fidelity as they happen among us get their nature from this practice, Rawls argues, and so it is only through this practice, as it seems, that these actions can be brought into connection with any supposed ends of morality. Thus, Rawls supposes, acts of fidelity do not cross these ends even in what I have called the tight corner.

---

cedure" in "Assure and Threaten." I have opted to employ the word "disposition" throughout my discussion. It encodes less theory and it might be, and sometimes is, given in translation of the *hexis* and *habitus* of Aristotle and St. Thomas. The re-emergence of this traditional philosophical category in Gauthier's works is among their most striking and interesting features.

3. Two Characteristic Marks of Practices and Dispositions

The two tendencies are united at least in this, that each attributes the difficulty that arises about its particular form of 'tight corner' to a blinkered focus on the individual act of fidelity together with its outcome or consequences. The further element that makes sense of tight-corner acts of fidelity, and is so easily missed, simply does not belong to that order. Thus the peculiar appeal that our two tendencies make to the concepts of a disposition and a practice cannot come down to this, that individual acts of infidelity might lead to the *loss* of a profitable disposition or the *weakening* of a beneficial practice, while acts of fidelity help preserve these principles. The suggestion might be rejected out of hand as hopelessly uncharitable to our theories: it seems quite implausible that faithful agents must reckon on such facts. But it is in any case clear that this reading would evince exactly the point of view under attack. According to it, the concepts *practice* and *disposition* are employed in an especially sophisticated analysis of the series of events into which the individual act of fidelity is fitted—a type of analysis that, each theory claims, must sometimes favor infidelity.[11]

If this interpretation of our two types of theory is uncharitable and unsound, then how *are* we to interpret the role of practices and dispositions in them? And what exactly are these items supposed to be? These questions cannot, I think, be handled separately. The words "practice" and "disposition" are legitimately employed in any number of connections within and without philosophy, and it is clear that they often bear senses that are completely alien to practical philosophy. Consider, for example, the use of the word "disposition" in the philosophy of science. The hypothesis I have adopted is that some truth can be developed from each of our tendencies by a sort of immanent criticism: the aim of attaining this truth might thus act as our guide in seeking a suitable specifically practical-philosophical interpretation of their central concepts.

It will emerge, I think, that in their practical-philosophical employments the terms must be taken to bear a much narrower sense than is customarily attached to them. But I think that no questions will be begged if we insist on two very weak marks at the outset. On any

11. The idea is explicitly rejected by Rawls in his discussion of Ross ("Two Concepts," Part II), but it is equally plain that Foot and Gauthier must reject it.

legitimate interpretation of the terms "practice" and "disposition", the occupants of the intended categories must at the same time be, as I will put it, *general* and *actual*. I will explain these two features separately.

The first mark, generality, has already implicitly been introduced. It may be elucidated by contrasting (1) the relation an individual action might bear to anything legitimately called "the disposition it manifests" or "the practice under which it falls" with (2) the quite different relation an individual action might bear to a *further intention* with which it is performed, or a *more inclusive action* into which it is inserted, or a *plan* or *course of action* it helps to realize. A single further intention might govern a succession of individual actions, showing itself in each one of them, as a particular plan might also do. A more inclusive action would itself *be* such a succession of individual actions, as a so-called course of action would also be. Thus, as we saw in Part Two, I might successively *dig a foundation, pour some concrete* and *lay a few bricks* as so many parts or phases of a larger and more inclusive action of building a house. Similarly, I might *get out my rifle, walk across the street, take aim* and *fire*, all with the further intention of ridding the state of a tyrant. The further intention with which I act is a sort of red thread that runs throughout this manifold of individual deeds, just as the extended process of house-building maintains itself through its various phases. It is obvious that a plan or course of action might have a similar position. An item of any of these four types might 'unite' the actions of several agents quite as well as the actions of any one.

But the inner tendency of an occupant of any of these four categories is precisely to wind down under its own steam, to pass away with its execution or completion. The succession of individual actions governed by any such thing will thus constitute a limited whole. The succession is related to its members or parts, the subordinate actions, as an individual animal is related to its members or parts—and not as a species of animal is related to *its* members or bearers. By contrast, it is plainly a central characteristic of each of our two tendencies that the further element, the one supposed to favor action on the strength of a promise even in the tight corner, is essentially one and the same, unchanged, unexhausted, and not merely similar, through a potentially unlimited series of individual acts of fidelity. A practical disposition must be something that might be exhibited in a potentially infinite series of acts of a *single agent*, all of them sharing a common description. A social practice must be something that will characteristically be exhibited in indefinitely many acts of indefinitely many agents. Thus, whatever else may be true of them and whatever exactly they are, practices and dispositions do not come to a limit in any action or event or in any totality of actions and events that could thereby be said to *satisfy*, *execute* or *complete* them; they can only be said to be *manifested*, *instanced* or *exhibited* in any such thing. This is the peculiar 'generality' that is our quarry.[12]

But if the element that sides with fidelity in the tight corner, a so-called practice or disposition, is supposed merely to be 'general' in this sort of way, how does it differ from, say, an appropriate *general concept?* Consider the general concept *act of fidelity* and the narrower concept *one of X's acts of fidelity:* any of X's individual acts of fidelity will "instance" or "fall under" either of these concepts alongside indefinitely many other individual actions. Of course, no one will suggest that we can *understand* how X's acts of fidelity might be rational or morally good just by pointing out that X's acts of fidelity fall under one or the other of these concepts. But more interesting ideas are available. If our two tendencies propose to accredit individual acts of fidelity by bringing them into relation to something general, how do they differ from a so-called deontology like that of Ross, or a realism in Christine Korsgaard's (polemical) sense, whether about rationality or moral good-

---

12. Of course this should not be understood to mean that an agent cannot lose a disposition or that a practice cannot die out; it is just that this cannot be the work of the disposition or practice itself.

It may be objected, as a point of interpretation, that in "Assure and Threaten" and other recent works Gauthier does make the rationality of promise- or assurance-keeping turn on the existence of an antecedent *intention*—namely, the intention allegedly expressed in the (sincere) assurance itself. It is not in that respect, though, that "Assure and Threaten" exemplifies the first of our two tendencies, but rather in its appeal to the idea of an agent's *deliberative procedure.* That Gauthierian deliberative procedures exhibit the generality that interests us will be seen later.

It may also be objected that some intentions or plans do appear to bear the generality we find in dispositions and practices. But this generality can at best belong to the *content* of the intention or plan, and not to the form of the 'further element' itself—and the latter is what will be at issue in the 'transfer principles' discussed later in this essay. It is in fact not clear, though, that an intention or plan *never to visit New York* or *always to return blows with bullets* has a genuinely general content. The particular event that would realize or satisfy it—*going to one's grave never having visited New York*, say, or *having lived one's life always having returned blows with bullets*—is simply of a very peculiar sort.

ness?[13] On a realist or a deontological conception, the element that swings things to the side of fidelity in a tight corner might be a certain general "relation of fitness", for example, or a norm inscribed in the nature of things, or the truth of a substantive general 'principle' of morality or rationality that forbids infidelity. That the outward act accords with such a thing will make it 'right for the agent to do' or 'what she has most reason to do'; that the agent somehow adverts to it in acting will make her act genuinely morally good or rational. A potentially infinite succession of actions might bear these relations to some general norm, principle or 'relation of fitness'.

Our second weak mark, 'actuality', is meant to capture the intuitive difference between any such conception and our two tendencies. In the two tendencies, the element that sides with fidelity, the practice or disposition, bears some kind of actuality in, or among, the agents whose individual actions it is supposed to accredit. For example, a practice, however we are to understand such a thing, evidently does not exist except through people's acting and being disposed to act in accordance with it. And on any account a disposition must have some sort of explanatory standing in respect of what happens when it is manifested in an individual action. By contrast, the character of realist relations of fitness or deontological 'principles' can be summed up in Hegel's ironic formula: they are "something far too excellent to have actuality, or something too impotent to procure it for themselves."[14] Such things could, for example, only 'act' through an agent's granting them significance—that is, in a way in which even non-existent relations of fitness and false or imaginary principles could.

On each account under discussion, then, the real presence of something somehow 'general' is among the conditions of the possibility of the individual act of fidelity, that is, of the truth of the thought that X

---

13. The notion of a deontology, which I employ for purposes of exposition, is notoriously obscure: see Barbara Herman, "Leaving Deontology Behind," in *The Practice of Moral Judgment* (Cambridge, Mass.: Harvard University Press, 1995). For Korsgaard's use of the notion of practical or normative "realism" (which she opposes), see, for example, *The Sources of Normativity* (Cambridge: Cambridge University Press, 1996), pp. 28–48. The idea of a "deontological" theory of rationality might seem a bit surprising, but in "The Normativity of Instrumental Reason," in *Ethics and Practical Reason*, ed. G. Cullity and B. Gaut (Oxford: Oxford University Press, 1997), Korsgaard contemplates but in the end rejects the possibility of a realistic or "dogmatic rationalist" interpretation even of the principle of instrumental rationality (see especially the third part of the essay).

14. *Hegel's Logic*, trans. William Wallace (Oxford: Clarendon, 1975), p. 9.

did A because she promised Y she'd do A—just as something like an intention or wanting or other will to do B is presupposed in the truth of
it that *X did A because it was a means to doing B*. The nexus of action
and consideration that is characteristic of the act of fidelity can only exist as the phenomenon of something that might equally be exhibited in
indefinitely many other instances of the same nexus.

4. Forms of Judgment in Which Practices and Dispositions Are Caught

No interpretation of the concepts central to our two tendencies, *practice* and *disposition*, can be taken for granted. My hypothesis is that some
truth can be developed, by a sort of immanent criticism, from each of
our tendencies, and I will take this as my guide in attempting to interpret their respective central concepts. The terms that are meant to express these concepts thus appear for the better part of this essay as
more or less empty tokens, and the effort is to supply them, by stages,
with suitable content. It will emerge, I think, that in their specifically
practical-philosophical employments the terms must be taken to bear a
much narrower sense than is customarily attached to them. Thus far,
our information about the intended categories is restricted just exactly
to this, (A) that an occupant of either can be instanced or manifested in
an unlimited series of individual actions that fall together under a single concept, a concept through which the practice or disposition is itself described,[15] and (B) that the thing thus instanced or manifested has
some sort of actuality in the agent or agents to whom it pertains. These
conditions are obscure as they stand; an apt interpretation can, I think,
only be found by considering certain of the abstract shapes of thought
and speech through which practices and dispositions can be represented.

Practices and dispositions are among the many things that *can* be described in so-called *generic* and *habitual* propositions, respectively—or
rather in interconnected ensembles of generic and habitual propositions. The simplest of such propositions have the outward forms "They
do A" (generic) and "She *does* A" (habitual). The next simplest have the
forms "They *do* A in circumstances C" (generic) and "She *does* A in cir-

---

15. We may grant, and will later insist, that practical dispositions can *also* be instanced or
manifested in things other than action, for example, in feeling and in practical thought.

cumstances C" (habitual). But propositions of these forms can exhibit any degree of internal complexity, as in "They do A in C, unless also C', in which case they do B . . ." (generic), and the like. The disposition to fidelity, or part of it, might be attributed to an agent with the words "She keeps her promises" or "She takes a promise to do something as a reason for doing it." Similarly, the practice of promising, or part of it, might be assigned to a population with some such words as "These people perform such actions as fall under descriptions that they have previously voiced in a certain special way (which *might* involve something like prefacing the descriptions with the words 'I promise'), and they perform them on that ground."[16]

Unlike any practice or disposition that it might instance or manifest, what I am here calling an *individual action*, taken as something present, is reported in propositions of a very different form—namely, in progressive propositions like "She *is doing* A."

The variable signs ("she", "they", "to do A") that I have employed in exhibiting these three crude propositional shapes (generic, habitual, progressive) suggest that practical content is in view. But as we saw in Parts One and Two, all manner of content can enter into them. Anything that can be called an event or process can receive *progressive* formulation—the melting of a bit of lead, for example, or the blossoming of a cherry tree; and I might use a *habitual* proposition to assign a particular sort of climate to some place, as in "Vancouver gets a lot of rain"; a *generic* proposition can be employed to assign a breeding season to a species of bird, or to attribute a melting point to a chemical stuff— to take two comparatively interesting examples from a very large class. At the present incredibly coarse level of resolution, then, we have to do with three *very* abstract ways of linking a subject and a predicative expression in speech. The three shapes of proposition are more adequately schematized as: "S's V" (generic), "This S Vs" (habitual) and "This S is Ving" (progressive)—or, to include the possibility of a condition or typical circumstance: "S's V in C," "This S Vs in C" and "This S

---

16. Because, as Rawls teaches, the practice of making and keeping promises already enters into the constitution of any individual act of promising and is implicitly adverted to in any use of that expression, the simpler sentence "They keep their promises" would make for an infelicitous formulation of the practice we mean: it suggests that we intend something *more* than is contained in the mere existence of the practice. (Nevertheless, I do not think it would be strictly incorrect.) It is thus natural to employ a more complex formulation than we do in the attribution of the corresponding disposition, which can take the practice for granted without any danger of misunderstanding.

is Ving, now that it's in C." In the transition from the first to the second, the subject is 'particularized', as we might put it; in the transition from the second to the third, the predicate is 'particularized' as well. I will take it as obvious that these three grammatically given modes of combination of a subject term and certain types of predicative expression correspond to (at least) three logically different forms of judgment. The same judgments might be expressed in other ways—for example, a generic judgment about a class of agents might be expressed by describing 'what is done', 'what one does', 'what we do' and so forth—but the inner connection and diversity of the three forms are rendered plain in these simple schemata.

Even where the contents joined refer to an agent or agents and to a type of action, and are thus intrinsically practical, there is scope for a further distinction. Our three ultra-abstract forms of connection of subject and predicate might take more determinate forms, and some of these more determinate *forms* might themselves be specifically practical. Consider first the progressive. Since I am an agent and *telephoning one's aunt* is a type of action, any judgment about me that is expressed in the progressive proposition "He's telephoning his aunt" might be said to be *practical by content*. But the judgment expressed might or might not be *practical by form* as well. If, for example, these words were given in answer to the question why I am picking up the phone, or if they were themselves folded into a sentential question of that reason-eliciting type, then the *same* underlying judgment might equally have been expressed by "He is *intentionally* telephoning his aunt," though this would have been overkill in the context. But, of course, not *every* judgment legitimately expressed by the words "He is telephoning his aunt" could also be expressed by "He is intentionally telephoning his aunt"; I might be mistaking her number for my niece's. The proposition "He is intentionally doing A" merely makes explicit what is already contained in "He is doing A" when it enters in one way or another into the rational explanation of action. It expresses a *more determinate form* of the type of judgment we express in "He *is doing* A" and more generally in "This S *is* V*ing*"—and, of course, a specifically practical form of such judgment.

Now, the judgments our authors express in such words as "It is their practice to do A" and "Her disposition is to do A" evidently bear a similar relation to those expressed with generic and habitual trappings. Consider that anything a philosopher would call a "regularity" in the behavior or activity of an agent or class of agents might get a habitual or generic representation. This representation would be practical by content. But it is clear that our authors would deny that just *any* such thing would rightly attract description with the words "practice" and "disposition" as they intend them. That our authors nevertheless shift back and forth from propositions of the shapes "They do A" and "She does A" to propositions of the shapes "It is their practice to do A" and "Her disposition is to do A" (and we have seen this already in Gauthier's use of the habitual) shows once again that the latter modes of connection of signs are meant to express *more determinate forms* of the abstract type of judgment we clothe in generic and habitual grammar. Like the word "intentionally", the words "practice" and "disposition" make explicit a shift of these abstract forms into a specifically practical gear, a shift that was present in our authors' use of merely generic and habitual propositions but was left to be carried, implicitly, by the practical-philosophical context. The trouble, of course, is how we are to understand this shift of a gear.[17]

Now, to return to our starting point, the 'generality' and 'actuality' we have so far noticed as characteristic of the 'further elements' on which our two tendencies turn are really features of *anything* that can receive generic or habitual expression. Propositions that come to us in generic or habitual trappings—whether or not the thing attributed is a kind of action and whether or not the underlying determinate form of attribution is specifically practical—are intuitively tailored to record something positive, real, present and 'actual', and thus something that meets our second criterion. They are no different, in this respect, from propositions that come to us in progressive trappings. They are all properly categorical and not merely normative or modal or hypothetical propositions. Where they have practical content, they tell us what agents are actually doing or actually do, not what they ought, might or would do.[18] On the other hand, whether it is practical in content or not,

17. Genuinely nominal uses of the words "practice" and "disposition" must be explained by reference to their appearance in propositions like "It is their practice to do A" and "It is her disposition to do A," and thus in terms of the more abstract generic and habitual forms of speech and thought. But the nominal uses are a bit more robust than that: typically, as we will see, what we think of as the *same* practice or disposition will be associated with a number of connected propositions of the appropriate sort. Some of the propositions that enter into such a connected complex will attribute things other than types of action to the agent or agents at issue, for example, certain modes of thought, the possession of certain concepts, and so forth.

18. Since the description of a disposition or practice will often contain a condition, it is im-

the truth of a progressive proposition like "She *is doing* A" or more broadly "This S *is* V*ing*" must come to a *limit* in the truth of the perfective "She *has done* A" or "This S *has* V*d*"—which expresses the existence of a complete or perfected individual event falling under the description "A" or "V". The truth of the corresponding generic and habitual propositions can of course outrun any number of the associated merely particular perfective comings-true. Thus the 'generality' we have found in practices and dispositions is a feature of anything that can be captured in habitual and generic forms of thought.

Like any general claim, any generic or habitual statement can appear as a subordinate element in what might be called a *statement of exemplification:* we can say things like "S's V—in fact, this S Vd yesterday" and "This S Vs—for example, it is Ving right now." It is the same with their expressly practical forms: "It is their practice to do A—for example, she (who is one of them) did A a couple of days ago" or "Her disposition is to do A—in fact, she's doing it now." This apparently trivial form of combination of propositions, one 'particular' and one 'general', is evidently the source of our access to the relations of *instancing, manifesting, falling under,* and so forth, which join an individual action to a practice or disposition. Note that this sort of combination cannot be reduced to mere logical conjunction: not every true statement in which "S" and "V"—or "(one of) them" and "A"—are linked through one of our 'particularizing' propositional forms (progressive, perfective) can be thus conjoined with a statement articulating the same signs through one of our 'generalizing' forms (habitual, generic), even supposing the latter is true. Not every individual action that falls under a concept through which a practice or disposition is described and has an appropriate subject can be said to *fall under* that practice or *manifest* that disposition.[19] I

---

portant to see that where it does, the result is no more a conditional or hypothetical proposition than is the description of someone as having a conditional intention. Such a condition belongs to the content that is joined to the subject by the employment of the habitual or generic forms, or, in the other case, by the interpolation of the verb "intends".

19. On the other hand, "All S's are F," together with "This S is F," really does entail "All S's are F—in fact, this S is F." Likewise for "Some S's are F." A statement of exemplification becomes a trivial conjunction if the generality expressed is of these familiar formal-logical types.

It is interesting that "This S was F five years ago" could not illustrate "Some S's are F" or "All S's are F." "F" must have the same tense in the exemplifying and exemplified propositions. By contrast, as the examples above show, instances, exemplifications or manifestations of *present* practices and dispositions can be formulated in a *past* tense. It is the same with anything expressible in generic or habitual propositions. The point should be compared with that made in ch. 8, n. 12.

will not labor the allied point that the truth of a proposition deploying either 'generalized' grammar, whatever its more determinate interpretation, is consistent with widely varying distributions of truth value in respect of propositions deploying the other, 'particularized' grammars. We have seen this already in connection with natural-historical judgments. However we are to understand them, the propositions "She keeps her promises" and "Her disposition is to keep her promises" are plainly consistent with the claims that she often hasn't, in the future sometimes won't, and even now is failing to keep some promise. Similarly, the attribution of a practice of promise-making and promise-keeping to a population is consistent with the claim that many members of the population have never kept very many of their promises.

Where a number of different 'particularized' propositions can follow one of our "generalized" propositions in a true statement of exemplification, the item expressed by the general proposition may be said to *unite* the things—the events, in the case that most interests us—that are registered by these several particularized propositions. Thus I will sometimes say that our search for specifically practical interpretations of such general propositions, and through it for correct interpretations of the concepts *practice* and *disposition*, is a search for certain specifically practical *forms of unity* of one event or action with another.[20]

20. Though our argument does not depend on any special view of the linguistic data, a few further remarks may be warranted. Where all three of "S's do A," "This S does A" and "This S is doing A" are possible, "A"—a specific type of predicative expression or verb—may be said to have the nature of a general event- or process-description. Extending received usage slightly, and also the different use of Part Two, all of these propositions may be grouped together as deploying forms of *imperfective* predication: in each an event-description is joined to a subject in a categorical affirmation, but neither present nor past forms of such an affirmation can be represented as naming or quantifying over complete or perfected events—as the perfective propositions "This S *has done* A" or "This S *did* A" can be. Most languages express the habitual and generic combination of subject and predicate with the least marked form of the verb possible—as in English we use the simple present tense. English is apparently somewhat unusual in having a past tense—that formed with "used to"—which forces a habitual or generic interpretation onto propositions it governs.

   Propositions exhibiting either a generic or a habitual form are frequently convertible into the other one. For example, the conditional habitual propositions "She does A when C happens" might be rewritten as a *generic* statement about occurrences of the condition, for example, as "Occurrences of C occasion her doing A." Despite the obvious connections, the division of linguists' labor has nevertheless tended to keep the two types of judgment apart. For evidence of this and for the data mentioned above, see Bernard Comrie, *Aspect* (Cambridge: Cambridge University Press, 1976), which treats the habitual and compares it with the progressive, and G. N. Carlson and F. J. Pelletier, *The Generic Book* (Chicago: University of Chicago Press, 1995).

~ 10

Practices and Dispositions as Sources of the Goodness of Individual Actions

1. Two Types of "Two-Level" Theory

Though it is not usual in practical philosophy to speak of a "two-level", "two-tier" or "indirect" theory of *rationality*, it is clear that all of the doctrines under discussion may reasonably be brought under that familiar moralist's heading. It is to Gauthier especially that we owe the idea of a 'two-level' theory of rationality, though he does not speak in these terms. But our theories are two-level theories of a specific type; indeed, they might be contrasted with what is brought under that heading rather than brought under it themselves. This fact will place some further constraints on the apt interpretation of their central categories, practice and disposition.

Any two-level theory is marked by two central propositions, a *transfer or transparency principle* and a *standard of appraisal*, as I will call them. Thus the transparency claims contained in our two tendencies, roughly expressed, are respectively these: that *a good practice makes the actions falling under it good*; and that *a rational disposition makes the actions manifesting it rational*. The light that falls on either sort of thing is supposed to pass through it to the individual action that comes under it. The associated standards of appraisal are supplied, roughly speaking, by the principle of utility and the idea of the agent's own good or interest or profit: these respectively govern the attribution of the relevant type of goodness to a practice or disposition.

167

But where *our* doctrines appeal, in their transparency or transfer principles, to the concepts of a *practice* and a *disposition*, another account might speak rather of a *rule*, a *principle*, a *set of principles for the general regulation of behavior,* a *practical identity*, an *intention*, a *plan*, a *plan of life*, a *course of action*, a *motive*, a *maxim* or the like. We may speak of these as so many categories of *mediating element*. Thus, for example, Rawls elsewhere makes the rationality of individual action (and much else) depend on the rationality of a larger *plan of life;* Christine Korsgaard might perhaps be seen as making the rationality of at least some individual actions turn on the merits of a superordinate *"practical identity"*.[1]

The transparency principle characteristic of a given theory will also refer to some *relation of expression* that individual actions may bear to occupants of the mediating category: *executing, falling under, manifesting, realizing, acting on, according with, being part of* and so forth. It will also of course refer to the particular normative or evaluative quality that the doctrine represents as 'transferred' from occupants of the mediating category to the individual actions that 'express' them—the particular sort of light that is supposed to be refracted by the transparent mediating element. This might be *rationality, moral goodness, moral rightness, fairness, reasonableness* or any number of other things. In a more complex case, we might need to refer to a suitably related pair of such properties.[2] The proposition that expresses this transparency should also involve a certain explanatory direction, so that it tells us something like this: if an occupant of a mediating category has the appropriate normative or evaluative property, then an individual action that bears the expression relation to it *thereby* also acquires that property (or another suitably associated property). Various qualifications might be admitted into such a thought without affecting its standing as a transfer principle or an affirmation of transparency.

Though the separation is sometimes artificial, the question of what *standard of appraisal* to apply to occupants of the mediating category

---

1. See Rawls, *A Theory of Justice* (Cambridge, Mass.: Harvard University Press, 1971), ch. VII, pp. 395–452; and Korsgaard, *The Sources of Normativity* (Cambridge: Cambridge University Press, 1996), ch. 3.

2. To handle a still more general case, we ought to speak not only of a pair of normative qualities—one appropriate to the mediating element, another appropriate to individual action—but of something broader than a relation of expression. Then we can handle such 'transfer' claims as that *the goodness, morally speaking, of a rule makes the actions that flout it morally wrong* and so forth.

can, I think, always be distinguished from the question of the transparency of the mediating element. How does a practice come by the excellence it is supposed to pass along to the several individual actions that instance it? In "Justice as Fairness," Rawls replaced the utilitarian standard of appraisal contemplated in "Two Concepts" with a subtle contractualist standard, all along deploying, or intending to deploy, the same underlying practice-to-action transparency principle.[3] Which standard is right? Similarly, we might consider a variant of Foot's or Gauthier's doctrine in which the disposition-to-action transfer principle mentioned above is retained, but the agent's profit or interest is dropped as the standard of appraisal for the dispositions in question. It might be replaced by some standard of agreement with the agent's 'nature' as human, say, or with his deepest practical self-conception, or with the principle of universalizability or anything else. I mention these possibilities to set them aside: in the rest of this essay the emphasis will be on the question of the transparency of the mediating elements, or on the interpretation and validation of our principles that express it. I will assume that our authors are right in supposing that the practice of making and keeping promises and the disposition to fidelity meet the correct standards of appraisal, whatever they are.

These distinctions having been made, we can isolate four features that, in spite of the obvious differences, put our two tendencies in the same neighborhood within the larger space of two-level theories. We have already remarked on the "generality" and the "actuality" of the mediating elements, and on the consequentialist or maximizing character of the standard of appraisal—a matter we are proposing henceforth to ignore. Instead I will emphasize a fourth feature, or rather an ensemble of related features, all pertaining to the status implicitly attached to the transfer principles themselves. First, the transfer principles characteristic of our two tendencies are intended to possess a merely *formal* or *non-substantive*, perhaps even analytic, character. Further, they are meant to express neither possible *principles of action* nor anything internally related to 'principles' in that sense. Finally, their justification (in the sense of a defense of their truth) is meant to be independent of the justification of any particular standard of appraisal. That the under-

---

3. See especially pages 47–48 and 50–51 of "Justice as Fairness," in John Rawls, *Collected Papers* (Cambridge, Mass.: Harvard University Press, 1999), and the associated footnotes, 1 and 4.

lying affirmation of transparency is to have the position implied by these features places further constraints on the apt interpretation of our tendencies' central categories, practice and disposition. To make the intended status clear, I will briefly describe a few two-level theories in which affirmations of transparency have a quite different place.

Of course, not all transfer principles are of the general-to-particular type characteristic of our two tendencies; that is, not everything that has been put forward as transparent in respect to good is *general*. It will help bring out the importance of principles that *are* of our general-to-particular sort if we take as our first illustration the chief thesis of Professor Gauthier's essay "Assure and Threaten." Gauthier argues there that the rationality of an *intention for the future* tends, with certain qualifications, to be communicated to the individual action that finally executes it—even where, apart from the antecedent formation of that intention, the action would have to be judged irrational. Such an intention, he thinks, is contained in the sincere 'assurance' one agent might give another (principally one given in exchange for a present good). The principle will thus underwrite the rationality of some acts of fidelity or something like some of them.

This intention-execution principle is clearly a transfer principle, and the essay as a whole may be said to propound a "two-level" theory of rationality: Gauthier's *standard of appraisal* for intentions looks to the contribution the intention itself might make to the agent's life's going as well as possible. But of course this pair of propositions does not, by itself, manifest the Gauthier-Foot tendency under investigation. The mediating element at issue, an intention for the future, is not intrinsically general or unlimited in our sense, though it is certainly 'actual' in our sense. An intention for the future, like the later progress of the action it is an intention to perform—reaping someone else's corn, as it might be—is potentially *completed, carried out* or *executed*, whereupon it passes out of existence, winding down under its own steam.

Now, as Gauthier is thinking of the matter, his rational assurance-keeper acts *on ground of* the fact that he has previously formed a suitable intention. The new particular-to-particular transfer principle provides one way of making articulate the connection the assurance-keeper himself sees between the past formation of an intention and the individual action he later performs. It either is, or is internally related to, a proposition with which the agent implicitly operates, and one he might reasonably be called on to defend. Gauthier is proposing to supply the necessary defense. Indeed, "Assure and Threaten" might at first sight be read as an attempt to bypass the difficulty of defending a disposition-to-action transfer principle and the associated demand for an elucidation of the obscure concept of a disposition. The concept of intention has the advantage of being perfectly clear, and Gauthier may actually prove his intention-to-execution principle.

But a closer study of Gauthier's argument will show that he makes his defense of this particular-to-particular transfer principle turn on a deeper principle that *is* of our general-to-particular type. Here is the principle: if a *deliberative procedure* is rational—if, that is, a given agent's 'employment' of it makes her life go as well as possible (to apply Gauthier's standard of appraisal *for deliberative procedures*)—then any individual action the agent arrives at by use of that procedure is thereby also made to be rational. The substantive 'deliberative procedure' Gauthier mostly contemplates is of course precisely that of sticking to one's prior rational intentions, subject to certain qualifications. But if Gauthier's defense of assurance-keeping is to work, the reference to the 'employment' of a deliberative procedure in the statement of his principle must be heard, as usual, in the right register. On his own account, after all, the whole interest of the subject resides in the fact that *individual* 'employments' of the deliberative procedure he praises will often make the agent's life go *worse*. It is evidently the 'employment' of a deliberative procedure *taken generally*—or taken habitually or dispositionally—that is supposed to make the agent's life go as well as possible. And so, on Gauthier's account, it is the rationality of *the disposition to employ this particular deliberative procedure*—or, equivalently, the disposition to reason practically in a certain way or the disposition to act on a certain sort of consideration—that makes its indefinitely many *individual* employments also to be rational.[4]

Thus the familiar general-to-particular transfer principle of *Morals by Agreement* and Foot's "Moral Beliefs" underwrites the special particular-to-particular transfer principle of "Assure and Threaten." That no attempt is made to justify the transparency of deliberative procedures or dispositions is a sign of the purely formal character Gauthier seems to assign to that claim and, I think, must assign to it. Once it is

4. See especially Gauthier, "Assure and Threaten," *Ethics* 104 (1994): 701–702.

joined to a suitable standard of appraisal, what it yields is precisely the general principle of a 'pragmatic' or 'Gauthierian' defense of *substantive* principles of rationality. It is a fixed point around which all such arguments turn: its own defense, if it needs one, must thus be of another kind. This defense will presumably be independent of the defense of any particular standard of appraisal for deliberative procedures, for example, one in terms of what will make one's life go as well as possible.[5] By contrast, Gauthier's justification of the intention-to-action transfer principle of "Assure and Threaten" goes hand in hand with a defense of the associated standard of appraisal for intentions (which is also, of course, a matter of what makes for the best life possible for the agent); they are defended as a package.[6]

Consider now this familiar proposition, the formula of so-called rule utilitarianism: if a rule of action maximizes utility and is thus (by the proposed utilitarian standard of appraisal) morally good or right, then any individual action that accords with it is also morally right. The word "rule" can be interpreted in a number of ways, but on any view it will be *general* in some sense. On standard interpretations, though, the rules intended are merely hypothetical and our *actuality* criterion is not met. (We will see that Rawls mentions a non-standard interpretation.) Now, on the textbook understanding of its justification, the rule utilitarian combination of a rule-act transfer principle and a utilitarian standard of excellence for rules is advanced as a doctrine of morally right action that squares best with our tutored or untutored moral judgments. It satisfies our supposed utilitarian intuitions, we say, while avoiding the unpalatable consequences of their act utilitarian expression. This form of argument could not be further from the one we found in "Assure and Threaten." But the result is much the same. First,

---

5. In fact, Gauthier appears not to commit himself to a standard of appraisal in terms of the agent's 'life going as well as possible'. He takes the phrase over from Parfit, apparently conscious that a similar argument might be run with a different standard of appraisal. See especially Gauthier, "Assure and Threaten," pp. 690–691.

6. See "Assure and Threaten," again especially pp. 701–702. Warren Quinn's essay "The Puzzle of the Self-Torturer," reprinted in his *Morality and Action* (Berkeley: University of California Press, 1995), pp. 198–209, has the special interest of defending a very Gauthierian intention-to-action transfer principle without appeal to the "strategic" or interpersonal illustrations characteristic of Gauthier's work. Principles of the intention-to-action type are also given extensive study in Edward McClennan's *Rationality and Dynamic Choice* (Cambridge: Cambridge University Press, 1990).

there is a fusion, in point of justification, of the transfer principle and the standard of appraisal for the mediating element. There is no question of an independent justification of the transfer principle, a justification divorced from substantive moral considerations. Further, once a good rule utilitarian has been furnished with an ensemble of meritorious 'rules', she will tailor her actions to fall into line with their formulae, at least on the most straightforward interpretation of the theory. She will act *by reference* to the rules, and the *principle of her action* will be expressed in the rule utilitarian transfer principle or something internally related to that thought.

The situation is unfortunately much the same with the practice-to-action transfer principle envisaged in Rawls's *A Theory of Justice*, namely, H. L. A. Hart's so-called Principle of Fairness.[7] This claim is, I think, very different from any envisaged in "Two Concepts," and is in fact evidence of decline. A like principle is advanced in T. M. Scanlon's *What We Owe to Each Other* under the title of the Principle of Established Practices.[8] According to either teaching, a suitable form of moral soundness in a *practice* will make the individual actions that accord with it also to be morally sound. It will also of course make the actions that run counter to the practice morally wrong. But what is the status of the principle itself in either case? How is it defended? And what are we to do with it? In *A Theory of Justice*, Hart's Principle of Fairness is imagined as put directly to the parties in the original position. In this respect its status is no different from that of the Principle of Mutual Aid or the famous Two Principles—the latter of which supply the *standard of appraisal* for the practices at issue.[9] Similarly, Scanlon's Principle of Established Practices is defended in just that way that all substantive moral claims in the book are defended, including even a sort of Principle of Fidelity: no one could reasonably reject it, given certain aims, though someone or anyone could reasonably reject any opposed principle. Scanlon's *standard of appraisal* for particular practices is again a

7. The Principle of Fairness is expounded in sec. 18 of Rawls, *A Theory of Justice*, pp. 108–114, and defended in sec. 52, pp. 342–350.

8. See Rawls, *A Theory of Justice*, section 52, pp. 342–349, and T. M. Scanlon, *What We Owe to Each Other* (Cambridge: Harvard University Press, 1999), pp. 338–342. Scanlon outlines the differences between the two principles on p. 406, n. 14.

9. The Principle of Mutual Aid is explained on p. 114 and defended on pp. 338–339; the two principles of justice are explained at length in ch. II and defended in ch. III.

matter of surviving a test of reasonable rejection. There is thus again no question of detaching Scanlon's transfer principle from the *substantive* point of view articulated in his book. We might speak of a pre-established harmony of good practice and good action, rather than of a genuine transparency of practices in respect of moral goodness. Further, in each of these accounts—middle Rawls's and Scanlon's—the ideally respectable agent is plainly to be depicted as *responding to* the practice and its merits as an external element of the situation in which she is operating. In this respect, she is related to the practices under which she lives as a faithful agent is related, on any view, to the past promises she has made. Rawls's and Scanlon's hero acts *by reference to* the practice she faces, in consideration of its merits, but the practice itself in no sense governs her operation: her action is at best governed by the Principle of Fairness or of Established Practices, taken now as a principle of action that she has internalized.

By contrast, it is plain that our transparency principles do not themselves correspond to principles or *archai* that might be imputed to the agent in the explanation or understanding of her action. *That* position is occupied rather by the particular practices and dispositions to which this transparency is attributed. On the sort of account under investigation, a practice or disposition is *itself* a "principle," if you like: we are contemplating the merits of action falling under such general *archai* in the individual case. If an agent were somehow to 'act on' one of *our* transfer principles—and thus *in view of* the merits of one of the practices or dispositions she herself bears, considered as a mere circumstance of her action—then her action would surely merely *simulate* action that genuinely instances *that* practice or disposition. If anything, it would manifest a very peculiar 'transfer' disposition and perhaps an even more peculiar 'transfer' practice. The proof that *such* an action, founded on *such* a consideration, is good, as moral or rational, would require a second (and proper) appeal to the appropriate transfer principle and would turn on the doubtful merits of that strange meta-disposition or meta-practice. It is clear that any such reading would be a parody of the texts that manifest our two tendencies.

2. The Transparency of Practices

An argument for a non-substantive and non-action-guiding practice-to-action transfer principle is plainly among the desiderata of Rawls's

"Two Concepts of Rules." He briefly considers the possibility of a non-standard practice-related rule utilitarianism: "One might be tempted to close the discussion at this point by saying that utilitarian consider-ations should be understood as applying to practices in the first in-stance and not to particular actions falling under them except insofar as the practices admit of it. One might say that in this modified form it is a better account of our considered moral opinions and let it go at that."[10] But this path is rejected. Rawls's preferred 'logical' account is intended precisely to divorce the idea from any substantive norma-tive theory, rendering it an independent element that can be rede-ployed, without further discussion, in the presence of a non-utilitarian standard of excellence for practices—as happens straightaway in "Jus-tice as Fairness."[11]

Let us return to the act of fidelity: our agent, X, did A for Y "pre-cisely because" she had promised Y that she would. We do not spoil the understanding of an action as an act of fidelity if we enrich this commonsense description a bit, saying that the deed arose from the agent's implicit acceptance of a certain 'rule'—that is, from her practi-cal judgment that promises are to be kept, *pacta sunt servanda*. It is not clear what is gained by saying such a thing either, of course, or how ex-actly we are to interpret it. But it is plain that we could not thus enrich our description of an act of promise-keeping that was founded on an ulterior motive. Rawls's approach to the question of the moral good-ness of an individual act of fidelity proceeds indirectly, by way of a search for the correct interpretation of this sort of 'rule' or general practical judgment.

On what Rawls calls the "summary" interpretation, which is closely bound up with the utilitarian background of the paper, a thought like *pacta sunt servanda* is understood simply to register the fact that a type of action has often been found good or right *independently* in individual cases (as productive of utility) and to recommend it on that ground. It would clearly be absurd to carry such a thought or 'principle' into a tight corner, genuinely recognized as such. Anything on the order of a transfer principle would plainly be out of the question.

Searching for an alternative interpretation of the large general thought upon which the act of fidelity (for example) may be said to

---

10. "Two Concepts of Rules," in John Rawls, *Collected Papers* (Cambridge, Mass.: Harvard University Press, 1999), p. 33.

11. See n. 3 above.

founded, Rawls argues that certain types of action can only take place given the "background" of what he calls a practice:

> Striking out, stealing a base, balking, etc., are all actions which can only happen in a game. No matter what a person did, what he did would not be described as stealing a base or striking out or drawing a walk unless he could also be described as playing baseball, and for him to be doing this presupposes the rule-like practice which constitutes the game. The practice is logically prior to particular cases: unless there is the practice the terms referring to actions specified by it lack a sense.[12]

A number of familiar features of (early) Rawls's conception of a practice are joined in this passage. The claim that "the practice is logically prior to the particular cases" means that some of the types of action some tokens of which instance a given Rawlsian practice can only be 'tokened' at all in actions that instance this or some other similar practice. The action-types *X promises Y she'll do A* and *X is doing A precisely because she promised Y she'd do A* would be examples.

Another feature of Rawls's conception is implicit in the idea that certain "terms" "lack a sense"—and not just an application—apart from their association with a suitable practice. This means (1) that a Rawlsian practice is instanced not only in *actions* but also, in another way, in certain *exercises of concepts,* and (2) that certain such concepts can only exist to begin with where they have an appropriate practice-instancing exercise.[13] Examples of such *concepts* are *X promises Y she'll do A* and *X is doing A because she promised Y she would.* Note that each of these concepts is implicitly deployed by any agent X who falls under it.[14]

12. Rawls, "Two Concepts", p. 164.

13. Of course, once these concepts do exist, an observer might legitimately be said to come to possess them without becoming a bearer of the practice she observes—and she might continue to possess them after the practices that constituted them die out. Similarly, the bearers themselves might use the concepts in non-practice-instancing judgments—for example (as we will see), in false accounts of their own practice.

14. Though Rawls does not emphasize the fact, we may note that the concept-constituting or concept-interpreting feature of Rawlsian practices makes it possible to avoid the ungroundedness that seems to attach to any attempt to explain the concept of a promise. We count it among the essential conditions of the formation of a promise that the parties to it think of themselves at least implicitly as giving and receiving *a promise.* But how do they come

Finally, in speaking of a "rule-like practice," Rawls means that the above-mentioned practice-instancing exercises of concepts must include a certain type of general 'deontic' judgment. The faithful agent's large background judgment that *pacta sunt servanda* would be an example. Take that sort of thought away and the practice falls to the ground, taking everything else with it—acts of promising, promise-keeping and promise-breaking, for example, as well as exercises of the concepts of these things. Thus the choice the faithful agent faces, whether to keep or break his promise, presupposes the presence of a "rule" that favors keeping it, as her promise already did. It is clear that where deontic judgments have this standing they cannot be interpreted on the summary model. The general reception of the rule enters into the constitution of the phenomena to which it pertains; it thus cannot be founded on a long run of experience dealing with these phenomena.

Rawls's conception of a practice is thus much narrower than any that might arise within, say, sociological theory; there is thus some hope of showing that such practices might exhibit the transparency that would give them moral significance. But let us grant that individual promises and acts of fidelity presuppose the presence of just such a thing and that the practice of making and keeping promises satisfies whatever standard of appraisal is to be accepted, utilitarian or not. Does any of this entail that individual actions "specified" by this practice are *themselves*

---

by the concept they are supposed thus to deploy? It seems that any explanation will have to refer to the concept explained. The answer, crudely, is that just as the presence of a suitable practice can turn a few seconds' worth of standing upright into a case of *drawing a walk* and a peculiarly shaped piece of wood into a *baseball bat*, so can it turn a concept into the *concept of a promise* and a thought into the *thought of a promise*. (The problem of "ungroundedness," as I am calling it, is of course Humean; an especially clear formulation can be found in Elizabeth Anscombe's essay "On Promising and Its Justice," reprinted in her *Ethics, Religion and Politics* [Minneapolis: University of Minnesota Press, 1980].)

Scanlon, in his recent attempt to explain the obligation of promises without reference to a "practice," rightly sees that he must expel the concept of a promise from the formation of his promises. In formulating the conditions under which his principle of fidelity (F) kicks in, he avoids ungroundedness by using only concepts like *intention, expectation, knowledge, cause*, etc. In my own view, which cannot be defended here, any such theory must get the casuistry wrong: no one is ever bound in fidelity except by exercise of the concept precisely of a promise. Scanlon's theory, if I understand it, comes dangerously close to turning almost any felicitous expression of intention, even the expression of an intention formed weeks earlier, into a promise—for felicity seems to require the hearer's interest in knowing what I am going to do and the speaker's intention to gratify that interest. See Scanlon, *What We Owe to Each Other*, ch. 7, especially p. 304.

thereby made to be 'morally good'? Rawls comes closest to a defense of this claim in the following passage:

> It follows from what we have said about the practice conception of rules that if a person is engaged in a practice and if he is asked why *he* does what *he* does, or if he is asked to defend what he does, then his explanation, or defense, lies in referring the questioner to the practice. He cannot say of *his* action, if it is an action specified by a practice, that he does it rather than some other because he thinks it is best on the whole. When a man engaged in a practice is queried about his action he must assume that the questioner doesn't know that he is engaged in it ("Why are you in a hurry to pay him?" "I promised to pay him today") or doesn't know what the practice is.[15]

But what seems really to follow from Rawls's ideas is that some sense of the question "Why are you doing A?" might be answered, and some form of defense or justification supplied, by "referring the questioner to the practice"—that is, by referring the questioner to the considerations that make the action something that is to be done under the 'rules' of the practice. We may grant that the existence of a practice in Rawls's sense is coupled with the legitimacy of forms of explanation and 'justification' of action that are distinct from the association of an action with some prospective good or wider objective. It does not seem to follow, however, that no *other* forms of explanation and justification can apply to the individual act. After all, a player who has drawn a walk might continue her progress toward first base—"because she has drawn a walk"—even though she anticipates heart failure, or even as an earthquake rumbles and the stands begin to fall; this activity can evidently be queried with several forms of the question "Why?"[16]

15. Rawls, "Two Concepts," pp. 38–39.

16. It is clear that Rawls is moved by features of games that have no analogy in connection with promises. For example, it is possible to restrict the idea of *playing game G* so that no activity falls under that concept unless it accords with the rules associated with the underlying practice. "If you're not following the rules," we might say, "then you're not really making a move." Action in accordance with the rules of games could then be viewed as *instrumentally* necessary to continued play. And in that case, action in accordance with the rules (considered just as such) would be rational or morally good, so long as continuing to play were rational or morally good. Rawls's confidence in his transfer principle is funded, I think, by this sort of thought. (See, for example, his reference to executing a will and the surrounding text on p. 38 of "Two Concepts.")

Despite Rawls's intention, the "justification" of an individual act of fidelity is nowhere itself bound up with or colored by the necessity of the underlying practice or of the good it serves. The reason is plain: the conception of a practice with which he operates has been forcibly rendered thin enough to cover the case of *games* and anything else to which his great 'logical priority' thesis will attach. The only forms of justification of individual action at issue must also attach to this wide genus and must therefore find application in connection even with games. Though Rawls argues that the practice of making and keeping promises is a good one, he is impeded from arguing that the 'reasons' that the practice underwrites are genuine moral reasons or that the agents who act on the strength of are thereby acting well, morally speaking. Though moral considerations make contact with the practice, they do not manage to break through to the actions themselves.[17]

We may note first that here it is not the practice that is evaluated, but associated instances of play. Furthermore, where the concept of *playing game G* has not been so restricted, the conclusion clearly fails to follow. This happens wherever *playing* is understood to be consistent with *cheating*. I take it that this is how things stand with the primitive notion of play and that the restricted concept is a rather sophisticated and optional development.

However it may be with games, *this train of ideas is completely out of place in connection with the practice of promising*. For in that practice what corresponds to the proposition "I'm playing game G" is the proposition "I promised Jones I'd do A"; that's what makes the practice-governed necessities kick in. But the continued truth of "I promised to do A" is not affected by what I later do, as the truth of "I'm playing G" might be supposed to be. The "necessity" of the corresponding action thus does not admit the evasive instrumental construction we can imagine in connection with the play of games.

17. We can only suppose that Rawls later came to see this and that the account of the obligation of promises in *A Theory of Justice*, sec. 52 (pp. 342–349), is meant to supply the deficiency. For there he systematically distinguishes between *two* readings of the proposition "promises must be kept" and the necessity expressed in it. On one reading it formulates a mere "constitutive rule" of the practice—something in the nature of a rule of a game—and expresses the concomitant merely practice-internal necessity. On another reading it formulates a genuine moral principle, the Principle of Fidelity, and the necessity expressed in it is that of moral requirement. "Two Concepts" might be diagnosed as having fused these readings—"the tendency to conflate [them] is particularly strong" (p. 349)—though its considerations properly pertain only to the former. (I suspect that the reference to conflation is autobiographical.) As we have seen, though, the later theory surrenders the earlier hope of a purely formal, non-substantive account of the relation between *the moral goodness (however judged) of the practice that contains this "constitutive rule"* and *the moral goodness of the individual actions that accord with it*. Or, equivalently, it surrenders the hope of a purely formal account of the relation between the moral goodness of the practice the 'rule' helps to constitute and the *truth* of the Principle of Fidelity.

3. The Transparency of Dispositions

If we pass now to the exponents of our other tendency, it will immediately strike us how little attention is devoted to the question of the transparency of the mediating element, a practical disposition, in respect of rationality. Gauthier and Foot are principally interested in showing that justice as a disposition makes a better fit with the agent's good than any of the alternatives and thus meets the standard of appraisal they propound. This fixation of attention is understandable, since that result would suffice to refute many traditional forms of skepticism about justice. The question of a transfer principle, of demonstrating that *individual acts* of justice are thereby shown to be more rational than *their* alternatives, thus appears less pressing.

In Foot, the matter is left completely implicit, but Gauthier addresses it in at least two places. In *Morals by Agreement* a section is devoted to the question "whether particular choices are rational if and only if they express a rational disposition to choose," which is precisely the question of a transfer principle.[18] But what follows appears rather to be a defense of the view that dispositions *can* be called rational, and also of the conception of rational agents as "choosing" among dispositions in accordance with the maximizing conception: "For we suppose that the capacity to make such choices is itself an essential part of human rationality. . . . At the core of our rational capacity is the ability to engage in self-critical reflection. The fully rational being is able to reflect on his standard of deliberation, and to change that standard in the light of reflection."[19] On the face of it, though, we can agree with Gauthier that it is a noble thing to have rationally appraisable dispositions or standards of deliberation and still deny that the rationality of a disposition inevitably extends to the individual actions that manifest it.

The matter arises again in "Rationality and the Rational Aim," Gauthier's response to the skeptical remarks made in Derek Parfit's *Reasons and Persons*, Chapter 1—remarks I have just been imitating. Parfit argued there that it is no objection to a theory of rationality or morality that it is "indirectly self-defeating". Applied to theories of rationality, this doctrine amounts to a rejection of the transparency of

18. David Gauthier, *Morals by Agreement* (Oxford: Oxford University Press, 1986), p. 183.
19. Ibid., p. 183.

dispositions: for a theory is indirectly self-defeating when the individual action the theory favors is sometimes not the act of the favored disposition or, equivalently, when the disposition *always to perform the favored individual action* is not the disposition that the theory "tells us to have".[20] Parfit's argument was simply this, that *every* theory of rationality must make room for such disharmony: situations like this just do arise. The official illustration was inspired by Thomas Schelling: with the help of a suitable drug, a prudent father frightens off a dangerous criminal by inducing a state in which he says things like "I love my children, so please kill them" and otherwise acts "irrationally". Since the criminal now has no hope of gaining access to the family's safe, he does best to cut his losses, leaving the children—the potential witnesses— unharmed.[21] Of course, the father's strategy might equally have been implemented with a fast-acting soporific, as happens in the movie *Kiss Me Deadly*. The same wild statements might then have been uttered somniloquently. It seems plain that nothing the father does in either case has the status of a voluntary action, and thus that none of these acts can be appraised as "rational" or "irrational" in the senses that interest us. Parfit's argument appears, then, to rest on a simple equivocation, construing "rational" first as we understand it in practical philosophy, but then psychologically, as mere *sobriety* or *sanity*.

But even if we drop the drugged state of Schelling's prudent father's brain, we will still, I think, find that the term "disposition" is completely unanalyzed and tends, in Parfit's discussion, to take over the whole extension of the word "motive"—including, for example, habitual states of passion, appetite or affect. A taste for chocolate, or an aversion to it, would make a respectable occupant of the category Parfit has in view. It is, however, not too surprising to be told that even where circumstances make it irrational to alter such a state, still the individual actions it prompts might yet sometimes be irrational.[22] That a narrower understanding of the concept *disposition* might be available; that Gauthier might have intended it; that it could not find instances in a taste for chocolate, much less in Schelling's father's drug-

---

20. Derek Parfit, *Reasons and Persons* (Oxford: Oxford University Press, 1984), p. 5.

21. Ibid., pp. 12–13. The example derives from Thomas Schelling, *The Strategy of Conflict* (Cambridge, Mass.: Harvard University Press, 1960).

22. Parfit does not distinguish systematically between the claim that a disposition is itself rational or profitable and the claim that it would be rational or profitable *to act to cultivate it*.

addled state; and that it might be associated with a true transfer principle—*Reasons and Persons* appears to give us no reason to doubt any of
these things.

It was therefore open to Gauthier to accuse Parfit of a second and
more fundamental equivocation. But, strangely, this is not the path he
takes in "Rationality and the Rational Aim." There Gauthier levels two
charges against the doctrine of *Reasons and Persons:* "On Parfit's view
not only are some persons cursed by rationality; others are condemned
to irrationality."[23] Suppose we are given a Parfitian 'disposition' that is
always manifested in rational individual actions but nevertheless itself
works to the disadvantage of its bearer through its other effects. There
are two further possibilities: that the bearer can't change the disposition and that he can. If he can't change it, he's "cursed by rationality,"
Gauthier thinks. If he *can* change it, then of course he is irrational if he
doesn't; but then even if he does change it, he will often act irrationally
later. So he's "condemned to irrationality"—a conclusion Parfit himself
draws explicitly.[24]

Gauthier's (rather un-Gauthierian!) thought is that these consequences offend intuition and that a theory that lacks them—a theory
incorporating a doctrine of transparency—will have a better claim to
our allegiance.[25]

But can Gauthier's first charge be made to stick? It does not seem
clear that a theory like Parfit's must apply the name "rationality" to the
disposition always to do what's rational, if there is such a disposition.
Where other dispositions are better and would be more rational they
would seem to have as much a claim to that title. The second charge
will certainly stick, but we may wonder about its own merits as a charge.
Gauthier is, I think, misled by Parfit's delight in what he takes to be a
novel, exciting and counter-intuitive result. A theory would perhaps be
counter-intuitive if it entailed, for example, that some particular action
was at the same time inevitable and irrational. But it seems in fact to be
a traditional *platitude* that reasoning animals developing from infancy
will inevitably act irrationally *somewhere*. As St. Thomas puts it, we can
all avoid *any given* "act of sin", but it would take a miraculous interven-

---

23. David Gauthier, "Rationality and the Rational Aim," in Jonathan Dancy, *Reading Parfit*
(Oxford: Blackwell, 1997), p. 32.

24. Parfit, *Reasons and Persons*, pp. 13–17.

25. Gauthier, "Rationality and the Rational Aim," p. 37.

tion for anyone to avoid *all* of them.[26] If there is a genuine difficulty, it must surely arise from the way this comes about in a given theory. If I understand him, though, Gauthier points to no repulsive feature of Parfit's account apart from its reaffirmation of this bit of the *philosophia perennis* and (I think) common sense.

In his controversy with Parfit, Gauthier is led deep into Parfit's territory and, it seems, away from properly Gauthierian positions. Where Parfit had denied that 'dispositions' are generally transparent in respect of rationality, on the irrelevant ground that drug-addlement and habitual states of passion, appetite and affect aren't, Gauthier is now forced to confess the transparency even of *those* states. He thus commits himself to an implausibly broad transfer principle on what appear to be very slender grounds. The correct path is surely to develop the insight latent in *Morals by Agreement:* to make articulate its conception of a disposition and to defend a doctrine of transparency that is framed in terms of it.

4. Other Practices, Other Dispositions: An Indirect Articulation of the Specifically Practical-Philosophical Conception of Practices and Dispositions

In the act of fidelity, the agent's word figures as a consideration upon which she acts—that is, it figures as a sort of 'explanatory reason'—but in a specific way. The constitution of any given case of this sort of efficacy no doubt has many conditions, some somehow within the agent and others extending beyond her. Each of our tendencies fixes on one of these conditions, the presence of a disposition or a practice. The status of the action as a case of acting on sound reasons simply or as a case of acting on morally sound reasons is then supposed to turn on the merits of the associated 'general' condition. The trouble, as we have seen, is to say why the intended items should be transparent in this sort of way; certain features of our writers' use of the concepts practice and disposition have seemed to impede our making this out.

Consider the moral philosopher's favorite piece of casuistical wisdom: a promise to meet someone to discuss trivial matters must come to nothing if a party to that promise can save his daughter's life by

26. See, e.g., *Summa Theologia*, I–II, q. 109, art. 8.

breaking it. In "Two Concepts of Rules" and more extensively in *A Theory of Justice*, Rawls claims that such justifications for failure to do one's word are *a part of our practice*, somehow written into it, and thus also a part that might be written out.[27] My suggestion in this section will be that the aspect of his conception of a practice that finds expression in this apparently natural idea impeded his defense of transparency in "Two Concepts" and later forced him to the quite different type of transfer principle we found in *A Theory of Justice*. But it is an aspect of his conception that might be dropped. I will briefly mention a possible Gauthierian parallel.

Elaborating this thought, Rawls suggests that there might be a practice of promising that is unlike our own in that it rejects the familiar battery of permissions and holds us to *any* promise "come what may". And it might belong to another alien practice of promising, he says, that its bearers are held to 'promises' they have formulated in their sleep.[28] It is only if we can imagine several possible practices distinguished in such ways that we will have any use for the idea that the excusing conditions *we* recognize are a 'part' of our own particular practice: only then would mention of these excuses have to enter into any complete description of it.

Let us then imagine three empirically given aggregates of people, three communities, each realizing one of the three sorts of practice Rawls describes (one corresponding to our own). A practice, Rawls says, "exists in a society when it is more or less regularly acted upon."[29] In the community with the peculiar principle about sleep, then, suppose that nine out of ten people, or ninety-nine out of a hundred, can be described as accepting the thought that somniloquent promises bind and as acting accordingly. They have often been found keeping their own sleep-promises and criticizing others who have failed to keep theirs. In the other alien community, the legalistic one, nine out of ten accept the proposition that one must keep one's promises though the heavens will fall, and in most cases in which *we* would take ourselves off the hook these people have done what they promised to do, though

27. Rawls, *A Theory of Justice*, p. 345; "Two Concepts," pp. 31–33.

28. Rawls, *A Theory of Justice*, p. 345. Rawls reasonably rejects the suggestion that the description of these practices as "practices of promising" is usefully ruled out as "inconsistent with the concept (meaning) of promising".

29. Ibid.

from time to time the heavens have thereby fallen. Apart from this, the general facts about the making and keeping of promises, and about the criticism of breach, are the same in each alien community as they are among us.

One apparent consequence of Rawls's account in *A Theory of Justice* is that since each deviant practice violates certain principles of justice, *no* promise falling under either of the poisoned practices can bind. Since "it would be wildly irrational in the original position to agree to be bound by words uttered while asleep," the Principle of Fairness never gets a grip even on promises falling into the central range of cases in which alien opinion mirrors our own.[30] Something similar would hold for the "Two Concepts" account. This seems a fairly counter-intuitive result, and I will return to it, but it is not what principally interests me.

The notion of a 'practice' that is implicit in a description of the use of *language* must be quite different from the 'practical' conception of a practice we are hoping to understand. But since they must fall under a broader genus, something might be learned from a brief detour, for purposes of analogy, into some old-fashioned considerations in the theory of meaning. Consider, then, a pair of alien *linguistic* communities employing expressions pronounced as our word "gold" is. In one community the word has only been applied to pieces of *gold*, and whenever the question "Gold or not?" has been raised about a given bit of gold, speakers have almost always declared: "It is gold." It is presumably *their* (linguistic) practice, then, to call gold "gold"; gold is "what they call 'gold'". In the other community things are mostly the same, but some other substance, a fool's gold, is also occasionally found, and we will suppose that individuals have called *it* "gold" in nine out of ten cases in which the question has arisen. Let us suppose further that their word "gold" is unlike our "yellow" or "valuable" in that it is fitted to be given in answer to a certain sense of the question "What *is* this stuff?"—that is, it is what was called a "natural kind term". It was a favorite suspicion of a certain line of thought that it is mere prostration before the facts to insist that it belongs to the (linguistic) practice of this second community to apply the word "gold" equally to gold and to the other stuff. A more likely story is that the practice of employing the word "gold" should receive the same description in *either* community: it is just that

---

30. Ibid.

in the second community there is widespread error about the fake gold, a frequent mistake with no bearing on the internal description of the practice itself.[31]

Let us return, then, to the three different social formations—one of them corresponding to our own—that we imagined as fitting Rawls's three different descriptions of possible 'practices of promising'. Putting the original practice-descriptions out of the picture, let us view the imagined communities as would a foreign traveler bent upon learning the customs of each place. What will immediately strike us, I think, is the impossibility of our making a confident attribution of the two deviant practice-descriptions.

We have, after all, no difficulty supposing that an individual member of our society might be inclined to perform its sleep-promises when informed of these. And we are actually familiar with the legalism that sometimes leads a child to stick to the formula of its promise when circumstances have made this unreasonable, and to criticize people for not keeping promises even when they can marshal decisive justifications. It is easy to imagine an adult who thinks and acts in one of these ways, and even brings up his children in accordance with these ideas. If we find such a person among us, the verdict will be that he does not grasp the practice, that he has a false opinion about it, that he is in error and leads his children into error. We will say all of this even if there are quite a few such people. But if we imagine, as we have, a whole community of persons thinking and acting in such a way, then we are apt to suspect a transition from quantity to quality and to cave in before the thought that, after all, this is their practice, that promising is something different for them and involves different excusing conditions. But what reason can be given for dropping our resolve? What reason can be given for rejecting a parallel with the example of words for gold? If we do hold fast, then we will say that the inner constitution of the practice itself is in all three cases the same. It is just that it is *associated*, in the deviant communities, with a widespread error or a superstitious religious conviction or something on the order of a fad—a disturbance, at all events, and mere dross—propagated perhaps through mutual scandal.

It might be said that we wouldn't have any use for the notion of a

31. This is a rather idiosyncratic rendering of some of the points of Hilary Putnam's "The Meaning of 'Meaning,'" reprinted in his *Mind, Language and Reality* (Cambridge: Cambridge University Press, 1975).

practice, and wouldn't understand it, if the facts about the alien communities were not adequate for the imputation of Rawls's divergent, deviant practice-descriptions. What else could a practice be? I want, predictably, to recommend the opposed thesis that we won't have any use for the notion of a practice if we *do* construe it this way. Consider again that if we adopt this conception of a practice and attempt an account of the tight corner along the lines of the Rawlsian tendency—claiming that it is only the excellence of the practice that can make sense of keeping one's word in the face of a greater possible good—then we will have to accept the unsettling consequence of Rawls's doctrine mentioned above. Tight-corner acts of fidelity will not be morally justified even in the central range of cases, namely, those in which the agent was awake and the sky does not threaten to fall. Contraposing, if we insist that such ordinary acts of promise-keeping *are* justified over there, then we will not be able to appeal to the goodness or justice of the practice to make sense of tight-corner fidelity: for the practice as a whole is clearly defective.

Suppose that, hoping to avoid this consequence, we reject the practice *as a whole* as bad or unjust but attempt to divide cases. *Part* of the practice of each deviant society is good and just. This respectable portion will cover ordinary tight-corner cases, but not the ultra-tight-corner emergency situations and sleep-promising cases in which, in the alien communities, 'fidelity' is still expected. This will yield the right result, but it will require a more complicated transfer principle and an account, not only of the notion of a practice, which remains obscure, but also of the notion of a *part* of a practice.

But more importantly, any development of this appeal to a felicitous sub-practice will enable us to draw a sort of objective line through the cloud of particular instances of 'fidelity' and criticism of 'infidelity' that have occurred in each alien community: only *some* of these will be expressive of the respectable sub-practice and hence themselves good. It will seem to us that the particular acts of promise-keeping that fall under the benign alleged sub-practice all 'belong together', in some sense, and that the deviant acts in each community are something 'fundamentally different' from these. It will thus again become difficult to reject an analogy with the linguistic community in which the word "gold" appeared to name a kind of stuff covering both gold and fool's gold. Why should we not dispense with the epicycle of the sub-practice and understand this relation, the *belonging together* that joins any two instances of ordinary promise-keeping, to be the relation *falling under the same practice? That* is the 'unity' we intend in the practical-philosophical employment of the concept of a practice. The difference between common or garden acts of fidelity and the deviant cases will consist again in this, that the latter do not express the practice exhibited in the former.

It might be objected that such a position would contradict an opinion held universally, if implicitly, in either alien community: namely, that the self-same practice is exhibited in all of these cases; or, equivalently, that a single sort of account of action by reference to the agent's past word is found in the uncontroversial and the deviant cases alike. It's all the same to *them*. But the principle of charity implicit in this objection has little force against the account I am suggesting, for widespread error will remain even on the opposed account. There will still be the universally held false opinion that 'fidelity', thus construed broadly, is morally good (the corresponding opinion will come out true on my account) and the consequent false belief about each deviant act of fidelity, that *it* is morally good.

It might further be objected that the account I am imagining must be circular: we want to say that individual acts of fidelity are morally good "because the practice is", but then, apparently, let the goodness or badness of an individual action determine whether or not it falls under the practice. But we need not accept the second clause. We need only say that if the practice makes some action good, then any action the practice cannot make good does not express the practice. This is evidently consistent with the view that such acts of promise-keeping as *are* good are only made to be good by the practice.[32]

The same objection would be implicit in the idea that our remarks involve a retreat from a 'practice conception' of promising—the sort of account found in Hume and Rawls and the main body of analytic

---

32. Similarly, it was because nothing with the status of a so-called natural kind term could be *true of* both gold and a fool's gold, that we had to hold that people failed to accord with their (linguistic) practice either whenever they called gold "gold", *or else* whenever they called the fool's gold "gold". It is consistent with this that the individual predications that *are* true, are only true "because of the practice" like any other predications of conventional linguistic expressions. Given that the practice makes actions of predicating "gold" of *gold* true, it cannot also belong to the practice to apply "gold" to a fool's gold.

moral philosophy. Again, it is not true: we can accept that promising must rest on a 'convention' and still insist that not just anything can be 'convened upon'.[33] No one will hold that just any series of individual actions performed by some number of agents can intelligibly be reckoned to display the sort of unity we intend in bringing things under the concept *practice* or *same practice*. We must also reject the somewhat weaker idea that any general schedule of action can be fitted into a possibly denoting phrase of the form "the *practice* of doing A in circumstances C, but B in C', unless . . . , etc."—and that to any subtle distinction among such schedules there must correspond a possible distinction of practices.[34]

If what is 'convened upon' in our three imagined communities and exhibited in ordinary acts of fidelity is the same in each case, then there can be no reason for supposing that the so-called constitutive rule of our *own* practice needs any more elaborate formulation than is contained in the proposition "promises must be kept," *pacta sunt servanda*. No closer description of the practice could be supplied by introducing qualifications, for it would mark no distinction among practices. The thought that there is something loose and inaccurate in the formula is thus an illusion, unless it is combined with the view that the practice is pointless and realizes no good or that it has something like the position of a game.

The concept of a disposition as it arises in the Gauthier-Foot ten-

33. If the position recommended here is correct, then Stanley Cavell is wrong to think that an objection to a practice conception like Rawls's can be expressed in the question "But what might it mean to urge a reform of the practice of promising?" See *The Claim of Reason* (Oxford: Clarendon, 1979), p. 295. In any event, Cavell's doctrine of promising seems much too extreme: "The very existence of human society, and the coherence of one's own conduct depend on it. . . . [P]romising is not *an* institution, but a precondition of any institution among persons at all" (p. 298). For interesting *a posteriori* counter-evidence, see F. Korn and S. R. D. Korn, "Where People Don't Promise," *Ethics* 93 (1983): 445–450.

34. The sensible substitutions for *A* and *C* in the formulas "Everyone always does A in C" and "The rule is: to do A in C" are vastly more wide-ranging than in "It is their practice to do A in C," where it is read as I am proposing we might be able to read it. The notion of a 'rule', for example, is extremely abstract, and can, as we have seen, be deployed in connection with *games*. Rules of games can exhibit almost any degree of complexity possible for Fregean universal generalizations. The distinctions among games can thus be as subtle as you like. This is why it was possible for David Lyons to produce his famous reduction of 'general' and 'rule' utilitarianism to 'act' utilitarianism in *The Form and Limits of Utilitarianism* (London: Oxford University Press, 1965). This is also why the notion of a 'rule' fits poorly with the idea of a practice in the sense that interests us.

dency evidently invites a similar treatment, though I will only outline the point here. No one will hold that just any series of actions of a single agent can exhibit the sort of unity we intend in bringing things under a single practical disposition. And there is no reason to imagine that just any *general* schedule of action might be employed to describe such a thing, or, equivalently, that to any subtle diversity of such schedules there must correspond a possible diversity of dispositions. Let the facts about a pair of agents be tailored to meet those subtly diverse disposition-descriptions: questions of rationality may again lead us to wonder whether they were correctly described after all. Suppose, for example, that I return a deposit someone has made to me, a book for example, thinking "It is his: I must give it back"—thus manifesting a fraction of justice distinct from fidelity—and that I have often done this sort of thing. Later, though, I return some autumn leaves that have blown from someone's red maple onto my lawn, again thinking "They are hers; I must give them back." Need we hold that the practical disposition manifested in my earlier acts must or could have shown up in an act of leaf-return? Need we hold that the disposition that was manifested in those sensible earlier acts is any different from that displayed in the like acts of a more reasonable person who would have let the leaves go? That returning the book and 'returning' the leaves struck me as 'the same', that I didn't *feel* any difference, cannot be supposed to establish the identity. The disposition that operates in my intuitively reasonable acts of return, we might think, is no different from the one that operates in *all* the acts of return of a person who lets leaves blow by; something else is at work in me in cases where I busy myself returning them.

My effort in this section has merely been to excite the intuition that we do operate implicitly with *such* conceptions of practice and disposition. I do not mean to deny that we are also in possession of more generic conceptions that would cover, say, a sociological regularity or a game or—in the other case—a habitual state of appetite or whatever 'disposition' characterizes those who 'grasp the rules' of a given game and apply them. I have approached the question of a narrower conception of a practice or disposition indirectly by considering the classes of actions that might 'instance' or 'manifest' such a thing. Much metaphysical labor would be required to make the conceptions themselves articulate and to defend them against skeptical doubts. But if there is anything in our two tendencies, then such results as these can hardly come as a surprise. If the only available notion of a practice is a purely sociological one and if the only available notion of a disposition is purely psychological—if, that is, practical philosophy can find no interpretation of these phrases that is proper to it, if it can find no other way of thinking a 'general' and 'actual' connection between an agent or agents and a form of action—then it is too much to expect that occupants of either category will be transparent in respect of good. Though items of either type *may* be ranged alongside possible objects of sociological or psychological knowledge in a wider class labeled "practice" or "disposition", the workings of *this* sort of member of either class will be invisible to any resolutely 'value-free' inquirer. Where we judge that a practice or disposition lays hold of some good—or, rather, where we judge that some good apt to be realized in a practice or a disposition *is* realized in such a thing—then, it seems, we take leave of the purely sociological or psychological domain. We reckon then with a different and specifically practical form of unity of one individual action with another; we grasp, that is, a different form of "general" element in human practical reality.

~ 11

Practice and Disposition
as Sources of Individual Action

1. Practice, Disposition and the Explanation
of Individual Action

On the traditional construction of the phrase "act of X", where X is the name of a putative virtue like "justice", "courage", etc., it was more than a merely classificatory expression. Fidelity, for example, was understood as a potency of sorts, and an act of fidelity as its act, its work, its actualization. In bringing an individual human action under a description like "act of fidelity", one thus already purported to give *some* kind of explanation of it. Though today we may no longer think of it as encoded into these phrases, we are nevertheless happy to think of a practical disposition as supplying an account of action, as a cause of action in some sense.

But how are we to understand this "etiological" aspect of the concept? If a disposition is named after the thing it is a disposition to do, then, for one thing, the problem arises how we can appeal to it in a serious attempt to explain these operations. The virtue of justice might look to be in the position of the *vertus dormitiva* of Molière's doctors' opium. The received solution is to depict the disposition as an underlying "state", one only indirectly captured by a reference to the associated individual operations, as whatever accounts for them all. But this picture raises a number of further difficulties in our own specifically practical context. It ought, for example, to make us wonder why there should *be* some one underlying account, of the intended occult type, of a given person's individual acts of, for instance, promise-keeping. Whence our confidence that some one something is behind them all? The picture seems moreover to commit us to the view that the disposition to keep one's word, or the thing that is that disposition, might have effects quite unlike an act of fidelity when conditions alter or when a further disposition is present.

And further, given that for us the whole essence of the matter is that, while itself remaining single, a practical disposition must be able to enter into a potentially unlimited series of individual actions, the underlying state invites a hopeless regress. For if we attempt to explain the phenomenon of a long run of promise-keepings in terms of a common cause in a state of this nature, we are still left with the problem, how to understand the equally long run of days or months in which the agent (or her soul or her brain) continued to manifest that state. The fundamental problem is merely deferred, and in the process translated into terms that must be alien to practical consciousness. The suspicion forms that it could never be the business of a practical philosopher to employ such a concept.

Still, there is no question that in bringing an action, or a nexus of thought and action, under a practical disposition we do supply a certain sort of account of it and perhaps even bring it back to a certain sort of "cause". I mean only to suggest that we do not understand the etiological aspect of the matter. I will now argue that this feature attaches as much to *practices* as to dispositions. Here too, though, we will meet with a number of difficulties of understanding. In the next section I will articulate a model that I hope will make sense of the etiological aspect of a practice as I develop it here. In the final section I will show how this model might be used to reconstrue the etiological aspect of certain dispositions as well.

Let us briefly consider Rawls's discussion of what he calls the conditions for the existence of a practice or "institution" in *A Theory of Justice*.[1] The rough account, of course, is that a practice and its rules exist in a society when they are "more or less regularly acted on".[2] In Section 10 of *A Theory of Justice* the thought is sharpened: a bona fide practice

---

1. The word "institution" often replaces "practice" in *A Theory of Justice* (Cambridge, Mass.: Harvard University Press, 1971). In his general discussion (sec. 10, pp. 54–60) Rawls uses the former, but in the application to promising (pp. 344–350) he uses the latter.

2. Rawls, *A Theory of Justice*, p. 345.

or institution must meet the further condition that the actions are "regularly carried out in accordance with a public understanding that the system of rules . . . is to be followed." What is this "public understanding"? How does it tie the agents together as bearers of a single practice? In attempting to unpack the thought, Rawls tells us first that there must be a "reciprocal recognition of one another's understanding that their [actual] conduct accords with the rules they are to comply with," and second—in respect of the normative or deontic component—that "[each] knows what the rules demand of him and the others" and that "[each] knows that the others know this and that they know that he knows, and so on."[3] In the text these appear as separable elements: some of them might be found, though others are not; where all are found, we have a practice or institution.

If we look no deeper into Rawls's intention, then, it will appear that a body of persons bears a practice or institution if the following conditions are met: each person believes that each person ought to adhere to a certain formula of action and accept it as a "rule"; each has herself adopted it as a rule and follows it; and each person is aware of these facts-about-all-of-them, including this fact, etc. Consider, though, that it is possible to gather *from experience* that everyone else acts and believes that people ought to act in accordance with a given formula, and further that once each person does gather this from experience, each might further gather that each has thus gathered. It is also possible for a person to arrive at the conviction that people generally *ought* to act in accordance with a particular formula by an entirely private calculation—from subtle moral first principles, perhaps, or from an astrological hypothesis, or by guessing; and it must *also* be possible for any such person, perhaps acting from a certain high-minded idealism, to adopt the rule thus reached as his own, and follow it. It must therefore be possible for *everyone* in a given society, by one route or another, to hit one day upon a certain formula for acting, the same in every case, and adopt it as his own. If the 'rule' is something that is obeyed in public, then we can suppose that a few days or weeks later, the evidence for 'reciprocal recognition' will have piled up. It seems to be a consequence of Rawls's view that *as soon as all of this happens* the formula may be given in a true description of one of their practices.

3. Ibid., pp. 55–56, emphasis added.

One reason this consequence is intuitively absurd is this: the story does not show how the underlying convergence of action (and opinion) is anything but *accidental*. If we are to find a single practice, then, as a bare minimum, we must suppose that the coinciding actions exhibit a common *source* or *account*.

But how are we to understand this? If we were simply to complicate Rawls's list of conditions with the further provision that the underlying convergence of action and opinion is "no accident"—that is, that the convergent acts and thoughts exhibit a common source—we would surely still lack a set of intuitively sufficient conditions: the notion of things' being no accident is too abstract and covers too many types of account of the things that come together. Suppose, for example, that an especially talented moral teacher comes to town, appears to each of us individually, and convinces us all of her novel ideas about the apt prosecution of life and social relations. Each of us puts the code into practice, each at first thinking that no one else does. In time, though, 'reciprocal recognition' will again come to pass, and it will all be no accident, in a sense: the convergent acts and thoughts will find a common account in the awesome rhetorical powers of the teacher. But the common account is intuitively of the wrong kind: we see only a guru and her disciples, not a practice and its bearers, to paraphrase Rousseau. It would certainly not help to suppose that, instead of making her pitch to each of us separately and individually, the preacher appears instead on cable television, and that we all know that this is how we came to share these ideas. Intuitively, no feature of a particular teacher's method of procuring conviction could have the desired effect, short of her taking the position of a legislator—a status that would itself intuitively need to rest on some antecedent custom or practice.

We might attempt to rule out the preacher with a more specific complication of our conditions: we might insist that facts of the sort we have mentioned add up to a practice *only where the 'reciprocal recognition' itself enters into the origination of the facts recognized*. In a genuine practice, each agent acts according to the 'rule' precisely *because* he sees that all of these conditions are met (including perhaps this one). Similarly, each believes himself to be bound by the rule only *because* all of these conditions are met. In that case, our convergence in action and normative thought would have a common cause or source of a very special type—one the preacher can't herself instance, though she might hope to trigger it. The convergence in action and thought would be self-reproducing in a certain sense; our 'reciprocal recognition' would enter into the circuit. Here the thought that practice-instancing action is "in accordance with a public understanding" acquires a richer sense, and itself supplies a determinate interpretation of the idea of a *common account* or *source* of our convergence in action.

But, of course, that I *see* that these large conditions are met will only affect *my* action on any given day if something operates in me that will underwrite a connection between this bit of contemplative knowledge and my actions. And *everyone's* seeing that such conditions are met will only have the property of maintaining what is seen (and thus the seeing of it, and so forth) if *everyone* is *habitually* affected by a form of consideration that takes an interest in such a fact. That each person *is* habitually moved to act by such a thought might of course be a complete accident, an inexplicable act of God.[4]

Though we may grant that this pileup of conditions attaches a perfectly legitimate sense to the word "practice", we must reject it as beside the point. Any theory that represents the existence of the practice as a *circumstance* and *condition* of the agent's acting in accordance with it—as a datum to which she *responds*—must, we said, appeal to something else as the principle that directly governs the agent's compliant individual action. The theory must find in the agent a power to be moved that has nothing to do with the particular given practice, but only takes such a practice into account when the agent happens upon it. The merits of the individual nexuses of thought and action must turn on the merits of *that* source (which, of course, might happen to take not just the practice but also *its* merits into account). But practices and dispositions in the senses that have interested us govern precisely

---

4. Thus, for example, in David Lewis's *Convention* (Cambridge, Mass.: Harvard University Press, 1969), the maintenance of a convention presupposes that the agents under it habitually form the preferences that put them again and again into the coordination problem to which the convention supplies a salient solution. The thought is that habitual convergence of *preferences* can translate itself into a conventional convergence of *action*, given suitable jumpstarting. But the convergent preferences and their habitual character are a surd exogenous fact as far as the system is concerned. This is of course not an objection to Lewis's doctrine. It has no application within the present problematic, in any case, since actions founded on practices and dispositions, in the senses that interest us, are precisely not chosen on instrumental grounds: we can as well say that they govern the formation of preferences as that they govern individual choices.

the connection between the agent's circumstances, as she sees them, and what she does. A disposition contains the agent's "deliberative procedure" or "standard of deliberation", as Gauthier puts it, and it relates circumstances to action; the "circumstance" to which fidelity in particular responds is of course nothing but the past promise itself. A "Two Concepts" practice is likewise intended to set up the connection between the agent's action and anything in her circumstances to which she might refer in "defense" or "justification" of it. Our thought was to accredit *this* original or un-derived reason-connection, from the point of view of rationality or morals, by considering the disposition or practice it manifests. A practice that enters an agent's thoughts as a datum to which she responds cannot be a practice in this sense.[5] The question, then, is when convergence on primary or un-derived principles of action amounts to community of practice and, in particular, what kind of common account this convergence must involve. We are back with our preacher: why must we reject the convergence that springs from her powers as of the wrong kind?

Let us recur to the position of "Two Concepts." It belonged to this doctrine that we advert implicitly to a practice when we bring things and events under certain concepts and apply certain forms of account to them. In the judgment *He's promising her that he'll do A*, for example,

---

5. Consider that a "practice" of sorts might find a *substratum* in everyone's internalizing something like Hart's and Rawls's Principle of Fairness. The situation could be much as it is with Lewis's conventions, which find a substratum in an appropriate distribution of habitual preferences. As long as the "practice" exists, any given adherent of the Principle will *see* this, and the principle will provide the ground for the nexus of action with the consideration that it is "in accordance" with the "practice". If it happens that *everyone* adheres to this Principle, then the "practice" will maintain itself. Convergence on such a practice is a shadow of a prior convergence on principles. But only the underlying convergence on *principles* could add up to a practice in our sense. (Rawls comes close to painting this picture in *A Theory of Justice*, p. 350; I have already remarked in ch. 10, n. 17 on the distance between the account there given and that intended in "Two Concepts.")

To see how different such a 'practice' would be from any object of our interest, consider that a *'disposition'* of a similar sort might be maintained in an individual agent if he somehow also habitually maintained appropriate ideas. He holds, for example, that people ought not to be surprised by what one does, or that a true man of character maintains a certain regularity in his action. Given that an appropriate 'disposition' has been started—a sequence of precedents, presumably—the agent will act "on" it *because of his other idea*, and thus the supervenient 'disposition' or succession will be maintained as long as that idea is. The case is exactly parallel with that just mentioned and with Lewis's conventions, but no one would confuse such 'dispositions' with the objects of Gauthier's interest.

we bring the two agents under a common practice of promising and see what they do in that light. In the judgment *He's doing A because he promised her he would*, it is the same.[6] Such judgments might of course be framed by an anthropological observer. But it also belonged to this doctrine that the *exercise* of such practice-dependent concepts and the *employment* of such practice-dependent forms of account are themselves among the phenomena of the practice. Thus, to give another fiduciary illustration, commonsense casuistry tells us that it is a condition of the formation of a promise that each of the parties to it *believes* that the one is *promising* something to the other and indeed *intends* or *wills* this; similarly, if someone does something "because she promised *y* she would", in the ordinary sense, she must evidently grasp the connection herself. We do not have a practice in Rawls's "Two Concepts" sense unless we suppose it is instanced in exercises of some such concepts and in the deployment of some such forms of account. Thus we do not have an early-Rawlsian practice except where it is instanced in *implicit adversion to itself*. If a bit more traditional philosophical vocabulary is permitted, we can infer that for the Rawls of "Two Concepts" a practice is something of which its bearers are or can become *conscious* in an emphatic sense; articulate knowledge of it can come to them by *reflection*.

But, as we have seen, where we advert to a practice we must also advert, at least implicitly, to something that can act as a common account or cause of manifold thoughts and operations of a manifold body of persons—something that can make their practical convergence or homogeneity 'no accident' in some appropriate way. The thing—whatever it is—that potentially operates as such a common account must *also* be something that is available to the bearers in whom it does operate; it too must be something any of them can reach by a kind of reflection, something already contained in her practice-instancing application of practice-relative concepts. But, now, anything a thinking subject can thus reach by reflection must surely be present or contained in the subject herself in some sense; anything outward or external could

---

6. It should be noticed that the connection posed, in such a judgment, between a promise and the promised action involves a *second* "look to the practice." The case is evidently not to be compared with one in which, say, I *tell* you that I promised X that I would do A and part of the "reason" for my telling you this is precisely that I *did* promise X that I would do A. *That* reason-connection is not founded on the practice of promising.

be reached only by empirical and speculative inquiry. Thus the source or account we seek must be the *same* for all of the bearers and also contained *in* any one of them. This is why the suasive potency of a preacher must be inadequate for the formation of a genuine "Two Concepts" practice.

2. Excursus for Purposes of Analogy: How a Thing's Life-Form Might Be Thought to Figure in an Account of What It Does

How, though, are we to understand the idea of a cause that can be said—if such language is permitted—to be *immanent* in the subject of its supposed effect but nevertheless the same, and not just similar, for many subjects that yet exist *outside* or *alongside* one another? Such a causality must be associated with any practice adequate to the idea implicit in Rawls's "Two Concepts." But we know more about that conception of a practice, and this complicates our problem. Where such a practice meets the conditions specified above—where it involves *that* kind of unity of one action with another and is thus the core object of our attention—it must be or involve something that can act as a *standard* or *measure* of genuine good and bad in the individual operations of the agents who bear it. But, finally, we also know that anything that can count as a "Two Concepts" practice must be joined to an *interpretative structure*, as I will put it: something that can affect the inner character of particular operations of its bearers; something to which we advert in describing the individual agent in certain terms, though not as something to which the agent is externally related. The question is whether we can find an interpretation of the category of a practice that meets these three conditions, or whether we have simply painted ourselves into a metaphysical corner.

But these three features are not so unfamiliar. We have already found them also in the workings of the special conception of a *life-form* or *"species"* that enters, frequently only implicitly, into ordinary, natural or pre-scientific thought of things as alive. This conception of a species is no doubt different from and less determinate than any likely to be deployed in a developed biological science (thus my preference for the word "life-form"), just as our practical-philosophical conception of a practice must be distinguished from any likely to be deployed in a social science. Each relates to an aspect of the "manifest image" of the world, in Sellars's phrase, and thus to a possible object of what he called *philosophia perennis.*[7] *Given this restriction to the 'ordinary',* my thought is that the category of a practice is a determinate form of a more abstract category, a genus that takes a different shape in the category of a *life-form.* The three features retailed in the last paragraph really attach to the genus. The specific difference is to be found in the different relations occupants of these categories bear to thought or representation. For, as we have seen, one kind of representation of a practice is always implicitly present in the practice itself: it is in the nature of a practice to be somehow conceived by its bearers, that is, by those whose practical lives it informs. The constitution of a life-form or species evidently does not depend on anything like this.

Let us begin a comparison of the objects of Part I and the present Part II by mentioning a fourth shared feature: like a practice, a life-form—the sort of thing we catch in folkish concepts like *white oak, vampire bat, date palm, blue crab, "man"*—is, we saw, something that can be represented through generic judgments of a particular type.[8] It too is something 'actual' and 'general', something that can be instanced or exemplified in a potentially limitless number of individual organisms and operations of these. The associated generic judgments are simply those that would enter into a "natural-historical" description of that sort of life—judgments that tell us *what they are like at this or that stage of development* or *when they breed* or *when they bloom* or *where they grow* or *how many teeth they have* or *how many tentacles are on the left side* or *how the glucose is split* or *where the adrenalin is stored* or *how it is synthesized* or *at what temperature the milk is kept*—that kind of thing. Any life-form will be the subject of indefinitely many judgments of this type, judgments describing the 'character' of the life-form or what 'belongs' to that kind of life; all of them ideally fit into a sort of theory of that particular form of life and how it hangs together. Though the contents predicated may be *recherché* and scientific, the mode of predication it-

---

7. Wilfrid Sellars, "Philosophy and the Scientific Image of Man," in *Science, Perception and Reality* (New York: Humanities Press, 1963), pp. 1–40. Though the word "image" is especially inept in this context, it is clear that practical philosophy as a whole operates entirely within what Sellars calls the "manifest image."

8. See ch. 4 above.

self is very primitive—as is the parallel *practice*-expressing predication contained in "this is what they do" or "this is what is done."

Like practices, life-forms are implicit objects of thought in much of what we say and think about individual organisms as we come upon them in experience—indeed, in almost everything we say and think about them.[9] We saw this in considering concepts like *breeding, blooming, shedding, eating, eyes, legs, petals, teeth* and so forth. It is clear that in otherwise sufficiently different forms of life, or among bearers of sufficiently different species, materially very different things might come under any one of these concepts; more importantly, anything that does come under any of them in some one type of organism might yet be found in another kind of organism and not come under it, as cell division is a form of reproduction among bacteria but not among us. Thus, in applying such concepts to the parts and operations of an individual organism given to me here and now, I make an implicit claim about the organism's form: in saying of an animal that *it is eating*, for example, I claim that *what it is doing amounts to eating for such as it is*. In applying and misapplying such concepts in ordinary experience of things as alive we bring an "interpretative structure" to bear on the individual organism before us: a possibly mostly wrong understanding of the character of the organism's life-form or species, the "such as it is". This understanding would be made explicit in natural-historical judgments mentioned above. This "interpretative structure" is applicable to other individual organisms—other bearers of the same form, other members of the same "kind"—and thus to things outside and alongside the organism we are describing. Nevertheless, in applying it to the individual organism we evidently do not look beyond it to these other individuals. The life-form is evidently not something to which the individual bearer is *externally* related; it is in some sense present in any individual bearer.

Like a practice, a life-form is of course associated with a standard or measure of good and bad—here, typically, of sickness and health, of deformity and defect, of what is missing and what is there in excess, and so forth. The deployment of such concepts is an essential part of the representation of things *as alive*, but the application of any of them to an individual organism once again presupposes a look to its species or

9. See ch. 4, sec. 4.

to the natural form of life it realizes: legs that are perfectly sound in one kind of animal would be grossly deformed in another, body temperatures that are "normal" in one would be feverish in another, and so forth.

Now, our present effort is to understand the type of common account of the convergence of a number of agents in action and practical thought that is associated with a *practice* in the sense that interests us. And here too, of course, I want to say that we find a model in the concept of a life-form. Where the operations and features of an individual organism are characteristic of its kind and predicable of that kind in a natural-historical judgment—indeed, precisely where the operations are "good", non-defective and sound—then a certain sort of account is already contained in the life-form. Since the life-form itself is shared by many individuals, this sort of account will of course apply to all of them. I will attempt to elucidate this aspect of the ordinary conception of a life-form by means of a simple series of contrasts with what I will (very crudely) call "merely mechanical and chemical" kinds of thing. This aspect of the concept of a life-form really attaches, I am suggesting, to the underlying abstract genus—and thus to the category of a (practical-philosophical) practice as well. This aspect of the matter was less developed in Part One.

Though we recognize that ice is water, or a form of water, and know that people have produced *liquid* oxygen, we are nevertheless pleased to call water a liquid and oxygen a gas, and this so to speak *sans phrase*. A sensible account of this lapse might perhaps run as follows. In itself, oxygen is of course neither liquid nor gas, but only either in certain circumstances; or equivalently, it is an accident of oxygen, as far as its mere nature goes, whether it is found at one temperature or another, and hence it is only *given* a certain sort of temperature that it will be "no accident" that it is a gas. But still, the sensible account would continue, in the circumstances that typify mortal judgment, including these judgments themselves (namely, room temperature or thereabouts), water is a liquid and oxygen is a gas. Furthermore, the stuffs are necessarily in these states whenever they enter into the most typical and natural relations a human being bears to them—respectively, drinking and breathing. And so, if one *human being* tells another that oxygen is a gas or that water is a liquid, *simpliciter*, her statement may be granted a certain objectivity; she does not presuppose room temperature out of mere naiveté. But it is intuitively a sort of half-objectivity: the mode of representation associated with either concept makes room for the possibility of a profounder understanding of the things thus conceived, one in which we do away with the presupposition that they are operating in such special circumstances as our own life presupposes.

This account of our lapse is a bit indeterminate, but it seems clear that some way of clarifying it would contain the truth about the matter. Let us now pass, though, from oxygen and water to living kinds of thing. We saw that here too we find ourselves coming out with such general propositions as that *human beings are a two-legged sort of animal* and *domestic cats are four-legged*. And here again the things are said without qualification and in the face of experience with, for example, three-legged cats and peg-legged men. It is evident, though, that in connection with representations of this second kind the "sensible" account we gave above must lose its intuitive attraction. We can find no place for a distinction between the half-objectivity possessed by the general judgments *sans phrase* ("man develops two legs, the domestic cat four"), and the full objectivity of the same judgments relativized to suitable circumstances. Of course, certain circumstances will lead a human being or a cat to lack a leg, and others, perhaps, to its forming seven or eight. But no one will say that the special circumstances 'presupposed' in the unqualified remark are somehow *imposed* upon the subject matter, however understandably, by the inquirer: the circumstances necessary to the development of two legs in a human or four in a cat are rather 'presupposed' or 'marked off' by something in the thing itself.

The same point can be made in connection with generalities pertaining to *parts* of organisms and to certain associated *substances*. For example, though it is often frozen, cow's milk "is a liquid", we say, *and not just as water is*. In representing something as cow's milk, we join it with something—something expressed by the general term "cattle" or "cow"—which itself fixes a determinate range of temperatures as appropriate to the stuff. At temperatures within that range, cow's milk is a liquid. Cows can be said, *in the same sort of general judgment*, to *maintain* cow's milk at precisely such temperatures, as bats perhaps keep their milk a bit warmer. That by which the stuff comes to be at all is that by which it comes to be *a liquid*.

A subtle categorial difference seems intuitively to come between ordinary representations of our so-called merely mechanical or chemical sorts of stuff and ordinary representations of living kinds or species, and of the parts of such things and associated substances. Representations of these latter types can be linked, in the associated system of general proposition, with a special range of circumstances. If it is the whole organism that is at issue, and not just an associated kind of stuff or part, then these circumstances constitute the kind's characteristic environment—its habitat or ecological location, if you like. The essential point is that this range of circumstances is narrower than *the range of circumstances in which that kind of thing can be found to exist.* We can say that it is no accident if a bearer of that life-form is found in such circumstances. There is nothing comparable to this in the general description of a "merely mechanical or chemical" sort of thing. If a true description of water, as a kind, isolates a range of temperatures as somehow 'characteristic' of the stuff, it can only mean that these are the temperatures at which it can exist, as, for example, it cannot exist at the center of the sun. Of the range of circumstances in which such a thing *can* be found, no more determinate range is anything but accidental in relation to the kind itself.

Thus the vicissitudes of an acorn in deep space are of no interest to a student of oaks—or rather, if a student of oaks *does* take an interest in the matter, it is because the knowledge might yield information about how the thing operates in its characteristic environment. When cells of a higher plant are grown in exotic media, the point is to grasp, for example, the chemical processes involved in the operation of ordinary cells in their ordinary location (trapped in a leaf, for example) and not just to discover 'what they do' in these exotic media. If that *were* the point, then the more ultimate end would have to be something other than an understanding of oaks as oaks or vampire bats as vampire bats—pharmaceutical profits, for example. A student of merely mechanical things, or of things as merely mechanical, seeks, by contrast, such principles as operate wherever her subject can be found.

The intuitive difference I am attempting to mark between the ordinary representation of a 'merely mechanical' kind and that of a living kind is closely related to an intuitive difference in the way these representations occur in accounts or explanations of particular events involving the things that fall under those kinds. They are two sides of the same categorial coin. If we leave aside the prospect (long since realized) of reducing laws pertaining to oxygen to those governing its compo-

nent parts, then we can say that the 'nature' of oxygen, which is expressed in the formulation of these laws, can account for the physical
state of a particular sample of O_2, *hic et nunc*, but only given particular
conditions. We might perhaps call these latter conditions (the stuff's
being held at 20°C, for example) the *real cause* of the state (in this
case, its being gaseous), but in another sense it is that coupled with
the general 'nature' of the stuff. We have seen that the class of general propositions through which we describe a life-form—the class of
natural-historical judgments—includes an assignment of certain specific conditions, a specific 'environment', to the sort of thing that bears
the form. This fact must frequently militate against the application of
the sort of etiological picture just given, and it makes another possible.
Thus, to take an especially transparent example, it is inept to account
for the development of four legs in a given embryonic cat *hic et nunc* by
pairing the 'nature' of the thing, its life-form (something partly described in textbook generalities about feline embryonic development
and completely described in the connected totality of "natural-historical
judgments" about that kind of life), with, for example, a description of
the *particular* circumstances that have prevailed hitherto in the womb
of the particular mother cat that carries it—the chemistry of the surrounding fluid, say. No one would think that the character of that particular womb contains the whole story by any means, but from the
point of view through which we first apprehend things as alive it is not
even a part of a correct account. The attempted etiology is inept for the
simple reason that the facts that *the given organism was earlier lodged in a
womb of such and such character* (namely, the 'environment' characteristic
of the kind at that stage) and that *it now exhibits four legs* (the species'
characteristic number) *have a common account in the life-form itself*—
something general, and something to which we appeal even in the account I am calling inept. The contrast will perhaps better emerge from
a comparison of the three sentences implicit in this discussion:

(I) Given the nature of water, or the general laws of its operation,
together with the fact that this stuff *hic et nunc* is water *and has been
brought down to* $-60°C$, we can say: it is no accident that the stuff
has turned solid.

(IIa) Given the nature of the domestic cat, or the aspect of it that
might be expressed in general principles of feline developmental

biology, and the fact that this being *hic et nunc* is an embryonic cat—*and nothing else*—we can say: it is no accident that the thing is developing in an environment of such and such type.

(IIb) Given those principles of specifically feline developmental biology, and the fact that *this* is an embryonic cat—*and nothing else*—we can say: it is no accident that it is developing four legs.

The nature of this stuff here as water can be said to underwrite the connection between the stuff's *being held at −60°C* and its *being solid*, and our inept account would have to appeal to generalities about the feline life-form to underwrite the connection between the given embryonic organism's *having been in these circumstances* and its *having developed in this way;* but this is an appeal to something that can *already* underwrite both its being in those circumstances *and* its developing in that way. In the natural-historical representation of the life-form, attributions of leg number, of womb character, and of any connection between these things, would all have the same character. The operations that instance a given life-form and are attributed to it generically in natural-historical judgments *include* those that put its bearers into the circumstances necessary for such further operations as instance that same form.

It may be thought that we have made things easy by contemplating a womb, a "circumstance of development" that is transparently linked to the life-form borne by what it carries—for this form is also borne by the mother. But it cannot even be called accidental that a particular dandelion seed or cherry pit falls on soil appropriate for its development, even though only a tiny ratio actually do, most of them meeting with rocks, water, deep shade and so forth. The life-form has provided for this, and thus made it no accident, by producing so much seed, as we have seen, and by providing means for its distribution.

Features of individual living beings are of course frequently rightly brought back to particular antecedent facts. But the truth of such claims presupposes that the feature at issue is precisely not itself characteristic of the kind and thus not rightly attributed to this type of thing in natural-historical description. It might be deformity, defect, disease or faulty operation, but it might equally be a determination of something the species leaves open, like eye color in humans—and, of course, most truths about individual organisms fall into the latter class. Even here generic propositions about the forms of operation characteristic of the life-form or kind will figure in the account of the 'abnormal' or more determinate development. Again, none of this is a matter of the complication of the 'pragmatics of explanation' by 'our expectations'. The circumstances that go unmet where the 'normal' development fails are not a subjective imposition on the subject matter. They are expressed in a type of judgment that is essential to the representation of this kind of kind to begin with. If we must speak of expectations, they are those of the life-form itself.

⌒ IT IS NOT THAT 'the development of four legs' is in *no* sense to be brought back to the appropriate environment, whatever it is, as one among many conditions. This is precisely the sort of understanding that would be supplied in a treatise of feline embryonic development, if anyone cared to write one. But what would be explained there is again precisely 'the development of four legs', *taken generally*. Likewise, the antecedent conditions that figure in the account—in our example, a certain state of the womb—would again be *taken generally*. It does not at all follow from the possibility of such a natural-historical account of a natural-historical fact, that an understanding of the origination of any corresponding *particular* quartet of legs *hic et nunc* should also inevitably involve a description of the *particular* conditions that prevailed in some particular womb.

What makes the origination of a particular collection of legs, paws and claws 'no accident' is something somehow general, something that accounts for other collections of legs, paws and claws as well—unless, again, these things are somehow out of line, whether in number or quality, or some more determinate feature of them is in view.

3. Fidelity as a Ground of Human Action: Practice and Disposition Identical as Practical Explanantia

In describing what is happening before me as *eating* or *blossoming* my thought moves in certain categories: among other things, I think of the organism before me as bearing a life-form, though perhaps I advert to the latter only in the demonstrative shape of *this kind of creature* and only implicitly. I represent this life-form as potentially instanced in other individual organisms, and as a measure of good and bad in whatever does bear it and as containing a special kind of cause of whatever is reckoned good according to that measure. Our Rawlsian reflections have led us to the thought that in describing what is happening before me as *promising*, my thought moves in certain parallel categories. Among other things, I think of the agent as the bearer of a *practice*, a 'form' of a different sort, but nevertheless something that is potentially present in other agents, something that acts as a measure of good and bad in what bears it, and something that can account for what is reckoned good according to that measure. One turn of the categorical framework gives us the concept of a life-form or a living nature; the other gives us the concept of 'form of life' or a 'second nature'. Of course the concepts of *good* and *bad* and of *account* will shift together with the associated conception of 'form' or 'nature' and the associated type of generality and general judgment; in *this* deployment, they are specifically practical.

Let us return to the concept of a disposition, in hope of some partial results. Let us say that *fidelity* as a disposition—the sort of thing Gauthier was talking about—is "what ultimately accounts" for each element in the long run of what are intuitively "acts of fidelity" on the part of some one person. This cannot stand as a complete definition, in view of the variety of possible interpretations of the notion of account or source. We know, for example, that we must take the appropriate type of etiology to be something quite different from that which joined the drugged brain of Parfit's cunning Schellingian father to his 'irrational actions'. Now, an individual human action cannot fall under the description "act of fidelity" or even "act of promise-keeping" except by bearing an appropriate relation to the appropriate *practice*. Thus fidelity itself, considered as a disposition, cannot exist apart from this practice.

In view of all this, the considerations of the last section suggest the proposal that we take the disposition of fidelity—the 'ultimate source' and 'inner basis' of a faithful person's many acts of fidelity—to be simply *identical* with the larger practice of promising, and nothing at all psychological.

For suppose we were to insist on littering the world with distinct *personal* bases for different peoples' several acts of fidelity. This is the picture Gauthier's remarks excite. But granting this picture, it would still follow from our Rawlsian reflections that the single self-same practice that is presupposed by each of these diverse bases and by the many individual acts they allegedly underwrite must itself either be, or contain, an account of the existence of each private spring of action. The practice thus either is or contains a more ultimate account of whatever it is that these several distinct personal bases were supposed to account for. For the ultimate source or account of *your* alleged private disposition must be the same as the ultimate account of my own: thus a more ultimate source of your keeping of a promise to someone, if it is an act of fidelity, is one and the same as a more ultimate source of my keeping of a promise to anyone else. The personal basis thus threatens to drop out of the account of the individual act of fidelity as irrelevant.

The conclusion becomes inevitable if we consider more closely the parallel with the concept of a life-form. The essence of the matter is that the special form of account or cause or non-accidentality that is associated with a life-form or a practice reaches all the way to the individual operations that instance the thing. That through which we understand the phenomena we collect as *this cherry tree's blossoming* in any one of the many years in which it blossoms is, we have supposed, precisely that through which we understand its blossoming in any other year, or any other cherry tree's blossoming in this or any year (supposing, as usual, that nothing is otherwise out of line). Considered as a cause or source of these things, the item to which we advert in each case is not a prior event, and it is in some sense contained in any one of the trees; it might be described in a detailed treatise about the workings of that kind of tree, if anyone cared to write one. *So also,* that through which we understand any one of a person's many practice-instancing acts of fidelity is precisely that though which we understand any other act of fidelity performed by him, or indeed by any other agent; considered as a cause or source of action, this item is not a prior event and is in some sense present in any of the agents; it might be formulated in a description of the practice. The practice occupies all of the available practical-explanatory space; there is no room to distinguish what Gauthier praised under the title of a disposition from what Rawls praised under the name of a practice.

This does not mean that an individual agent might engage in genuine acts of fidelity though she lacks certain familiar thoughts and intentions and desires, for example—no more than the parallel thesis about cherry blossoms suggests that an individual cherry tree might bloom even though five times as much of a certain vegetative growth hormone runs in its sap as does in any other tree, and no more than our remarks about cow's milk suggest that a bit of it might remain liquid at −60°C. It is just that apt thoughts, apt intentions and so forth, like apt soil, apt hormonal ratios and so forth, all admit the same sort of account that the action or blossoming does. In reaching for the "disposition" we reach for *that sort of account*—and thereby strike the practice. This is a general feature of dispositions that are associated with practices, and thus of any genuine "artificial virtue" in Hume's sense.

Just as mention of antecedent particular facts is typically only needed in an account, for example, of a cherry's *failure* to blossom, or of its blossoming in April and then again in June and September, so also mention of special facts about an individual agent will only be required if, for example, he does *not* keep his promises, or keeps them only when it strikes him as useful, or keeps them come what may, or keeps them even when they were mere cases of somniloquence. Thus the various forms of infidelity, considered as dispositions or vices, really *are* private attainments and private sources of action. They are local impediments to the apt instancing of a practice that the agent nevertheless bears and that is instanced minimally in his possession of the concept of a promise and in the individual promises he forms. It is just that there are other things going on with him. We might think of *fidelity* as a private attainment in a sense, as something that might distinguish one of the practice-bearers from another, but as such it is simply the *negation* of infidelity or the absence of those impediments. Thus, so considered, it is precisely not itself a source, account or ground of action. Considered as a *source* of action, fidelity is the practice under another name and the same for everyone. Where agents keep promises from fidelity, their actions have different sources only in the sense that they have made different promises. Apart from that, they act not just on similar or parallel grounds, but on the same ultimate ground and not just on principles with the same content, but *on the same principle.*

Acknowledgments

I am grateful for permission to use revised portions of my previously published work. Material that appears in the first chapters of Part III is drawn from "Two Forms of Practical Generality," in *Practical Generality and Preference*, ed. Arthur Ripstein and Christopher Morris (New York: Cambridge University Press, 2001), and material in Part I is drawn from "The Representation of Life," in *Virtues and Reasons*, ed. Rosalind Hursthouse, Gavin Lawrence, and Warren Quinn, © Oxford University Press, 1995, by permission of Oxford University Press.

I am again and again grateful to Lindsay Waters of Harvard University Press for his incredible patience and inexplicable cheer in overseeing the publication of this book—if it is a book—and to Liz Duvall and her colleagues at Technologies 'N Typography of Merrimac, Massachusetts, for editing, indexing and typesetting the manuscript and, again, for many acts of the virtue of patience.

I am grateful too to my revered teachers Rogers Albritton, Philippa Foot, Montgomery Furth and Warren Quinn. My fortune and that of my fellow students at UCLA in that period is something that astonishes me more and more as I gain greater perspective on it. Other philosophers to whom I must express gratitude, especially for their criticism, would include these: Robert Brandom, Ronald Condon, Steven Engstrom, Anton Ford, Matthew Hanser, Michael Kelar, Douglas

213

Lavin, Gavin Lawrence, John McDowell, Sidney Morgenbesser, Sebastian Roedl, Kieran Setiya and Candace Vogler. This gratitude extends to many others, of course.

To my wife, Wendy Kobee, I feel that I owe everything. I dedicate this book to her, hereby, with the words of Sonnet 29 sounding in my imagination.

Index

"Act and Intent" (Chisholm), 120–121n1

action: concept of, 1; description of, 106; ethical theory and, 27; intellectual aspect of, 93–96, 95–96n14; intentional, and wanting, 1, 11, 22, 86n3, 91–92, 95–96n14, 98–99n2, 104–105n12, 112–113n12; naive explanation of, 1, 86–89, 86n3, 89n6, 114, 124, 132; preliminary formulation of central claims about, 89–93, 89n7, 90n9, 91n10, 92nn11–12; relation between reason and, 90, 90n9, 95–96, 95–96n14; sophisticated explanation of, 85–89, 92, 97; as specific form of life process, 27; and wanting, 2–3, 22, 87, 97–98, 98–99n2. *See also* individual action; intentional action; naive action explanation; rationalization of action; time and action

action explanation: described, 88, 99, 128, 132, 151. *See also* naive action explanation

"Actions, Reasons and Causes" (Davidson), 87, 90n9, 95–96n14

Anscombe, G. E. M.: Aristotle's theoretical philosophy and the doctrine of, 6, 7, 12, 13; "Authority in Morals," 89n7; on concept of morality, 5, 7; on description of action, 106, 109–110, 110n7; *Ethics, Religion and Politics,* 89n7; "The First Person," 120–121n1; on the first person, 120–121n1, 127n10; *Intention,* 6, 77, 89n7, 96n15, 104–105n12, 109n6, 112n10, 132n15, 136n17; on intention, 104–105n12, 107; on mediate character of vital description, or its wider context, 53–54, 58; *Metaphysics and Philosophy of Mind,* 120–121n1; "Modern Moral Philosophy," 5–6, 7, 29n6; "On Promising and Its Justice," 176–177n14; "Practical Inference," 89n7; on relation between reason and action, 95–96n14, 96n15; on sense of the question "Why?", 47–48, 78, 79, 85–86, 90, 112n10; on temporary retreat from ethics, 7; on unity of straightforward rationalization, 132, 132n15; on wanting, 104–105n12; on wider context as species, 58–60;

215

Frege, Gottlob *(continued)*
  with, 121–122, 122n4, 127n10; state
  or properties vs., 122, 122n4
Fregean/post-Fregean method, 13–22
"Frege's Theory of Predication"
  (Rumfitt), 120–121n1
"Function and Concept" (Frege),
  122n4, 131n13

Galton, Anthony, 123–124n6, 141n22
Gaut, B., 160n13
Gauthier, David: "Assure and
  Threaten," 155–156n10, 159n12,
  170, 171, 172, 172nn5–6; infidelity
  rejected by, 157n11; on justice as
  disposition, 9, 189–190; *Morals by
  Agreement*, 150, 154n7, 155–156n10,
  171, 180, 183; on rationality of
  fidelity, 152–156, 152n4, 153n5,
  154n7, 155–156n10, 159n12, 208,
  209; "Rationality and the Rational
  Aim," 180, 182; "Reason and
  Maximization," 155–156n10; on
  standard of deliberation, 170–172,
  172n5, 197, 197n5; transfer
  principles of, 159n12, 169, 170–173,
  172n6, 183; on transparency of
  dispositions, 180–183; "The Unity
  of Reason," 154
Geach, Peter, 122n4, 143n25
Gegenstand (object), 14, 18, 26, 95–
  96n14
generality, role of, 149–150
The Generic Book (Carlson and
  Pelletier), 166n20
gold, and theory of meaning described
  with use of term, 185–187
goodness concept: described, 80–82,
  80n16; moral goodness of acts of
  fidelity and, 152–156, 152n4,
  162n16, 168, 168n2, 175–179, 176–
  177n14, 178–179nn16–17, 188;
  practices and dispositions as sources
  of goodness of individual action and,
  167–173, 168n2, 172nn5–6, 177–
  178, 179, 180–181, 182, 188, 191
Graham, Daniel, 124–125n7

Grice, H. P., 102–103, 104–105n12,
  145n29
Groundwork (Kant), 32
Grundlagen (Foot), 34

habituality, topic of, 125–126, 126n9
Harman, Gilbert, 102–103, 145n29
Hart, H. L. A., 173, 197n5
Hegel, G. W. F.: Aristotle's theoretical
  philosophy, and view of, 13; on
  forms of judgment, 16; on logic and
  life, 25n1, 25–26, 27, 33, 160; on
  sameness in sphere of living concept,
  53; *Science of Logic*, 25, 25n1; on
  teleology concept, 12–13
Heidegger, Martin, 13
Historia animalium (Aristotle), 63
Hornsby, Jennifer, 101
Human Genome Project, 56
Hume, David: *An Enquiry Concerning
  the Principles of Morals*, 114n13; and
  fidelity, act of, 188, 210; naive action
  explanation and, 113–115, 114n13,
  115–116n15; practical-philosophical
  approach, and concepts of, 8;
  practices and dispositions
  tendencies, and concepts of, 4
"The Humean Theory of Motivation"
  (Smith), 115–116n15
Hursthouse, Rosalind: *On Virtue Ethics*,
  7, 29n6; *Virtues and Reason*, 89n7

image, manifest, 10, 92, 92n11, 200,
  200n7
individual action: explanation of, 192–
  199, 193n1, 196–198nn4–6; fidelity,
  and explanation of, 192; and fidelity,
  act of, 192; practices and dispositions
  as sources of goodness of, 167–169,
  172, 173, 177–178, 179, 180–181,
  182, 188, 191; rationality of, 168,
  170, 171, 180. *See also* action
individual substance category, 2, 22,
  55–56
infidelity, act of, 153, 153n5, 157,
  157n11, 160, 187, 210. *See also*
  fidelity, act of